THE PROVOCATEUR

The PROVOCATEUR

HOW A NEW GENERATION OF LEADERS ARE BUILDING COMMUNITIES, NOT JUST COMPANIES

LARRY WEBER

CROWN
BUSINESS
NEW YORK

Published by Crown Business, New York, New York.
Member of the Crown Publishing Group.

Random House, Inc. New York, Toronto, London, Sydney, Auckland
www.randomhouse.com

CROWN BUSINESS and colophon are trademarks of Random House, Inc.

Printed in the United States of America

Design by Robert C. Olsson

Library of Congress Cataloging-in-Publication Data

Weber, Larry.
The Provocateur : how a new generation of leaders are building
communities, not just companies / Larry Weber.
1. Executive ability.   2. Leadership.   3. Executives—Attitudes.
4. New business enterprises.   I. Title.
HD38.2 .W43 2001
658.4'09—dc21   2001042482

ISBN 0-609-60826-6

10 9 8 7 6 5 4 3 2 1

First Edition

To Dawn.

Good thing we gave the business world a try.

ACKNOWLEDGMENTS

Community-building is the basic premise of *The Provocateur* and it was truly a community of colleagues, friends, and family who helped me create this work. The idea began to germinate in the 1980s and I am grateful to the many early "Weberites" and Weber clients whose thoughts and ideas helped clarify my thinking on marketing and management. I owe special thanks to Lois Kelly for finally spurring me into action and helping me, along with Hannah Hosom Roveto, to shape my thoughts into a coherent theme. My agent Jill Kneerim's thoughtful guidance was invaluable in turning my proposal into a reality. My editor John Mahaney was unwavering in his enthusiasm and I am thankful to him and the entire team at Crown Business for their assistance. I would also like to thank John Dooner and Phil Geier at Interpublic for their support of my intellectual endeavor.

This is a book about leadership and I would like to thank those leaders who shared their stories with me. I truly enjoyed my conversations with Stewart Alsop of New Enterprise Associates, George Colony of Forrester Research, Akamai's George Conrades, the late Michael Dertouzos of MIT's Lab for Computer Science, David Hayden of Critical

Path, Philippe Kahn of LightSurf, former Verbind president and CEO John Kish, Tom McMakin, former COO of Great Harvest Bread Company, Bob Metcalfe of Polaris Venture Partners, Patrick McGovern of IDG, Groove Network's Ray Ozzie, V. A. Shiva of EchoMail, Jeff Taylor of Monster.com, Chuck Vest at MIT, General Motor's Rick Wagoner and Donnee Ramelli, and David Wetherell of CMGI.

In addition to my parents, who fostered my love of learning, I am deeply indebted to four people, without whom this book would never have been written. First is my assistant Karen Clark, who finally broke my record as the "Murphy Brown" of the public relations industry. Second is my writer, Wally Wood, who turned my thoughts into words and contributed many stories and anecdotes of his own. Third is my "brain" Rebecca Oddsund, who was with me every step of the way, from the initial shaping of the book through editing, production, and marketing of *The Provocateur*. Last, and certainly not least, is my wife Dawn, who is my partner in every sense of the word. Her insight, guidance, and support were invaluable. I thank all of them from the bottom of my heart.

Finally, I would like to thank my family for their love and their loyalty. They are my most important community.

CONTENTS

INTRODUCTION

Many of the ideas in this book grew out of the journal that, early in my life, my grandmother suggested I keep. Once I became involved in business, I began jotting notes on my observations of executives and their behavior.

Around 1984 I noticed a change starting to occur. The 1960s flower children were moving into management, saying, "We've got to make money" while simultaneously trying to maintain their ideals. Technology was starting to creep onto executive desks, improving productivity and creating a new way for people to work. Though the traditional model of how to run a business had worked for decades, it seemed to me the executives that were starting to succeed were doing something else. This came home to me most powerfully when I first met Mitch Kapor, the CEO of Lotus Development.

I had been working for Harry Figgie, the founder and CEO of Figgie International, which became a *Fortune* 500 company while *Fortune* also named Harry one of "America's Toughest Bosses." I found Harry brilliant, blunt, and a bit of a bully. He believed in command and control; Figgie International was his company and you never forgot it. People who told him "no" tended to lose their jobs.

Introduction

Harry held quarterly financial update meetings with each division. Figgie International had 30 to 35 individual companies at the time I was working as one of the marketing people. I remember waiting with the executives of the next company to go into meet with Harry; they often would be physically distraught. Harry created a culture riddled with fear, yet demanding excellence.

The people who rose to the top were the ones who had self-confidence to the point of arrogance, but they had to regularly produce. There was no love lost between Harry and his executives. Also, now that I look back, Harry's style impeded innovation. Executives wanted to get out of those meetings as quickly as they could.

Harry was successful at the time, but the times started to change around the early to mid-1980s. Figgie International began to lose a lot of talented people who didn't want to work in fear of whether they could keep their jobs. I left to work in Boston, and shortly afterward, I was sitting in the offices of a new software company called Lotus Development. It had just gone public and was hot because it had realized the value of the new IBM personal computers, using them to run software that made your job easier with a product like 1-2-3.

My meeting was with Mitch Kapor, and in the middle he jumped up, went out of his office, grabbed three other people, and said, "Come on in here." Eventually he said, "There's not enough room in my office, let's go in an office with more room." Two guys sat on the floor, one sat on the table. We discussed with lots of back-and-forth exchanges how we could market 1-2-3 to accountants and the importance of marketing Lotus as a friendly and wonderful place to be.

In a way, Mitch was building a community, not a company, and I began to see the contrast between the Harry

Figgie style of management and a new style of leadership in Mitch Kapor. Harry focused on building a company, mainly by cutting costs, and Mitch—it was clear in our first meeting—was pulling people in, asking questions, walking around the offices, and laughing. Mitch knew that if we built the community around solving people's problems, we were going to build a cool company, and if we built a place where people really liked to work we would have our pick of this new industry's best people.

When I started putting these observations in my journal, I thought about the differences in style. Harry was quiet, he was brilliant, but he reminded me of an Army general who thinks through a strategy and implements it bluntly and directly. Mitch, like Harry, had an architecture in his mind, but he was open to and engaged other people in its development.

Around the same time, I encountered two other contrasting executives: Ken Olsen and Steve Jobs.

I met with Olsen, the CEO of Digital Equipment, and his executives in a company conference room. White businessmen in white shirts, ties, and blue suits ringed the table. They seldom said anything and when they did, they first looked to Mr. Olsen for his reaction. Olsen sat quiet, stoic, and skeptical of developments to come in the technology industry. This was around the time when he told the press, "The PC is a toy" and "Marketing is what you do when your product is no good."

A few weeks later I was at Lotus for a presentation by a young new CEO named Steve Jobs who was demonstrating his new Apple computers, what they could do, and why Lotus should develop programs for them. He was mesmerizing, an evangelist, someone for whom one would drop everything and follow wherever he led.

Olsen, like Figgie, was trying to build the company. Jobs, like Kapor, was determined to build a community—whether they be the people who developed software or the ones who bought the computers. After that first exposure I wrote, "Jobs is an entertainer. He educated us about the new uses of the personal computer. And he's really trying to guide us through what we think will be a difficult time. He's saying come with me down the Yellow Brick Road even though we don't know what Oz looks like."

Seeing and recording these contrasts in a short time planted the seeds that blossomed into my idea of the Provocateur, a manager who leads a company more as if it were a rock band, a theater group, an orchestra, or a circus than an army. A rock band still has a leader, but one who promotes the group, one who encourages individuality and innovation.

I offer this not as a book about specific individuals but as the beginning of a dialogue, a conversation about the natural evolution of leadership. It is not a field manual for managers who want step-by-step directions for supervising change. To write it, I had conversations with a number of the brightest executives I know, and you'll find their ideas throughout. The ideas—if the achievements of my own company are any indication—have hard-headed, practical, business value. I truly believe that executives who embrace them will enjoy ample business success and still have fun while shaking up business as usual.

THE PROVOCATEUR

1

THE PROVOCATEUR

Organizations today require a new kind of leadership because technology, the global economy, and the social landscape are altering the very nature of business. I call these new leaders Provocateurs to distinguish them from the Generals who successfully led companies in the past.

Provocateurs build communities; Generals build companies. Provocateurs put the relationship with the customer at the company's center; Generals put the product (or service) at the center. Provocateurs know that a brand is based on communication with customers; the stronger the communication, the stronger the brand. Provocateurs empower employees; Generals establish hierarchies with command and control. Provocateurs value openness, interchange, and innovation; Generals maintain secrecy, control communication, and distrust novelty.

In business, Steve Jobs, the president of Apple Computer is a Provocateur; Larry Ellison, the CEO of Oracle, is a General.

In sports, Phil Jackson, coach of the Los Angeles Lakers, is a Provocateur; Bobby Knight, former head coach at Indiana University, is a General. Phil Jackson has said that every successful coach needs "the intuitive ability to change a conflict situation into a team-building one." Knight, says Bill Walton, is a coach "whose success is based on bullying and intimidating people. His style is rooted in boorish behavior, with which he psychologically terrorizes his players for his own benefit."

In education, Charles Vest, president of MIT, is a Provocateur; John Silber, chancellor of Boston University, is a General. Vest recently announced that MIT will be making the materials for nearly all of its courses freely available on the Internet. In 1997, BU dropped its 91-year-old football program "largely through the efforts of despotic chancellor John Silber."

In media, Oprah Winfrey, chairman and CEO of Harpo Productions, is a Provocateur; Rupert Murdoch, chairman and CEO of News Corp. is a General.

Provocateurs, as we'll see, are riding the tide of history. They, not Generals, will build tomorrow's great companies. They will do so because their beliefs are more suitable for today's business realities than the Generals'.

CUSTOMER RELATIONSHIPS ARE KEY

Provocateurs believe that the relationship with the customer is at the center of the business, not The Product or The Service. The product is important, but so is after-sale service and delivery and labeling and financing and every other element of the customer's contact with the company. Provocateurs say, "Our goal is to build trust, to make the experience of dealing with us great." A Provocateur's goal is to have the customers so involved in the business they feel they are important players in the enterprise's success, which of course they are. Some people who purchased an Apple computer are so engaged with the Apple mystique, they put Apple decals on their cars. Some people who own Harley-Davidson motorcycles have the brand's logo tattooed on themselves.

Provocateurs believe they should build a community in which the members take care of each other. David Hayden, the founder of Magellan, the first search engine, as well as CEO of Critical Path, a San Francisco–based firm that provides email services to large companies, said, "I think leadership has changed in the last eight years in a marked way. Today's successful business world is about creating communities, which really ties into a collaborative ethic, rather than a competitive ethic. The issue that the CEOs or leadership teams in all new successful companies have addressed to some extent—and I think is tied directly to the extent of their success—is that they are more collaborative, not only within the company, but within the marketplace. They are community builders."

Generals believe that hierarchy, the chain of command, is the best structure. The General gives orders to the colonels, who give the orders to the lieutenant colonels, who give the orders to the majors, who give the orders to the captains, who give the orders to the lieutenants, who give the orders to the troops. In this order, the person closest to the situation—in business, the customer—has the least authority to make a decision.

Provocateurs believe that employees should make decisions themselves through dialogue and example. Patrick McGovern, the founder and chairman of International Data Group, told me, "We call our CEOs the Chief Encouragement Officer"—IDG has 105 companies (and more than 12,000 employees) around the world—"and their role is to encourage and empower people by the trust they have. I always observed that if you go through the 'Prove-this-to-me, prove-that-to-me' exercise, managers feel, 'Well, I guess my competency is distrusted here.' If you expect people to do well, they will believe they will do well. They actually execute in ways to get that success, so it becomes a self-fulfilling prophecy."

With the military as their model of organizational structure, Generals believe the way to keep people in line is through command and control. Since many Generals see people as motivated only by greed and fear (Napoleon's observation), they use bonuses and threats—with an occasional public execution—to maintain control.

Provocateurs believe that employees will be motivated if they understand and subscribe to the organization's goals and needs. As a result, the leader who is a Provocateur keeps very few secrets from employees or the outside world. (As a fringe benefit, Provocateurs tend to receive more and better press coverage for their businesses since reporters like straight-talking, knowledgeable sources.)

Generals believe secrecy is vital. Since loose lips sink ships, a General is disposed to be highly secretive about sales, product strategies, and every other single thing the company does. Former Ford CEO Alex Trotman was secretive and once became so angry that *Fortune* was going to publish an article identifying Bill Ford as a candidate for chairman that Trotman ordered the company's general counsel to find out if someone had leaked the story. "Company lawyers, along with attorneys from Ford's Washington law firm O'Melveny & Myers, formally interviewed members of the board, including Bill Ford, as well as some top executives. They also searched business and personal phone records looking for calls to news organizations." The investigation was inconclusive, and it is hard to believe these tactics improved Trotman's relations with his board.

LEADERSHIP CANNOT BE SEPARATED FROM MARKETING

Provocateurs believe the leader's most important task is marketing. Since the relationship with the customer is the business's center, one cannot separate leadership from marketing or marketing from leadership. In the world of the Generals, a business leader could have come out of finance, manufacturing, or operations; marketing was just a department down the hall. Provocateurs understand that a CEO's primary job is communicating with customers to benefit the company, the brand, and all their constituencies. The stronger the communication, the stronger the brand.

Leadership and marketing are no longer two separate facilities. They are entwined because you cannot separate a company's marketing from its brand and leadership. The relationship with customers is the essential company center now. The business builds on that relationship through a concept I call dialogue data, which involves collecting and analyzing information about customers to learn their wants and needs. A company can collect valuable data about its customers through ongoing dialogues across all communications media—online, phone, mail, surveys, focus groups, and more. This data goes beyond simple facts and figures (i.e., his favorite color is green; she is 37 years old) to habits and behaviors that can help determine how best to reach the customer. Provocateurs understand that these are not conversations just to build a relationship (although they help do exactly that); they are designed to pinpoint the needs, wants, and desires of a specific consumer or business customer.

Provocateurs believe that markets are more than their demographic characteristics. A 23-year-old woman and a 60-year-old man can share an interest in four-wheel-drive vehicles. A high school dropout and a Ph.D. can share an interest in woodworking . . . antique outboard engines . . . gardening. People are joined by their interests, values, hopes, and dreams, and any individual belongs to dozens of different communities.

Generals believe that business is a zero-sum game. If someone else wins a sale (or a client, or a patent, or a bid), the General loses. If he wins, someone else loses. The pie is only so big, and the bigger my piece, the smaller yours must necessarily be. It is a worldview that still makes sense in some situations, such as the competition between Sony's Betamax and JVC's VHS to set the standard for videocassette recorders, but those situations are far fewer than the General assumes.

Provocateurs believe that business is not always a zero-sum game. Because knowledge and ideas are abundant, it is possible for everyone—customers, suppliers, employees, and even competitors—to come out ahead. Provocateurs do not believe that if they win, someone else automatically loses; they believe the pie can grow. More competitors are cooperating to buy items like auto parts, office supplies, airline tickets, cleaning services, and other goods and services that do not affect the business's core competency.

Provocateurs believe that the farther you are from the scene of action the more difficult it is to know what's happening. A leader from the traditional military/church hierarchical structure risks losing touch with customers and their concerns. In contrast, the flatter the structure, the closer the business leader is to the customer, where everything happens. The Provocateur still recognizes the need for some hierarchy, but believes that the fewer the levels, the better for everyone.

The Provocateur still needs control. The orchestra conductor has to establish the beat and cue the timpani. The theater director has to tell the actor he's rushing his lines, tell the set designer the door is in the wrong place, tell the costume head the dress is the wrong color.

Provocateurs work continually to tear down the walls between departments and divisions within the company, between the company and customers, and between the company and suppliers. They thereby create an atmosphere in which employees trust themselves and their decisions. (How many executives complain, "I can't get my people to take any risks"? They don't take risks because the fear of punishment is greater than any expectation of reward.)

A Provocateur starts with a premise, such as

- Personal computers are useful (Apple)
- Women have questions about their health (iVillage)
- All-natural packaged macaroni and cheese is healthy (Annie's Homegrown)

and builds a community of customers, employees, and suppliers around that premise. A successful Provocateur acts like a great mayor for the community, creating excitement, momentum, and engagement. The community is inclusive rather than exclusive. It encourages more communication, not less. And, to a greater or lesser degree, it involves every stakeholder in as many elements of the business as possible.

Provocateurs are still capitalists. They embrace the idea that a capitalistic system is the best way we have found to harness human ambition, creativity, and greed. It simply works better than socialism or communism or statism. Provocateurs embrace the 1960s ideal of a shared openness and a democratic way of doing things, so they do not espouse unbridled capitalism with its attendant ills such as child labor, sweatshops, and environmental abuse.

ARMIES NEED GENERALS, BUSINESSES DO NOT

The General model of business leadership came out of the model provided by the military and the Catholic Church. To win a war, an army must have one General, a Napoleon, a Wellington. A ship must have one captain. The Catholic Church has one pope. Authority is structured in the form of a pyramid with the General on top.

During the Industrial Revolution and the rise of large business enterprises in the nineteenth century, corporate leaders took the General model as the only one that made sense. It was the only way to organize large groups of people for a common goal. Generals believe that business is a form of war, with enemies, strategies, victories, and troops. The role models and the social environment that these leaders knew were based on how armies win wars. If you were Ford, you set up your organization as if you were an army—and the enemy was General Motors, Chrysler, American Motors, Studebaker, Nash, Toyota, Nissan, Volkswagen, Volvo. What better model than an army led by a General in a battle in which we're out to annihilate our competitors?

Generals find new ideas and innovation uncomfortable. Generals are never sure what the flakes down in the lab or the wackos at the ad agency are going to come up with next. They take a literal approach to business, putting their faith in rules, regulations, and policy.

Because they are uncomfortable with creativity, Generals do not give innovation a high priority. They believe it is more important to produce a quality product with periodic incremental improvements and to keep employees lined up and ready to take orders than it is to introduce something radically new and, by definition, uncertain. To make up for the lack of innovation within the company, their businesses usually have had to buy it—hence the mania for acquisitions.

The General approach to business worked for a long time because both employees and managers accepted the model as the one that made the most sense. When they chafed, they changed companies rather than trying to change the system.

Unquestionably, Generals were right for their times. They built great companies. They were able to get results, organize and move masses of people in one direction for one goal, and were able to increase manufacturing, reporting, and financial efficiencies dramatically. Many of the rules, policies, and principles they established and lived by remain valid—instituting budgets and cost controls, being first to market, using just-in-time manufacturing, capturing market share, buying weak competitors, and much more.

That said, the Generals who lead companies today face an increasingly harsh and unsympathetic world. They will have to change (or be replaced) or eventually their businesses will face sickness, merger, or death. Because of the sea change currently under way, the future belongs to the Provocateurs.

A NEW WORLD REQUIRES NEW LEADERS

The world has changed. "Fundamentally, the psychology of business and the psychology of information flow is shifting underfoot," says John Kish, the former president and CEO of Verbind, a Boston-based company that tracks customer behavior. "Old-style companies that believe in the military point of view are going to say, 'No, it's all command and control, and if we don't see it, we can't own it . . . we don't want to deal with it.' The truth is, those companies are going to find themselves succumbing to the same problems that the long-distance carriers currently see, which is commoditization."

We are only beginning to see the effect technology has on the way companies sell and buy products and services, the way prospects learn about offers, the way leaders manage their organizations. G. Richard Wagoner Jr., president and CEO of General Motors, tells me that the GM model, which worked well 20 years ago, does not work today, if only because technology has changed how corporations operate. They can do satellite broadcasts, send email over the Internet, respond to email from around the world.

"The tradition of independent operating units throughout GM gets back to the very roots of the company, which was all by acquisition," says Wagoner. "Because our industry is integrating globally and leveraging globally and because we need economies of scale, we can no longer use that model." The model is now one of global cooperation and collaboration.

I spoke with Michael Dertouzos, the director of MIT's Laboratory for Computer Science, shortly before he passed away in August of 2001. He said that "the best companies in the world are those that empower their people by giving them a freedom that's nonspecialized. Henry Ford wanted human labor to be specialized. He wanted it exploited, like a cost that should be minimized, and it was expendable. If this part didn't work, you tossed it and put in another. That was his idea of mass production. The companies that emerged in the late 1980s discovered that human beings count. They said, 'You should be a shipping clerk, but we are not going to tell you what a shipping clerk does. You are going to make our company the best in the world by doing what is right for shipping, and we are going to empower you to go out and buy your own machines and broaden your outlook.' It was really a new discovery."

Into the 1970s, an implied social contract carried over from an earlier time that said, "I will work hard and be loyal, and in exchange the company will guarantee me a job." At a time when the big corporate armies were expanding, there was reason to be loyal because the company took care of its own. But the downsizing that swept corporate America in the late 1980s and the 1990s broke that contract. Employees began to realize that although they might be loyal to the corporation, the corporation was not necessarily loyal to them.

We're moving into a period when honesty and openness will create leadership opportunities for people at all levels. People are starting businesses at a record clip because creativity in leadership allows people to try many different things. True Provocateurs are pleased when an employee quits to take a bigger, more responsible job or to start her own business, if only because it tends to validate the original hiring decision. At the same time, Provocateurs tend to retain the people they've hired because they allow—indeed, encourage—them to start things within the organization.

With low unemployment, power naturally shifts from the company to the individual. But within the past five years or so, there's been a psychological shift as well from "I need a job, I want to be loyal, I'll do what you tell me" to "I want a job that makes the most of my abilities. I'll be loyal as long as I'm challenged and rewarded."

Power has also shifted from the company (or the retailer) to the customer, who has become even more important in driving what a company develops and what it does. The customer's power has grown because she now has access to so much information about products and services.

This is a key point. Power is shifting to employees and to customers, a shift driven by technology and by, I suspect, a human need to feel in control. In control of one's life, work, and purchases. We no longer have to rely on a salesperson's word; we can compare features, prices, and benefits in a way few people could even 10 years ago.

"The global reach of communications makes the individual finally very powerful, both from a sovereign state and a sovereign corporate power perspective," says David Hayden. "Leaders are now emerging who at least intuitively understand that and are working along those lines rather than along the older line, which is to annihilate your competitor and be secretive." The leader who does not recognize and embrace this power shift will become more and more impotent.

The World Wide Web is accelerating communication, and we can never return to a simpler time. The world has changed because communication among people, facilitated by the Internet, is so open and so immediate. You have friends in other companies, you email them, you talk to them, you are in the same communities with them whether they live in Detroit, New York, Boston, or across the globe. The walls between and within companies have become porous. So have the walls in the selling process. When you want to buy something, from a Palm Pilot to a week in Aruba, you can go on the Internet to find out what's best for you and who's offering the lowest price.

LEADING IN A FRAGMENTED WORLD

Our world today is more fragmented than it was 50 years ago. On a global level there are more countries now than there were at the end of WWII. At the same time, pictures from space reinforce that Earth is a single, fragile sphere in a vast universe.

In the West there has been a fragmentation of media as a few mass magazines and television networks have given way to the rise of special-interest publications, 500 cable television channels, and now the Internet. Likewise, business is less focused on groups or mass audiences. Instead, marketing has become a process of defining and reaching smaller and smaller market segments, a process that ends at some companies when each product or service is unique for each customer. It is therefore becoming increasingly difficult to move large groups in one direction, especially given the diversity of employees, managers, customers, suppliers, dealers, and regulators.

It is far more appropriate these days to build a rock band, a theater group, or a circus where no single performer is much more important than another, and the role each plays commands respect. With the growing sense of social and media fragmentation, people feel a sharper need for community.

But Generals do not build communities. They build proprietary companies. They build dictatorships. That is a far less effective management style today—and will be worse in the future—because, more and more, a firm has to rely on a network of partners who must cooperate to be successful. It must offer employees opportunities that are meaningful to them. It must build a relationship with each customer, not simply make a sale.

Like many things in life, leadership ranges across a continuum. At one end is the pure General, at the other the pure Provocateur, and there are probably few leaders who stand at either extreme. Rather, we all contain some elements of each.

Nevertheless, overwhelming forces— social, technological, economic—are turning the tide of history in favor of the leader as Provocateur. The more we think and act like Provocateurs, the better we will do in the twenty-first century. Provocateurs will be the ones who understand that the Internet is about communication, not information; that leaders must build a community rather than a company (and how to do this); and that customers have become nomads (and what to do about it).

Successful Provocateurs are a combination of educator, entertainer, Sherpa guide, and head concierge. The educator establishes the organization's mission clearly and visibly and uses every opportunity to teach through example, word, and deed. The entertainer creates an environment in which people feel connected; they entertain in such a way that people do not feel they are being passively amused. The Sherpa guide is able to conduct others—customers, employees, suppliers, even entire companies—along an uncertain path, developing individual skills and strengthening commitment at every step. The head concierge knows both what customers want and where to find it.

Different leaders reflect different mixes of these qualities. Some Provocateurs are more educator than Sherpa guide, just as some are more entertainer than concierge. But all share these elements.

Also, a would-be Provocateur who has *only* the characteristics of, say, the educator is not a business leader but an educator. In other words, business leaders must still manage their organizations; they must provide vision, goals, appropriate tools and training, and rewards. The real issue is how one manages in this age of the Internet and that, I believe, requires dexterity in all four roles. I'll show how leaders with these qualities create a provocative environment, find and challenge the best employees, and form an inner circle that can complement the leader.

By the end of our journey together, you will see why it is so important to become a Provocateur for your organization and for yourself. In the end, it brings not simply business and professional success, it offers a richer and more rewarding life.

2

COMMUNITIES –
NOT COMPANIES

We're . . . creating a community of geographically dispersed, highly linked entities that can rapidly learn and quickly innovate based on each other's experiences. We used computers to do most of that linking.

—Tom McMakin,
former Chief Operating Officer,
Great Harvest Bread Company

The Great Harvest Bread Company, founded in 1976 by Pete and Laura Wakeman in Dillon, Montana, is a wonderful example of building a community, not just a company.

Today, Great Harvest is a chain of 140 whole wheat bread stores in 37 states, all but one of which are franchises. Systemwide sales are around $60 million; the average store's sales are $450,000. The franchiser's sales from royalties and new franchise fees are around $3.5 million a year. The average profit per store is 17 percent before taxes and owner's compensation, while the franchiser's profits are 19 percent before taxes.

The Great Harvest franchise is unusual, to say the least.

The contract's cover page says, "Anything not expressly pro-hibited by the language of this agreement is allowed." Tom McMakin, Great Harvest's former chief operating officer, says, "Most franchises are built on the notion of command and control, where someone comes up with a mom-and-pop notion, a blueprint for a successful small business, and they stamp it out across the country. You're basically buying your-self a job if you've bought yourself a McDonald's because if, for example, you come up with a great new hot dog recipe, you're not free to install that in your store. We're pursuing something completely different. We're using franchising to create a competitive advantage by creating a community of geographically dispersed, highly linked entities that can rapidly learn and quickly innovate based on each other's expe-riences. And we use computers to do most of that linking."

McMakin says that Great Harvest has two basic tenets: "We have absolute freedom for our owners. Owners are encouraged to create little bread stores in their image and in the image of their communities. We feel that gives an authentic 'mom-and-pop' feel to the stores. But at the same time, we're a community of mom-and-pop stores that know what we're doing. That means we enable owners to stand on the shoulders of 140 other owners' experience as well as 25 years' worth of experience. We do that primarily through what we call an extranet—because it's remotely accessed. But still, it's in essence an intranet."

Great Harvest's extranet allows members of the commu-nity to participate in chat rooms and threaded discussion groups, and search archives of organized articles. "We find there'll be a great rush of enthusiasm about how to best bake chocolate cherry bread in November. Two years later a brand-new owner will be in the situation of baking chocolate cherry bread for the first time and will wonder what's the best way to do that. They'll log on and be able to find that old set of conversations between smart owners that gave tips on how to do it best."

The founders of Great Harvest have always been in love with the idea of freedom, although the Wakemans insist that each bakery plays music, has a friendly atmosphere, and observes certain production standards. "We've always thought that our product here at the franchise company was to sell the opportunity to create a business that belongs to the franchisee," says McMakin. "So our businesses have always been connected, but different. We've connected them using conventional means—newsletters and the sorts of things that other companies use to connect geographically dispersed locations. When the Internet was first born, we all had CompuServe accounts and then we migrated to GroupWare. Currently we use an Outlook-based and extranet-based system for connecting people. It was just a natural fit."

Milling wheat and baking bread are hardly new innovations. Great Harvest's phenomenal success has been based on technology to build a community of franchise owners who can share ideas and information. If one manager tries something and finds it successful, it spreads through the community and everyone benefits—Great Harvest, the individual franchisees, and customers.

Communities are where people go to find new ideas, seek opinions on issues, voice unhappiness, and exchange views. Indeed, organizations themselves are comprised of myriad communities fostered within their own departments, divisions, Web sites, extranets, and intranets. Customers in such a community are not an annoyance or a distraction but an integral part of the neighborhood. Employees are not lazy time-servers; they want to do their best for the company and customers. Suppliers are not con men, lying about quality and delivery schedules; they are part of the family. Reporters are not necessary evils; they are trying to find interesting stories for their readers and viewers. Clearly some customers are impossible, some employees are in the wrong job, some suppliers are cheats, and some reporters are hacks. But these are the minority, and the Provocateur deals with them as exceptions rather than the rule.

YAHOO BUILDS A COMMUNITY

Jerry Yang and David Filo (both of which carry the title "Chief Yahoo") never planned to start a company and build a community (if not a virtual city). As Ph.D. students at Stanford they thought they'd work for small companies involved in computer-aided design software for semiconductors. However, before they finished their degrees, says Yang, "The CAD industry grew up, consolidated, and had pretty much become the province of two or three big companies." So in 1993 they began looking for something else to do with their lives.

When they returned from Japan after a six-month academic exchange program, they discovered the World Wide Web and Mosaic, software that one could use to search for information stored in computers all over the world. Yang and Filo wrote software to go with Mosaic to collect statistical data on NBA basketball players so they could update the performance of an imaginary "rotisserie" basketball team. However, the Web was growing so rapidly it was becoming almost impossible for anyone to know what was available, and Yang and Filo began to create software that could organize Internet sites into categories ("Yahoo" is an acronym for "Yet another hierarchical officious oracle").

Once the company began to take off, Yang and Filo realized they did not have the background to run the enterprise and they began looking for a CEO. Tim Koogle, who they hired, and has since departed in the over-zealous Internet purge of the early 21st century, told *Fortune,* "Here were a couple of very smart guys who were genuinely passionate about what they were doing and not in it for the money or the ego or the fame. They also struck me as being well aware of what they didn't know. Then there was this thing they'd built called Yahoo!. And in spite of the fact that they had spent no money on promotion or branding, it was getting what we call strong organic takeup—people were finding it, and using it, and telling their friends about it. Whenever you see something like that, it usually indicates that it's something people really, really want."

Yahoo!, which started as a simple search engine, has added everything from online calendars to free email, online auctions, a travel agent, financial news, and a business-to-business marketplace. The company has attracted users into its community by being flexible. Yang has said, "If you use Yahoo! for mail, fine; if you use it for chat, great; if you use it for finance, who cares, as long as we get you into Yahoo!, because chances are we can keep you there a little longer. So there's not a set way for all of our customers to use our service. That flexibility in our product—that it does lots of things, that it's there and quickly responsive when you need it, and that it lets the user choose without censorship or being told what he ought to look at—all of that started as early as 1994. It wasn't a business decision we made later."

Savvy companies can create communities through multiple channels to provide constituencies with a place to communicate with the company and each other. The Internet aided this revolution, and through its evolution, has driven models for effective community building. Indeed, many would say that the millions of online communities—from Yahoo! investor chat rooms to AOL travel message boards to internal company message threads—are the true heart of the Internet.

Communities will exist whether the company participates in the process or not, and woe to the leader who chooses not to participate. In fact, every organization must nurture seven basic communities, including customers, employees, shareholders, partners, reporters, regulators, and competitors. Some companies are so serious, they are appointing chief community strategists to develop and manage all aspects of building a sense of community. "A chief community strategist is equal parts policy maker, minister of culture, ombudsman, and operation manager," *Business 2.0* has reported. "Matthew Bannick, vice president of customer support, handles this role for eBay, the site that is the ultimate in convergence of community and business. He is a direct link between eBay's 3.8 million community members and the company's top executives. He and his team develop reports for managers based on feedback from eBay message boards, customer email, and monthly face-to-face meetings with community members." All this feedback, of course, is what I am calling dialogue data.

Television created a culture of isolation as people sat passively in front of the set. Ads always show a family (Dad, Mom, son, daughter) watching together, but nobody talks with one another. After 50 years of television and urbanization, many people feel a sense of loss for small-town life even if they've never lived in a small town. They imagine a place where neighbors look out for one another, where the pharmacist on the corner of Main and Elm knows your allergies, the waitress in the diner serves your regular breakfast, and the banker will always help with a loan. It isn't New York or Los

Angeles or Chicago, and it certainly isn't Phoenix. It is the imaginary community of 10,000 TV shows and movies.

With the advent of the Internet and technology, there is a possibility for interaction. It is getting to know people's needs better from a business perspective, learning what kind of company community they want to be part of, understanding what they really want to buy from a company. As simple as this sounds, it marks an important transition from a marketing point of view because the company leaves the television set and drops the monologue. It stops talking *at* people and begins talking *with* them to make relationships better and, by extension, to make products and services better. The General would not have cared; his company is still on TV to announce, "Here's what we're selling. Buy it. It's good for you. You'll like it. Trust us."

If a business presents its ideas thoughtfully and clearly through all points of customer contact, the process actually allows customers to be innovative themselves and be part of the firm's innovation process. The process could actually point a company toward new businesses.

At the same time, a company does not want to oppress people with its environment. It wants a mix of possibilities and opportunities so prospects and customers feel it is a place in which they can reflect on whether to buy something, that it is not being pushed on them. How do you create an environment that lets customers and others feel as if they are in control?

A small example of what *not* to do: A friend changed the Netscape browser from his wife's name to his. In the process, however, either he did something wrong or the computer hiccuped, and now whenever he tries to open the browser, an error message pops up on his screen: "Talk to your network administrator." Since he works alone, he does not have a network administrator. He can reach Netscape's site, but he cannot figure out where to address his problem or even how to ask about it. Netscape has an area of frequently asked questions, but my friend's problem is not covered. He would send an email, but there is no obvious address. He would pay the typically exorbitant telephone service fee, but there is no telephone number. "I like the site," he says, "but I'm less and less patient with it because it won't help me."

HOW TO CREATE A COMMUNITY

What are the characteristics of building a community? I think you must have a general vision and idea of how the community is going to look first. This means sitting quietly to ensure that you have learned enough from customers and prospects to know the attributes they and you want to see in your community/company. They may have no interest in knowing how the server works, but they do want to know it will handle the traffic without delays and lost messages.

Real communities have an infrastructure: roads, water pipes, sewer lines, electricity. They have security: a police force, fire department, highway department. There are schools, a library, stores, restaurants. They may have a hospital, a college, factories, hotels, shopping malls, parks, and different neighborhoods. The communities I talk about in this chapter also have the various components that make them a true community.

On the simplest level, building a business is based on the different pockets of excellence that it will need—finance, marketing, operations, and so on. Just as a town has to hire teachers and police and sanitation workers, a company has to find the people who are best at specific tasks. Today's market requires employees at every level who can relate to customers on what a product or service should have in it, what it should do. Those points of contact create a dialogue to create a living, breathing community.

The longer you're part of a community, the more you know where to go for the things you want. If you're interested in art, you know where to find the art museum. You know where to find the bookstore, the town pool, the best restaurant. The longer people belong to a company's community, the more they know where to find the things they want such as the specials, the new products, and the financial results. Subliminally, customers develop loyalties the way people do to their hometowns.

"We've always said that the way in which people are connected is the easy part," says McMakin at Great Harvest. "The hard part is to create a culture of real sharing. It's not entirely obvious how to do that. People come home from the end of a day baking bread, in our case, and they're tired and they're a little bit scared. It's scary getting on a big community bulletin board and posting a thought or asking a question or looking stupid or something like that."

Great Harvest has done a number of things to create a sharing culture. The Wakemans, McMakin, and other managers explicitly tell their staff and colleagues that "we feel each of us has certain gifts and talents in this world. So if I opened a bakery," says McMakin, "I might be good at promotion or front-counter work. Someone else is going to be good at the back-office systems, the accounting, or maybe even the maintenance of the machinery that goes into the bakery. Together we're stronger than we are apart. At every convention I'll give a speech, and that's a strong part of that speech. We're stronger together than we are apart. We try to create a sticky environment. We try to make it fun. We do not have any prohibitions against using our extranet for personal purposes. Owners will develop friendships in a face-to-face meeting, like a convention or a peer group. We encourage them to use our extranet to talk with each other about how their kids are doing, that sort of thing. People post jokes on our extranet all the time. We're not bugged up trying to prohibit that kind of activity as in, 'Hey, that's not on task. We're not marching toward our annual goal with that kind of activity.' We say instead, 'That's what makes being on our extranet fun and interesting after a hard day's work.'"

Good communities are not monologues (the way totalitarian communities tend to be). They are not isolated. A General tends to view a company almost as a bunker, under siege from competitors, regulators, disaffected customers, and prying reporters.

In contrast, Provocateurs want to create a feeling there are no walls between the company and the outside world. The company has a constant interaction with other businesses, with prospects and customers, with suppliers and regulators, and with other communities, all of which tend to make it stronger.

"The speed of innovation has changed dramatically," says John Kish, the former president and CEO of Verbind, a Boston-based company that analyzes consumer Internet behavior through proprietary software. "Consequently, for any group to keep up with what is going on in today's business environment it needs to enlist the help of other people and of other firms, often who have different views of the market than yours. Without that, you can find yourself moving only so fast. You are going to be bounded by your own company's ability to innovate, or your own company's ability to perceive the market. Whereas if you built meaningful relationships—in our case, with people as diverse as advertising agencies, technology providers, and television stations—they all come together with a synthesized view of a customer. We have found it allowed us to begin taking a completely different point of view in terms of what is going to happen to the market."

Building a community also requires the willingness to listen to everybody. Michael Bonsignore, the former chairman and chief executive of Honeywell International, spent two days a week traveling to Honeywell plants and offices in the United States and abroad to meet staff. Not long ago he held a general "town meeting" in Honeywell's Freeport, Illinois, sensing and control unit and then met with 20 "high-potential" employees, answering questions and listening to their thoughts. "Since no other executive but me is present at those small meetings, there's an atmosphere of candor, and a chance to get a unique perspective I would never get if I stayed in my office" in Morris Township, New Jersey. Bonsignore understands that an employee far from corporate headquarters, who suddenly finds himself part of a large new enterprise, has to be asking, "Where do I fit in, and how do I stay connected?" It's reassuring if the CEO shows up eager to exchange thoughts.

FIND A COMMON MISSION

Most entrepreneurs with a product or a service have an idea of what customer need or want it will fill because they themselves have the need. Their ideas appeal to people who have a problem like their own. Answering that problem gives them a positioning, a target market, and an idea of where to advertise and what to say.

The entrepreneur's idea is similar to the base attraction of a traditional community. If I live in the Northeast and am tired of snow, a base attraction is the warm weather of Florida or Arizona. If I am a biotech researcher and look at a map that shows biotech firms and warm weather, San Diego pops up because it has both.

The big issue is how a company turns the initial attraction to a community into a long period of innovation. It must build on itself and create not just a larger customer community, but a tight-knit customer community, one that people feel so good about, so part of the environment, that they would not think of leaving.

In the early days of Microsoft, people felt a real sense of community when they could understand the DOS commands to run their PCs. Bill Gates, a General in Provocateur's clothing, was able to make people feel this was a good community to join. Then people woke up and realized they were locked in. They discovered they had no choice, and Microsoft was not listening to them anymore—indeed, it believed it did not have to listen to them.

Gates did build excitement. He caught the wave of a burgeoning new industry and while he was locking people into his system, they did not realize they were being locked in. Microsoft took advantage of a new category's excitement, and that is great. Gates did what any good businessperson would do. I don't think he was being completely straightforward with his customers, though, because they were not going to have a lot of flexibility. A business should, at the very least, create the feeling that the customer has choices.

The Provocateur understands that customers get excited by and attracted to communities with a common value system or common value chain. A good example is Saturn.

Saturn was a brand-new automobile company—new car, new company, new factory, new people, new dealers, new location, new everything. In the first five years of its existence, Saturn sold 1 million cars by marketing its relationship with customers as much as the cars themselves. It broke with all other automobile marketers by strictly observing a no-haggle price policy. And, among other community-building efforts, the company has the Saturn Extended Family Database. Owners fill out an online questionnaire that includes occupation, ambition, favorite book, favorite movie, favorite music, and so on. To search for kindred souls within the database, one types in keywords like "California" and "Shakespeare" and up comes a listing of email addresses of Saturn owners in California who love Shakespeare.

At the same time, there are subcommunities within the larger community. I live in a house, but I am out taking a yoga class, shopping at the grocery, visiting the pharmacy. New York City has Manhattan, Brooklyn, Queens, the Bronx, and Staten Island; Manhattan has Greenwich Village, Soho, Yorkville, Harlem, and Washington Heights. General Electric has dozens of subcommunities: aircraft engines, power systems, plastics, NBC, capital services, employers reinsurance, aviation services, medical systems, global consumer finance, industrial systems, lighting, appliances, and more. The issue is how they complement each other, work together, understand the vision of the larger community.

Provocateurs understand that as their companies grow, there will be niche communities within them and how they work together, help each other, and share ideas will ultimately determine their success. Great Harvest Bread Company, Harley-Davidson, Saturn, and others are doing it well. The company may someday become like a big city, but still have the intimacy and value proposition of a small community.

GET OUT ON THE STREETS

Generals have difficulty overcoming their aloofness and getting out on the street to see what is really happening. Jill Barad, the former CEO of Mattel, really thought that by buying The Learning Company in 1999 for $3.5 billion she was going to connect with the next generation of children because they wanted educational software instead of Barbie dolls. The Learning Company was responsible for "Where in the World Is Carmen Sandiego?" and "Myst," but by the time Mattel bought it, The Learning Company had not produced a hit title for several years. The purchase was a bizarre leap, and Barad made it without any real analysis of what children truly want.

Indeed, if Barad, who enjoyed spectacular success marketing Barbie dolls, had visited the nearest Toys "R" Us before buying The Learning Company, she might have had second thoughts about the purchase. Customers could cut the $30 price of the Learning Company's "Dr. Seuss Toddler" CD-ROM in half by mailing in a $15 rebate coupon. According to a Forrester Research report, many educational software publishers lose money on every sale. Publishers spend $100,000 to $2 million developing the software, allow the retailers a $7 to $10 margin on a $30 product, and, in some cases, have rebated the entire $30 to the consumer.

Under Mattel, The Learning Company's software sales fell for 11 consecutive months; at the end it was losing $1 million a day. Mattel's board fired Barad, and the new CEO handed over The Learning Company to Gores Technology Group for no money down and an undisclosed amount of "future consideration." Mattel still had to absorb a $440 million after-tax loss and was still on the hook for $200 million in Learning Company debt.

The Mattel example suggests that because they are removed from the customers Generals often misanalyze their communities. They often mistake what the community wants and needs. They decide to install art deco lights along the streets of Williamsburg. The lights may be beautiful, but they are out of place in that particular community.

Provocateurs work from the ground up and know exactly what's happening on the streets of their communities. They have a passion about what they are selling and feel a real connection with customers. The Provocateur's biggest job in building a community is keeping the power and cycle of innovation going—to keep the wheel going, to keep fresh talent. It is important to make sales, but the firm will make more sales if people view it as an innovator and if it responds to customers because they are part of the cycle of innovation.

A company might be driven to create an environment that attracts and gives the kind of presentation that addresses many of these issues. Much e-tailing to date (like most Internet advertising) has been coming at the Internet from the wrong direction. It is wrong to put nothing more than a catalog on a computer screen. A site should be infinitely richer, with links to all kinds of information and other company resources. It should not be so obsessed with The Product.

Generals were obsessed with The Product. Here is the car; are you going to buy it or not? Here is the outfit; do you want it or not? Here is the software; take it or leave it.

ENGAGE CUSTOMERS IN NEW WAYS

Those Provocateurs who are involved with e-tailing (clearly a minority) employ a different process. They attempt to engage customers in a way that was not possible before. They offer convenience (24 hours a day, 7 days a week, 52 weeks a year), selection (every book in print, every stock on every market, specifications on every product in inventory), competitive prices, or all three. One reason for Amazon's success has been its claim to have quick access to virtually every book in print. People were attracted by that original claim. Once customers began to buy, Amazon was able to focus on their interests and suggest other titles. You've bought Sylvia Plath's poetry; you'll be interested in a new biography of her. You've bought four Haruki Murakami novels; you'll want to know about the new one.

Toys "R" Us tried to replicate their store online. Here is the row of dolls, here are the cars, here are the games. If a Provocateur were leading Toys "R" Us, she would think that if people want to go to the store, they'll go to the store. If they want to shop online, they'll expect easy access, quick turnaround, and convenience. What can Toys "R" Us offer online that is better than our physical stores?

One idea would be the ability to group and regroup toys by customer-defined communities: toys for boys, toys for girls, toys for infants, toys for toddlers, toys for six-to-eight-year-olds, action toys, science toys, classic toys, safe toys, games, crafts for kids, fun toys based on a Toys "R" Us rating system, science toys under $15 for eight-to-ten-year-old girls. It is as if the customer can rearrange the store's layout and inventory at the click of a mouse. Rather than be overwhelmed by the physical store's volume and variety, each individual shopper can focus on just those relatively few items she feels are appropriate for her child. Customers should be able to rate and comment on toys the way readers rate books on Amazon.com.

A great e-tailing site is RedEnvelope.com. They can help a wife find a 25th wedding anniversary gift for her husband who has everything. But leaders will not stop there. They continue to gather information about the customer that will allow the company to retain her as part of the community. The firm sold her a package for their 25th anniversary and will now suggest birthday presents for her husband, so she continues to return. The company makes it easy and interesting to come back to the site. "We know from what you've told us and from past purchases that your husband likes wine; did you know the great new wines are just coming out of northern California?"

Where do you get that intimacy? Carry the community metaphor a little further. The local wine store down at the corner, where the owner's hobby is California wines and where you have been shopping for years, is now an online business. Rather than the owner's hobby and personal knowledge of your habits, the Web site has access to virtually every vineyard everywhere and has a record of your every purchase. Many of us tend to buy more in a shop—or Web site—that provides that kind of advice and selection than in one that does not.

DEVELOP CUSTOMER COMMUNITIES

An individual belongs to many communities. You live in a neighborhood in a town in a county in a state in a country and each of these offers different benefits: town water, county roads, state universities, national parks. But an individual also belongs to communities of interest such as a church, PTA, bowling league, quilter's club, or Rotary. The number of communities is limited only by the range of human interests. AOL has been able to build their total community by adding neighborhoods of common interests, much like a traditional community would have a little theater, yoga class, and a library book club.

Apple Computer has been able to develop a community among customers and employees. I remember going to Apple trade shows and finding it fascinating that people who had nothing to do with the industry would line up to pay money and get a badge to go to a computer trade show because they were so excited by the Macintosh.

The idea of community means one cannot always distinguish among the members. In the early 1990s, as Lotus began to prepare for the launch of Notes Version 3, the company realized that a groupware product needed a community to demonstrate the product's benefits and uses. Notes, of course, is the software that permits workers all over the country—all over the world—to share files no matter what computer they are using locally.

Lotus CEO Jim Manzi and Vice President Larry Moore said, in effect, let's grab some users who really need to work together, like a big accounting firm, and let them test and work with the product, then use them as part of broadening the community. We'll get those people enthused about this great new product and let them tell the story.

Price Waterhouse (now Price Waterhouse Coopers) was a major Lotus customer and was interested in the product. If Notes lived up to its advance billing, Price Waterhouse was going to buy a Notes license for almost everyone in the company after they tested it. Lotus management decided that rather than have Lotus talk about Notes, have a customer do so, which I believe takes marketing to the next level. In a real way, the customer becomes a part of the company, a part of the marketing effort.

When Lotus introduced Notes Version 3 in Boston, Sheldon Laube, who was the head of IT at Price Waterhouse, spoke about the firm's experience and did a better job of selling the products than the Lotus executives. At that point, the line between Price Waterhouse and Lotus almost vanished. They became a group of executives who had a common goal of streamlining processes, so the overall vision and mission started to dissolve the customer-vendor relationship boundaries.

Lotus itself was really a community. You didn't really feel like you were working for the big company. You felt you were part of changing the landscape of business. The employees connected to founder Mitch Kapor's original idea of changing the nature of business to harness the power of personal computers. A breakthrough product like Notes just kept the momentum going. People used phrases like "the family of Notes users" and "the Notes family."

Lotus then created Lotusphere in Orlando, Florida, an annual trade show/conference/seminar that is essentially a Notes love-fest. Lotus shares information about new versions of the product, and there are speeches, great food, and entertainment. Earth, Wind, and Fire performed at one Lotusphere. Lotus knew it wasn't going to sell Notes on its own; it needed a whole set of third-party applications to make it work. So they built a true community around Lotus Notes by incorporating the third-party suppliers into the company. They became an integral part of the organization. The success of this community building is reflected in Lotusphere registrations. Lotus limits attendance, and it took about two months to sell out the first Lotusphere in 1996. Five years later, it took two and a half hours to sell out the 2001 event.

One of the marks of a good community is a sense that one can influence it. One can stand up in a town meeting and be heard. If I truly believe I am a member of the Saturn, Schwab, or Snapple community as a customer, employee, or supplier, I believe I can have an impact. The effect may be tiny, but the community/company will listen to me. I will be a part of it. I will be more motivated because I want to make the community succeed.

In its early days, AOL attracted people with community-based content such as breast cancer rather than commercial content. Steve Case is a Provocateur who understood the importance of community-based attraction of customers. He knew people were roaming. They were growing disenchanted with big brands. They had less time. He saw that as a huge opportunity, and he felt what they were looking for was content around their lives. So he gave them information about things that interested them. The early AOL was communities around topics like breast cancer, sports, and gay and lesbian issues. AOL then built a commercial structure around these interests.

In a sense, AOL and portal sites like iVillage, The Globe, or The Street are like a good magazine that identifies an interest and attracts advertising because the advertisers want to reach the audience the site attracts.

The Provocateur, to lead a successful community, will have to know how strong an environment should be to attract and keep customers and when is the right time to introduce a different relationship. Amazon.com knows my profile from the books and the music I've bought from them. That is different from knowing the prescriptions I buy from Drugstore.com, the Amazon affiliate. If Amazon is smart, once I start buying prescriptions for my asthma, they will send me authoritative articles on the use of steroids in inhalers for asthma. They should not inundate me with emails on allergy-free pillow sales or books on herbal medicines, which would drive me away as a customer.

There is an element of educative marketing, of building the environment, and then using technology to send messages to people that will keep the dialogue going while they may be visiting other places. In some cases they may want a company to follow them with email, and in others they never want to hear from the company again and will resent any email.

The way to address this customer sensitivity is through permission marketing ("Do you want to receive email messages from us?"), and more and more sites are using it. But a company has the opportunity to be smart about building a dialogue. Instead of the almost annoying opt in or out question, the question should be far more specific: "Would you like more information about allergens?" "Would you like to know immediately about any design defects that develop in your new car?" "Would you like to know about new books by Danielle Steele?" Rather than bother the customer with distracting suggestions, what can you offer that the customer values?

BUILD EMPLOYEE COMMUNITIES

What are the elements of a communal company? It includes vision, communication, philanthropy, and incentive. Employees feel good about working for a company that is known for contributing to the community. Today many companies offer employees the opportunity to take time off on a regular basis to do volunteer work.

Incentives in building the community include creative individual philanthropy or a common cause that makes employees feel like they are in the right place and would not leave for a $100,000 stock option at another company. Because a firm needs to invest so much energy into creating a relationship with customers, it should spend as much energy building an environment that retains the employees who service those customers.

George Conrades is the CEO at Akamai Technologies, which, with its network of more than 12,000 servers in 62 countries, distributes, stores, manages, processes, and delivers data and applications using the Internet in a cost-effective and scalable way for robust electronic commerce and rich media experiences. Conrades believes that hierarchical command and control has traditionally characterized a make-and-sell environment, a "here it is, don't you love it? How many more would you like?" environment. In contrast, a service business is a sense-and-respond, a "what can I do for you now" environment, which "requires you to have a more collaborative process in your firm . . . people constantly interacting and talking to one another . . . working together to make it happen as quickly as possible. We foster a collaborative environment here to get at better ideas. We argue like crazy, testing one another's assumptions, then make a decision, and go. That is the epitome of a collaborative environment, but it has to do with the cycle time of today. Firms from Day One talked about their environment of collaboration, the importance of people, and good communications. They sent you to management schools for stuff like that—but that isn't the way they necessarily operated."

Provocateurs must understand the balance between technology and the need for human contact through meetings, celebrations (promotions, birthday parties, retirements), and other events. They almost become an orchestra conductor; the individual players are alone when learning their parts in a new piece, but come together when it is time to rehearse and perform. Provocateurs know when to physically bring people together, and that skill will become even more important in the future so that people do not feel isolated in their cubicles or home offices. As the Web evolves, people will be able to see each other as they talk or send a message, which will ease the sense of isolation.

PROMOTE A COMMUNITY OF SUPPLIERS

Companies have always had a community of suppliers. Some treated their suppliers as partners, even buying them to make the relationship closer. Others have treated their suppliers as serfs, demanding concessions, setting unreasonable deadlines, and squeezing them on price.

Provocateurs understand that even when it is possible to abuse a supplier without any immediate repercussions, it is a mistake. Suppliers should be valued members of the community, and the Internet can dramatically improve their value. General Motors, for example, is making its Supply Chain Data Warehouse available via the Web to more than 5,000 suppliers and supplier organizations worldwide. "One of the early reasons for data warehousing was to optimize your own business," says Ron Shelby, acting chief technology officer of GM. "Sharing data with suppliers is an extension of that. To be more agile, we have to have a supplier base that's equally agile."

GM is treating suppliers almost as if they are another division of the firm. GM suppliers can log on to a secure Web site via a browser and ask about quantities of supplies shipped, delivery times, and prices, helping them optimize their own product planning, ability to source materials, and fulfillment processes. North American suppliers are able to check warranty claims GM receives for the components they provide. GM now gives suppliers access to quality metrics stored in the data warehouse. "It will help them understand where they may have production problems," says Cherri Musser, business services process information officer at GM. "That means improved quality on their part and, in turn, improved quality on our part."

By making suppliers Internet partners via the Web, companies are able to cut costs because fewer people are involved in the purchasing process, improve efficiency because there are fewer mistakes in orders, and increase profitability because less money is tied up in parts inventory. Dell Computer's suppliers have direct access to Dell's sales and can therefore plan their own ordering, manufacturing, and shipping. The danger that a supplier will misuse such information is more than offset by the efficiencies the information provides.

ENCOURAGE A SHAREHOLDER COMMUNITY

Most people who invest in a company do not usually feel they belong to its community. To make shareholders feel (as much as possible) part of the community, Provocateurs look at all constituencies and the communication avenues and content that can be available on each. Shareholders obtain information from the media, company letters, email, and wireless access. (Japanese stockholders routinely check stock prices on their DoKoMo cell phones.)

Shareholders want information. Too often company management hides and then announces, "We didn't meet our numbers." With the Web, the opportunity exists to be completely open and make information available every day. Companies need to appoint spokespeople to address the shareholder audience. The CFO should speak in everyday terms, give examples, list what to expect. Shareholders ought to be able to access the same information as an analyst, be able to listen in on the conference calls the CEO or CFO has with analysts. That is already happening, of course, as more and more visitors can hear such calls—live or recordings—on corporate Web sites.

Shareholders should also have access to analysts' reports. The company should buy the rights to share that information—positive or negative—with shareholders. The goal should be to build trust so that shareholders retain the stock for a long time. It does not help the individual stockholder, the company, or the economy when investors look no further ahead than the current quarter's earnings, the situation the Generals have managed us into.

PROMOTE A COMMUNITY OF INFLUENCERS

The Web almost immediately became the largest vanity press in history. For a time, anyone could post anything on the Web and people believed it. Pierre Salinger, the former White House press secretary, thought he'd learned the truth behind the explosion of TWA Flight 880, obtained international coverage, and then learned that his source was an unverifiable Internet posting. Since the Web allows anyone, anywhere, to say anything, it is more important than ever to know the information's source.

Validation will be important in the Provocateur's world. Journalists have always been great third-party validators since they are (presumably) disinterested reporters. It is important to work with top journalists so that they can validate the company's story. Companies also should have third-party sources that people respect as a resource. Companies need to develop a whole validation family—journalists, third-party experts, and academics.

A company should develop strong ongoing relationships with the 10 to 15 most important third-party influencers to tell the company's story in good times and bad. These validators can help support a new product or service, or validate a new market. But validation is not only saying how good the company is or praising its products. Sometimes news will be unfavorable or negative. That's the price we pay for editorial objectivity. But if the company maintains a trustworthy relationship with its influencers, it will be able to make its position clear during difficult times.

Third-party validators are key when a company has bad news. For example, when a company reports poor quarterly earnings, a financial analyst can help explain the company's long-range mission and strategy for success. The goal is to create an ongoing narrative that is more than a knee-jerk reaction to today's bad news. In the case of a calamitous event—the Tylenol poisoning, the Intel chip flaw, the Pepsi syringe scare—third parties are a critical part of the community to help explain the news. "The worse the news, the more effort should go into communicating it," says Andy Grove, chairman of Intel Corporation.

If a Provocateur has built a strong community, it will usually come to her support. Customers will allow a mistake, especially if management is open and forthright and takes responsibility. Intel waited a bit too long to address its chip problem, but then it did explain publicly how they were going to fix it, sending that word by email, which largely defused the crisis. Automobile companies have come a long way in being far more open about product defects—perhaps because they have no choice.

DEVELOP A COMMUNITY OF REGULATORS
Legislation in a borderless economy will only become more important. If France can demand that Yahoo block French customers from Internet sites that sell Nazi memorabilia, why can't China demand that every site in Taiwan be blocked from Chinese computers? It is important that managers know about legislation that will affect what they do. Just as we have bellwether states in legislation—if a law passes in California, Connecticut will look at it—we are going to have bellwether countries.

Many high-tech companies have tended to view Washington as another sales opportunity, not as a source of legislation and regulation that can help (or hurt) them market their products and services. They send people to sell things to the government, rather than looking at ways the government could affect the way their customers view what the company is doing, or affect the way they will conduct commerce in the future. The technology industry only recently discovered Washington as a place that wanted to listen, wanted to learn, wanted to see how business and government can together keep the momentum and the growth while making sure that ordinary citizens get their due and their money is not wasted.

Dr. Charles Vest tells me that one of the things he has done consistently since he arrived as president at MIT is to build stronger understanding and support in Washington for U.S. science and research and advanced education. "When I first surveyed that scene," he says, "it was crystal clear that universities never worked well together. Each one was pushing its own area or its own project. My colleague Jack Crowley and I have worked together for almost 10 years to do two things: first, build coalitions. We worked together with all the major public and private universities. Second, to whittle the messages down to simple, fundamental, understandable things. I would like to think that we at least had some influence on what has been a dramatically better environment in Congress for our universities. I think no one representing a single institution's interests could have much impact."

It is important to reach out to government if only to protect the relationship with the customer community. Companies have points of view; they should not keep them to themselves. At the same time, wise executives are open to other opinions. They may agree Internet privacy is a serious concern and perhaps the company should change the way it gathers information. Just because government bureaucrats hold an opinion does not automatically mean they are wrong.

The government will always be there—not as an enemy, not as a friend, but as something management has to deal with. If Microsoft had addressed the government's concerns immediately when they arose in the early 1990s, it would not be facing a crisis as this book is written. Does Bill Gates believe, as a General Motors CEO apparently believed, that what's good for Microsoft is good for America?

It is also increasingly easy through instant message polling to discover how people view issues, which means the Provocateur can go to government meetings armed with information that can help in the decision making. The company becomes an integral part of policies that affect their communities. It creates a balance between the needs of business and the needs of citizens.

ENGAGE COMPETITORS

Provocateurs *want* competitors. Over the years, emerging company managers have told me, "This is such an original idea, we don't have any competitors." It is hard to keep my mouth shut at this naiveté. They should want competitors if only to validate their idea so they can raise some money and generate interest in their community.

Provocateurs always know their competitors and are always open to dialogue with them about certain initiatives concerning innovation and industry standards. This is not just for technology companies; it can apply to insurance, furniture, trucking companies—every industry. Provocateurs always search for how they can do better and be better. They know they can learn from their competition and are not worried that a competitor will learn something from them.

In my experience, many top executives personally resent their competitors; they feel their lives would be so much easier if the competitors just went away. That feeling is troubling because (1) competitors don't go away and (2) good competitors make a better industry. The related issue is management focus: "When you run a company, you can do it to serve your customers, or you can do it to damage your competitors," says Bob Metcalfe, the founder of 3Com and now a venture capitalist with Polaris Venture Partners. "The road to ruin is when you turn your attention to your competitors instead of your customers."

If you want to play at the top of your game, play someone better than you. Provocateurs understand that competition is actually healthy for their companies. Good competitors keep them from becoming complacent, lethargic, or unresponsive.

In today's world there are numerous examples where a business is a competitor in one area and a partner in another. It is important to keep a place open at the table. People learn from their competition, from playing, from working. General Motors, Ford, and DaimlerChrysler, while doing their very best to sell their own brand of automobiles, are cooperating to develop Covisint, an independent business-to-business online auto-parts market. The three companies spend nearly $250 billion annually on auto parts and supplies, and the site, which the FTC has approved, replaces each company's separate procurement site and will be open to other automakers.

MEET THE MATURE COMMUNITY CHALLENGE
The Provocateur's ultimate challenge arrives when a community matures. It is one thing to manage an organization that is growing and new opportunities are regularly opening for employees and managers; it is very different when the

company has matured—or shrinks—and the opportunities and challenges dry up.

One issue is size. In many ways it's easier to have fun when the company has 10 people than when it has 1,000. One suggestion is that when a unit grows to around 200 people, the company spins it off. I asked George Conrades what he will do when Akamai grows well beyond its current 1,000 employees. "I don't know," he says. "We'll learn how to be Jack Welch. But he's got a unique company in General Electric with the way it is structured. He really has a conglomerate, a lot of smaller companies."

I believe the number of employees is less important than the Provocateur's ability to rewrite the architecture on an ongoing basis to add smaller, more focused groups that are based on their core competencies and bring greater value to the community as a whole.

Everything hinges on the quality of the product or service. The only way to obtain that quality is through managing dialogue so that communications is at the core of everyone's job. Everyone has to understand the need for communications between employees within the company and between customers and suppliers and the company.

Through the Industrial Revolution, actual communities grew up around industries—for example, Detroit around cars, Akron around rubber, Pittsburgh around steel, Chicago around meatpacking, Battle Creek, Michigan, around breakfast cereal. (Anyone interested in why this happens should look at Michael Porter's book, *The Competitive Advantage of Nations,* The Free Press, 1998.) At the time, there was no marketing to speak of. Because companies were still meeting unsatisfied demand, few had to think about identifying customer wants and needs. They had to worry about manufacturing the product, training a sales force to sell it, and shipping the orders.

As the economy developed, however, marketing became critical. People lost a sense of community as companies became remote from their customers. Now there is an opportunity, through technology, to give people a sense of community, of being involved, of connectedness. This sense is perhaps more important now than ever before because customers have become nomads.

3

THE NOMADIC
CUSTOMER

Now you need to establish far deeper, interactive connections with customers if you hope to keep them.

—Eric Almquist,
Mercer Management Consulting

Power is shifting as customers have become nomads. They are no longer limited by geography. The Internet and new democratic governments have opened new worlds and new choices, allowing people to travel from one brand to another at the click of a mouse or auto dial on their cell phones. Sometimes they stay with one company's brand for a while— but only if the company provides value, quality, responsiveness, performance, and connection.

Customers become nomads for many reasons, but three seem basic:

1. Marketers train them to respond to price alone.
2. They have many more product and service options than in the past (and will have even more in the future).

3. They both know more and can learn more about products, services, and companies than ever before.

And, as always, they become nomads because companies abuse them.

My wife and I bought a small vacation house in Florida. The telephone company told me that only Sprint provides long-distance service in the area. I thought that with deregulation one could use any long-distance provider, but I signed with Sprint. Although its customers in this vacation- and second-home community are affluent, Sprint demands payment within 18 days after it mails a bill or it switches off the service. Restoring the service takes four to seven days and costs $15.

After Sprint switched off my service, I called the company to say my wife and I usually pay all our bills within 30 days and explain the situation: "You send a bill out, and it takes a few days to get from Florida to Massachusetts where I live. It might sit in the office for a week or more because I am traveling. By the time I get it to the people who write the checks, 25 or 30 days may have passed. In the meantime, you've sent a notice and shut off the service."

Sprint also sells telephones, answering machines, and fax machines, and I had bought $2,500 of equipment for the house. "I would think," I said to the customer service representative, "you'd look in your records and see that someone who paid for all that equipment and paid for the service for the first 90 days on a credit card is probably good for the monthly charge. But you turn off the service because the bill wasn't paid in three weeks? I don't understand that."

"I'm sorry sir," she replied, "but that's our policy."

I said, "How can we solve this right now? Can I just give you a credit card that you can use? Do you want me to sign something? Or send you an email? Just charge the card every month." She said they could not charge a credit card, but they could obtain direct payment from my Florida bank. "Fine. Send me the form."

Which she did and which looked as if it were printed in Chinese. I filled it out quickly, accidentally giving one wrong digit in our account number—so the form did not compute. Sprint then sent me a huffy letter that said I did not have such a bank account although I claimed I was going to arrange payment . . . blah, blah, blah. I realized I had made a mistake, corrected the account number, and returned the form. In the meantime, Sprint sent another we-are-going-to-shut-off-your-service notice.

I now believe that Sprint, which is supposed to be a cutting-edge marketing company, is a corporate bully. The moment another company offers long-distance service in south Florida, I am gone. I will be a nomad as soon as the chains come off.

MOVE PROSPECTS THROUGH DIALOGUE

Marketing's job has to be two-fold: It has to move prospects to buy through dialogue, and it has to encourage them to stay in the community by creating a better environment and relationship—an idea that not every executive grasps.

In the past, people bought things out of a certain loyalty. Your mother washed her face with Ivory soap, so you bought Ivory. Your father swore by Chrysler engineering, so you bought Chrysler. Your friends wore Levis, so you bought Levis. You were aware of certain brands, and for the most part, you saw no reason to change.

Marketers started to take that loyalty (or inertia) for granted. Some marketers feel that people will continue to buy their brands just because they've always bought their brands. At the same time, they believe they can attract people who buy *other* brands through price promotions, coupons, special offers, and giveaways. When every marketer bases its attraction on a price promotion, brands tend to become commodities and customers tend to look for the best price. As we all know, finding the best price now that we have the Web can be childishly simple.

In 50 years of talking *at* people through television advertising and other marketing communications vehicles—no true dialogues or building a strong relationship with customers—the Generals missed the opportunity to create the new communities. Instead, they created the nomadic customer we have today.

At the moment, advertising agencies (and most of advertising's client companies) cannot get away from the idea of a monologue; they talk at prospects through traditional advertising and banner ads, which are traditional ads pretending to be something new. Companies have one objective: to sell products. Once a person buys, the company does not much care about her until she's ready to buy again. For some customers and some products and services, that's fine; the customers do not want any more involvement or information, and the products—many package goods—do not require more.

But for many, many other customers and products and services, people *do* want more—more information, more service, more involvement—and the products lend themselves to offering more. "Now you need to establish far deeper, interactive connections with customers if you hope to keep them," according to Eric Almquist, an Internet expert with Mercer Management Consulting. One way to do that is through digital storytelling, combining multimedia technology, the Net's global reach, and the emotional appeal of personal stories. "By listening and sharing with your customers, you're essentially having them cowrite your brand," said Kit Laybourne, chief of Oxygen Media's digital storytelling project, which solicits stories about everything from diet nightmares to blind dates from hell. "And they're doing it for nothing or next to nothing."

As an example of how this can work, Coca-Cola sent an artist/digital storyteller to Oaktown, Indiana, to record Iris Bell's story. When Iris's father, Kevin, left the family farm the day after Christmas in 1944 for the South Pacific, he took six bottles of Coke with him in his duffel bag. The first time he got homesick, he drank one. He shared four more with fellow soldiers in Burma. He never opened the last bottle. He carried it back to the farm, where it sat for more than 30 years on the mantel in the living room. When the farmhouse caught fire in 1990, Kevin—by then an old man—rescued it from the burning building, the only material possession he fought to save. Kevin has since died, but Iris Bell keeps the bottle on her kitchen counter. "Daddy always said it was a good-luck charm," she says. "My daughters will get it when I'm gone."

Coke's chief archivist Phil Mooney believes "you simply can't buy advertising as emotionally potent as this. Digital storytelling helped us pop the lid on a lot of emotional ties that we just hadn't been able to capture in our marketing before the Net."

In 1996, a major brewer invited my interactive marketing company to make a presentation. The head of marketing said, "Come out; the Web is starting to be pretty interesting." This was a company that already had a following, the semblance of a community. College students would make pilgrimages halfway across the country to buy cases of their beer. As its reputation and sales grew, the brewer started advertising like all the other big beer companies, focusing on their home area. Their ad agency advised that there was an association between sports and beer, and so they created some of the dumbest commercials on television. Now the company wanted to do more.

When we met, I said, "The Web is a different medium. You have to understand how to communicate to your constituencies through different media at different levels. You don't want to say the same thing every time to the same people. Marketing has progressed beyond that. Let's build on your heritage. You have this cache, an excellently made regional beer that has a following all over the country, that's brewed in the middle of the most beautiful part of America. Why don't you do things on the Web site that you can't do on television? What are some cool places you've discovered to camp out? Where are some of the cool new trails? Have the company bring this whole world to people online. Demonstrate how to climb a mountain, how to rappel down a cliff . . . or follow some college kids around as they explore the national parks. One individual might be interested in hiking. Another might be more interested in the foliage in Joshua Tree National Forest. They can click and get a brochure on the foliage or the endangered species of the Joshua tree. Create an environment through an architecture that allows an individual to drill down into a particular interest and become part of a community. At the end of the day they have a beer and talk about seeing a family of moose, or being afraid of the bears. And while they're at it, visitors could download a coupon for a six-pack. Build on the community idea to the point where eventually the company can sell apparel or tents with the company logo on them. Once you set the architecture for community, you could keep going."

The head of marketing looked at me after the presentation and said, "You know, Larry, this Web things sounds important, but all I really want to know is can you put the advertising spots we run on the NFL onto our Web site so people can click and see them online?"

I said, "Someone would have to drink a case of your beer to click on one of your commercials." We didn't get the account, and the brewer missed an opportunity to involve customers, create a community, and build a relationship through personal interest. You want to create an environment in which a person wants to camp at your place one night. You want to be on his (or her) nomadic map.

The advertising industry has to get over presentation and into dialogue marketing, marketing that is communication centered and community based. Lawrence McNaughton, the managing director of Corporate Branding, a Stamford, Connecticut, consulting firm, said in March 2000 that some companies try the easiest approach to help a sinking corporate brand: "They throw some new advertising out there." But a brand is affected by media relations, internal employee communications, investor relations, local community relations, the company name, packaging, logos, even the architecture of the company buildings. Rather than telling passive consumers why a product is wonderful, companies should be talking with active customers, listening to their suggestions, gripes, and ideas.

Marketing based on a dialogue with customers will, I believe, grow only more powerful as the Web becomes even more visual than it is today, and as it does so, it will become more emotive. The CEO will talk directly to prospects, appealing to their heads and hearts. People will be able to pretend they are test-driving an SUV, watching the scenery change as they put the vehicle through its paces. They will hear stories from real people like Iris Bell who have had real experiences with the product.

Every purchase decision, of course, is a mix of intellect and emotion. People buy some products and services—new electronics products, major appliances, insurance, vacation tours—mainly after intellectual inquiry. They buy others— soft drinks, beer, cigarettes, haircuts, massages—mainly through an emotional attraction. Few purchases are purely intellectual exercises or the result of blind emotion; most are both. Today, the Web mainly offers information. As it becomes more and more visual, companies will be able to make more visual and emotive presentations. Rather than appealing only to customer emotions or only to the intellect, they will be able to touch both.

In the past, many consumer goods marketers depended heavily on emotional presentations to sell their products. Think of how little solid, useful information the average television commercial (or magazine ad) provides. The Web lends itself to furnishing much more information about products and services than was ever practical in the past. With it, marketers can in theory tell every prospect virtually everything she would ever want to know (and more) about a given product. A company can set up a kind of *Consumer Reports* online that will answer a question immediately or find the answer and, through email, send it in a friendly, warm, comforting way.

Although the Web will have color, sound, and motion like a traditional television commercial, it will be interactive. Click on the product during a demonstration and obtain more information about a particular feature or benefit that interests you. Fill in your interests, click on the screen, and learn what is available for someone like you. The possibilities are limited only by human imagination—in other words, endless.

There has been a migration of power from manufacturers to retailers (Wal-Mart, Best Buy, Circuit City, etc.) and from retailers to customers who, for the most part, do not need any particular manufacturer or retailer. In their effort to attract and retain these nomads, e-retailers will be offering a theaterlike, visual and emotive environment in the future. Customers will decide to give the company personal information or not. If the company establishes trust and creates a rich, emotional environment that touches the heart while it answers the head, it will be incredibly effective.

The world is moving toward a more narrative presentation, and Provocateurs are experts at the narrative. Ben & Jerry's is a great example of a narrative. The narrative is that two young guys wanted to make great ice cream, took a course, and began modestly. Their ice cream was so good they had to expand production to meet demand. But Ben & Jerry's was more than rich ice cream. Unlike a giant, faceless dairy corporation—Sealtest, Hood, Borden—Ben & Jerry's supported its Vermont community by buying milk locally. It bought brownies for its Chocolate Fudge Brownie ice cream from a New York City bakery employing homeless people. The nuts in its Rainforest Crunch came from the Amazon rain forest. It was donating 7.5 percent of its profits to worthy causes. When you spooned into a pint of Ben & Jerry's, you were not just eating ice cream, you were doing your bit to make the world a better place.

A great narrative tells a powerful story that engages the business's constituencies. It makes people want to talk to the company. It is not simply telling a story, it is involving people so they want to interact with the company because of the narrative. They want to make the company, its products, its service—even the world—better. The company that tells an incomparable story about its products, its people, and its community will flourish (always assuming the stories are true, the products do what they're supposed to do, and the people are engaged). These are narratives that touch your heart, as well as your mind.

As we move into the next era of marketing, if a business can encourage prospects and customers to stay and enjoy its environment, it will learn a lot about them. They will become an integral part of that community. John Kish, the former president and CEO of Verbind, tells me that his company assumes that real-time analysis of customer behavior offers marketing insights. Verbind markets services that companies can use to track customer behavior—specifically what action to take when the behavior indicates the customer is either doing something different or is considering doing something the firm wants to reinforce or prevent.

Kish gives a simple example from retail banking. A customer may interact with a bank 60 or 70 times a month, writing checks, using ATM machines, calling for balance information, making deposits, and so on. One Verbind product records every single activity so the firm can distill individual behavior. "We understand when she begins shifting those patterns and if the shift is significant," says Kish. "If she begins using a lot of ATM machines that aren't owned by the bank, it may indicate she is thinking about moving money to another bank. In the case of automatic payroll deposits, knowing someone always makes a deposit on the first and the fifteenth, and the fifteenth has come and gone without a deposit, you want a system that can understand that the lack of a behavior is every bit as significant as the behavior itself. If you did not make a payroll deposit, it means you are dead, you have lost your job, or you are changing banks. Bank marketers tend to only care about the third alternative, and the information gives them a chance to do something about it." Knowing that someone is thinking of leaving the community gives a company an opportunity to learn why and make a change before that happens.

TALK TO THE PEOPLE

Fifty years ago, Procter & Gamble introduced a laundry cleaning product that was better than soap, a powder detergent called Tide. (And who of a certain age will ever forget "Tide's In! Dirt's Out! T . . . I . . . D . . . E . . . Tide!"?) One product, one message.

Today, P&G offers New Tide with Bleach, Liquid Tide with Bleach Alternative, Tide Mountain Spring (powder or liquid), Tide with Bleach Mountain Spring (powder or liquid), Tide High Efficiency (powder or liquid), Tide Free (that is Tide with nothing as a powder or liquid), or New Tide with Activated Hydrogen Peroxide. Given that most of these come in a variety of sizes, a supermarket's Tide section can fill almost an entire aisle.

P&G justifies such brand proliferation on the basis that "individuals want different things from a detergent. Some people want convenience, while others focus on cleaning power. Sometimes people choose a detergent based on the fragrance (or no fragrance!), while other times, the type of water you have in your home determines which detergent works best. For all these reasons and more, we have developed an entire range of Tide products."

While it is true that individuals want different things, when the number of offerings starts to confuse the customer, it erodes customer loyalty. People begin to question whether P&G was taking care of or listening to them; they have so many choices and so little time, for many people it becomes easier to move on. Another brand may not be as good as New Tide with Activated Hydrogen Peroxide, but the moment a customer starts to waiver, to question her loyalty, the company has missed an opportunity. The idea that people will be loyal to the new product because it carries an old name borders on brand arrogance. It is a General saying, "Our customers are going to be loyal because they've been loyal for 50 years."

Procter & Gamble would probably argue that it exercised the typical marketing process, which uses focus groups heavily after the product was developed. But did it develop Tide Mountain Spring because people said they want their clothes to smell like a mountain in the morning? (And who wouldn't? But then, what does a mountain spring smell like?) Or did it develop Tide Mountain Spring because Lever Bros. had introduced Downy Mountain Spring? Was Tide's product in response to a genuine and growing customer want or to a perceived competitive threat?

(It could, of course, be both, in which case P&G's move was appropriate. But in my experience, companies often introduce a product not because its customers have indicated an interest but because a competitor has introduced one. It's the maybe-they-know-something-we-don't school of marketing.)

But even if Procter & Gamble is entirely correct that different people want different things from their laundry detergent and that each Tide product suits a large and growing niche of a gigantic market, every new version multiplies the communication challenge. What is the real difference to my dirty laundry between Liquid Tide with Bleach Alternative and New Tide with Activated Hydrogen Peroxide? And how does P&G tell me quickly enough and engagingly enough that I listen and not throw my hands in the air and reach for the box of All?

I have been loyal to Advil since a physical therapist told me it is one of the better anti-inflammatory drugs, especially for back problems. Recently I went into the pharmacy to look for my familiar little brown pill. There were only three bottles of the brown pills, but there was the giant green gel, there was the red-and-yellow coated, there was fever, cough, cold Advil, there was back pain Advil, there was a bigger tablet Advil. And I wondered whether they are really all that different. Maybe I should look at something else.

People become nomadic when they have choices, when the economy is in flux. Do I buy all my books online or continue to go to the bookstore? Do I call L.L. Bean or send an email? During this transitional period, the confusion creates some disconcerting feelings about how to buy and how to conduct commerce.

The company's connection with a customer weakens because it no longer understands his interests, concerns, and needs. How does it lose that contact? Through inattention, inertia, and ignorance. Gerber apparently lost touch with its customers and then market share when Earth's Best introduced "natural" baby food—no salt, no sugar added—and stormed onto store shelves. Had Gerber been listening carefully to its customers, it should have realized things were happening in America. The children of the 1960s began having children, and they are concerned about what they eat, what's in their food, and what they feed their babies.

With a little awareness, Gerber might well have cut Earth's Best off at the pass and come out with a new line of baby food, a product extension (as it eventually did) for this large and growing segment of the baby food market. It could have researched before it was beaten by the innovation of someone who probably talked to parents who were using Gerber and saying, "I really wish I could just have the time and the blender to cook the carrots and do it myself." Earth's Best probably went, "Bingo!"

Companies led by Generals in the old economy have been interested in customers mainly as consumers. They responded to customer complaints to sell the product, but they didn't aggressively try to build the relationship. Thoughtful customers wonder why they should be loyal if the company is not attempting to build the relationship but instead puts them on hold when they want to ask a question.

Unresponsiveness has created this nomadic customer and, I think, a redefinition of service. Pundits have talked about a shift to a service economy for years and warned that if companies didn't meet customer expectations—or better, exceed their expectations—people would start shopping elsewhere. This is why "levels of communication" have replaced "levels of service." The promise made determines the purchase. The promise may be general—"We'll be at your house on Tuesday the 19th"—or specific—"We'll be at your house on Tuesday the 19th, between 10:00 and 10:30 in the morning." The more specific the promise, the higher the price, which most people understand. The follow-through on the promise determines the satisfaction, which, if high, leads to repeat purchases and recommendations.

Failing to follow through, however, leads to communicating the bad experience to relatives, friends, and, thanks to the Internet, thousands of strangers. With more Americans getting online every day and chatting with strangers about whatever is on their minds, communicating a bad experience means broadcasting that experience to other people.

Generals tended to ignore customers' real interests in dialogue and interactivity, forcing them to become nomadic.

Generals believe they know what is best, and what's best for the company is best for the customer (a version of "What's good for General Motors is good for America"). What's best for the customer is a quality product at a competitive price—whether that's what the customer wants or not.

People sometimes become nomadic because companies create niches within niches. As they have options, people tend to want more choice. For example, 20 years ago few people would have thought of going on an extreme sport vacation or ecotourism safari. It was inconvenient and brutally expensive. There were certain common vacation options, and people called their travel agent who set up a vacation in Bermuda or the Caribbean or Europe. We now have a group of individuals who have found a new niche—hele-skiing or windsurfing or white-water kayaking. They became nomadic because of a society that has created individuals who want more diversity; who have interests they can now satisfy.

Customers also take control of what fills their interests. It is the individual drive to define oneself as a unit of one. I am an individual and have certain needs, and these are the things I will do to try to find the communities that best fulfill my needs. If I like ecotourism, I will find the sites that promote trips to the Galapagos. If I like quilting, I will find sites that tell me about quilt shows, quilting supplies, and quilting cruises.

International Data Group, among its other businesses, publishes technology-related trade magazines around the world. Pat McGovern, the founder and CEO, tells me that virtually everything his company has done successfully was suggested by a customer. For example, "Years ago we actually walked in and met Steve Jobs and said, 'We want to do an Apple II publication,' and he said, 'Don't be stupid! That's history.' He said, 'I have a secret project, the computer of the future, the Macintosh, and you have to sign a huge nondisclosure agreement, etc.' And then he said, 'I want you to do a magazine for this computer, and I'll subsidize the first year's subscription for everybody.' I ended up doing that."

McGovern says, "When we reacted to the customer's suggestions, we were very successful. And when we went ahead and did something on the basis of our internal planning and then tried to sell it to the market, it inevitably would not go well. People were saying, 'All right, sell me on this.' I realized the key to success was not in my being helmsman—the idea that I am going to control the big boat and make it go according to my navigational chart. The key was to set up a process that allowed for as high-frequency communications as possible with customers and then with people in the company, so we really did know what was happening and what people wanted."

WE WANT TO JOIN COMMUNITIES

People are smarter customers today, and they have less time than ever. They want to be part of a community that fits their lifestyle, their needs, and their budgets. The sooner corporate leaders understand this desire and the sooner they establish a dialogue with prospects and buyers, the better they will do.

Increasing access to knowledge has made customers more nomadic because they can obtain more information about whatever they want and can therefore think about buying virtually anything they can imagine (and can afford). At one time, if there were a Ford dealer and a Chevrolet dealer in your immediate area, you thought about buying a Ford or a Chevrolet. Today, people will buy virtually any brand of car from any dealer within a hundred miles.

The Web also means that smaller companies with specialized products have more opportunities to find customers.

Small toy makers, as one example, are finding customers on the Web. "Real estate in the big stores has always gone to the names that everyone knows, and the small companies have been banging their heads against the wall to get shelf space," says Chris Byrne, a toy industry consultant in New York. As the vice president of merchandising at one online retailer said, "These products are cool, but they never saw the light of day in the traditional stores. But we have an open toy policy here. Anyone can submit a toy to us, and if we think it is great, we will buy it."

One advantage an online retailer has over a chain (and this is true for fields other than toys) is that it doesn't have to stock hundreds of stores. Web sites can buy a few items and then gauge customer demand. If an item sells out, the e-tailer can order more. If it doesn't sell at all, it has not lost shelf space.

The point is that the Web makes it easier for a person to find the particular needle she wants in a global haystack. eBay is a good example. It offers auction excitement, but more significantly, it offers people a place to find things they could not easily or conveniently find before.

Provocateurs anticipate the prospect's need for knowledge and are open, honest, and direct in the environment they have built. Because of this, people will come back for more. If nomadic customers continue to receive the honest, direct, and forthright information about the company's innovations, and if they, no matter how marginally, are involved in the development of products and services, they will keep coming back to the community. They make it their home.

People are designing their own environments, and a company becomes part of that. Customers, if they are happy with their experience, become the company's best salespeople. If you truly reach out and educate and talk with the customer, then word-of-mouth, which hasn't changed in years, becomes even more powerful in today's environment. It does so because technology allows someone to pass along the word with the click of a mouse: If someone you know has a serious disease like breast cancer, you can send them to a Web site. The site may happen to be connected to four commercial sites, but the woman has gone there because of someone else; someone who has a common intellectual or emotional interest in her situation.

Great marketing makes customers wear something on their sleeves or caps. It is the feeling that a school or a fraternity or a club can engender, the feeling that it will always be *my* school. Even 30 years later an alumnae will write a check because she loved it. She has good memories and still has good friends from that time.

That is less about selfishness and more about connectivity, more about not wasting someone's time and really being able to connect you with the feeling and the information you want. The person chooses to come to your theater, and when she does it had better be the best theater possible.

Many Web companies are making the same mistake that traditional marketers make and ignore customers (or do not put the customer relationship at the center of the enterprise). Generals lead a number of Web companies; just because someone heads an Internet company does not mean he (or she) is a Provocateur—or even a good manager.

George F. Colony, chairman of the board and CEO of Forrester Research, interviewed a number of dot-com chief executives before the market and the companies collapsed. "There was a fanatical focus on valuation—getting public and liquid—while value—what the customer eventually gets—was a backseat discussion."

Compared with the traditionalists, "Many of the Web company CEOs lacked depth, experience, and common business sense," says Colony. "Their commitment was short-term—three years on the average. They talked about their highly fluid workforce—a constantly changing cast of characters, cashing in on the promise of more stock options and an IPO and then cashing out, post-offering, in search of another pre-IPO company. The business thinking of these CEOs centered on simplistic and cliché mental models: 'Be like Amazon!' 'Advertise, advertise, advertise!' 'It's a land grab!' 'We don't want to be profitable too fast.' 'B2B is the place to be.'"

Many of the Web company commercials on the January 2000 Super Bowl dramatized this corporate ignorance and hubris. Why spend $2 million on a Super Bowl spot? To build brand awareness? To flash a 60-second monologue at millions of people who do not know who you are, do not understand what you do, and do not care? That is not brand awareness. It is money down the toilet. The companies would have been better off giving $2 million to a charity and getting the publicity for it.

But they should have spent the money studying their prospect and customer base to learn how they could create an environment that will establish a dialogue and a platform for sharing information they could use to develop products and services.

Rick Wagoner at General Motors tells me the corporation's business model now revolves around the customer. "Our biggest advantage is that we have more automotive customers than anybody else, so our goal in life is to please them with our products and our services, and our expertise in those can lead us into other businesses that leverage and build on the expertise. The customer is really the centerpiece of our whole business strategy." Thinking about the customer relationship has become the litmus test GM is using to think about what businesses it should be in.

One may think the nomadic customer is a negative—our disloyal customers looking for something else. Actually it is a positive if you understand why people become nomads and what they are looking for. It is good that people look for other opinions. It means that companies have opportunities to attract customers while they're searching. But what are they looking for?

WE WANT COMMUNICATION, UNDERSTANDING, AND TRUST

Because customers are no longer limited by geography, they sometimes stay with one brand for a while—but only if the company provides value, service, responsiveness, performance, and connection. These basic demands, however, are a complicated order to fill. Consumers want value, but value is not the same thing as low price. Value is the right price for the product. A pair of designer shoes may cost $250, but if they are by the designer of the moment, the customer (certain customers) will perceive them as worth the price. A pair of sandals bought for the beach may be cheap, but if they fall apart when they touch the sand they're not worth the $2 they cost.

Value is in the customer's mind. It is not, unfortunately, something a company can mandate. Is a Volkswagen Passat GLS a good value at $23,800? Is a Honda Accord EX V6 a better value at $24,550? How about a Mitsubishi Galant ES V6 at $23,052? Or a Mazda 626 LX V6 at $24,445? These are all very comparable sedans, and the only answer is— everything else being equal: availability, dealer reputation, financing—it depends on the customer.

Most people would agree that a brand today doesn't equal a product. A brand is a promise. We grew up in an era in which the Generals ran companies and a quality brand equaled a quality product. One believed Mercury was a great brand because it sold a great car. One believed Compaq was great because it sold great computers. Hershey was great because it sold great chocolate.

Because the customer has become the center of an organization, the product has now moved into an orbit. In other words, the product (or service) is the fulfillment of a promise the business makes to the customer through dialogue. Therefore, the stronger the dialogue with the customer, the stronger your brand will be.

Obviously the company still has to produce a quality product; today that is usually the cost of entry rather than a differentiating advantage. But to me a quality product is way down the value chain. I expect that if I have a good dialogue with Ford, I will have a reliable, comfortable, safe vehicle as the end result. Obviously if Ford does not supply that, it's in trouble.

But the product has moved from the utmost importance to secondary. The customer's experience, dialogue, and interactivity with the company becomes the essence of a brand today. If customers are going to choose and live with a brand for the next 5, 10, or 20 years, they have to feel comfortable with and trust the company behind it. That comfort and trust grows out of the communication they have with the company. Therefore, the communication should facilitate a stronger dialogue that is at the center of creating great brands today.

With the advent of the Web and marketing's decreasing dependency on traditional monologue advertising—television, radio, print—branding has become interactive. The dialogue with the customer creates a brand position and conveys its strength. The issue is not one of privacy, although consumer advocates may say it is. It is about making the experience with the company the best it can be for the customer. And the stronger the dialogue, the stronger the brand. The weaker the dialogue, I argue, the weaker the brand.

As I pointed out in the last chapter, if a business cannot create an environment that is exciting and interesting and rewarding for the nomadic customer to visit, then it will not even be able to make its promise and its brand isn't going to be worth much.

We all know that communication has become far more personalized than ever before. As more and more people go online, a company's ability to communicate directly with and to hear from a larger percentage of its customers grows. The challenge is to treat the information people share with the company with respect and to use it in ways that benefit them and to show it does benefit them. Otherwise, businesses become insufferable snoops and gossips.

WE WANT SERVICE

Customers are looking for service, but not every customer wants (or needs) the same level of service. A properly-run company will offer different service levels for different people, levels determined by what the customer wants and what the customer is worth. It does not make business sense to provide a level of service that the customer does not want (so the customer decides one side of the equation), nor does it make business sense to provide expensive services to small and demanding customers (the business's side of the equation).

One level, for example, is a basic automated service like the email many companies use to notify customers it has recorded and shipped an order. At another level, Amazon automatically notifies a customer that a certain writer whose books she has bought in the past is coming out with a new title, and would she like to order it now?

Most people accept that automated level of service, but as purchases are more important or involve more dollars, they usually want more personalized service. At that point, the system should kick to a live human being who is going to be in charge of servicing the account or answering questions. The Lands' End site (www.landsend.com) offers customers the ability to talk directly and immediately to a person while on the site. Customers ought to be able to change the level of service they want. Some prefer to have a basic automated email relationship until they need something more personalized, and at that point, they should be able to let the company know.

Some customers exhibit nomadic characteristics when they want to be anonymous in the world of automation and online privacy. These are the people who search out the good communities. They become nomadic because they want to be in control. They say, "I want to see what's available, and the Internet lets me do so." Sometimes a person wants a relationship, and sometimes he wants a one-night stand. The company has to be sensitive to whatever the customers want: relationships for those who want them, transactions for those who want nothing more.

Companies also have to be careful to avoid their addiction to neon—garish Web sites with too much activity. They got addicted to neon when it was first introduced in the 1920s, and now whatever medium they use, they tend to flash: "Buy! Buy! Buy!" All right, already! I want something that allows me to move at my pace, at my need and comfort level.

WE WANT RESPONSIVENESS

A friend went online to research a new Chevrolet Suburban. She sent an email to the dealer: here's the color I want, the sound system I want, and so on. The system works because automobile dealers understand they have to sell their vehicles even if it means finding the right car on the other side of the state on another dealer's lot. My friend gets the color and features she wants. Now Chevrolet and the dealer have her email address and know we bought a new Suburban, the first redesign in several years.

One week goes by. No communication from Chevrolet or the dealer . . . no email. Two weeks go by . . . no email. Three weeks go by . . . four weeks. One would think that a company maintaining the email address of someone who has bought her second Suburban would have an automated email that says, "Mrs. X, are you enjoying the Suburban? Is the new design something you find exciting? Are you having any problems? Are you disappointed with anything about it? Is there anything we should consider changing in future models?"

Even if the customer is disappointed—or suffers from buyer's remorse—the company can establish a dialogue. Maybe the company can do something to cure the disappointment or reconfirm the customer's wisdom in making the purchase. Maybe the product isn't perfect, but with the customer's help and suggestions, the company will make it better next time. My friend would have told Chevrolet exactly what she thinks of the vehicle and probably had five suggestions for improvement. She would have entered into a dialogue.

At the same time, marketers walk a narrow line here. Debra Goldman wrote in *Adweek* that her new car manufacturer and dealer "sent us not one but three different consumer satisfaction surveys in the first months of our lease, plus a fourth letter asking us to return the third one. I finally did, writing over it in big red letters: 'For God's sake, we're satisfied! Leave us alone!'"

Goldman knows that the car dealer wants to cement "a 'relationship' that will lead to many happy years of us giving him our money." A computer-generated birthday card from the dealer "was nothing more than unctuous direct-mail hooey coughed up by an anonymous database. It felt about as warm and personal as that familiar junk-mail greeting, 'Debra Goldman! You May Have Won $10 Million!'"

The smarter companies are led by Provocateurs who say, "We had better be all over the customers in creating that environment—not bothering them—but creating an environment in which they want to be involved." Any marketing person will tell you that communication creates a relationship. Pat McGovern at IDG says, "Our customers should be our board of directors because they're the ones who have the ideas of where the markets are. Not only do they have the ideas, but they have the money to pay us to perform and fill those market needs. We set up a whole series of processes to do just that. We established a set of corporate values that said we are dedicated to keeping in close touch with all our customers and prospects. We want to be very flexible and keep changing and developing in the market. And we want to keep totally sensitive and very quick moving and reactive to the market."

This is communication with a purpose. The concept of dialogue data is part of the process of analyzing your customer's needs. As you look through your conversations and take out the nuggets, they can become "data." It is better than taking transaction data, which is what a General would do: "Let's rely on 'Are they buying it?' If they buy it, sell more."

Few companies are set up to respond to customer complaints or to customer suggestions creatively. But an enormous amount of innovation comes out of customer experience with your product or service, since some people find it doesn't work the way they'd like.

It's important that the customer never questions the company's authenticity or its goal to produce a quality product or service. I accept that GM is going to build a great four-wheel-drive vehicle, that Campbell is going to make safe, healthy soup, that FedEx is going to deliver my package on time.

A communication process conveys that goal. To build deep, strong trust takes time. The issue in our society is that everything is so fast, yet relationships of trust take longer than ever because people have learned to be skeptical, often cynical.

The Provocateur will say, "My goal is to build trust, to make our customer feel it's great." The problem in a lot of companies is that customers become a distraction. Then they become a pain in the neck as they whine for service, new features, better products, lower prices. Then they go somewhere else.

WE WANT CONNECTION

Provocateurs are immersed in dialogue in everything they do. Generals are accustomed to monologue. After all, 50 years of television is 50 years of monologue, and it shapes behavior whether you are the viewer or the creator of brand ads on television.

The advertising industry spent 50 years doing the research, then the creative work for commercials, and then broadcasting it at the viewer. A television commercial is no dialogue. You watch or not. The advertising industry's problem with the Web is that it has tried—probably because advertisers do not know better—to maintain the monologue model with banners and buttons. But few marketers have embraced the most important aspect of the Web—its ability to carry a conversation and to learn more about an individual prospect or customer. And the more you learn, the more effectively you can influence.

Provocateurs understand that the dialogue, the ongoing relationship with the customer, is at the center of the company.

Generals, including those in advertising agencies, keep the product or service at the center of the company. They believe that the product—its features, its benefits, its presentation, its price—is the most important thing but it's not, because people have so many product choices. The relationship with the customer is the most important thing.

The Web has shifted the balance of power radically. Buyers can say without raising their voices or being inconvenienced, "Wait a minute. If you're not going to keep me engaged, if you're not going to listen to me, I'm going to another environment." Instead of buying another Suburban in three years, maybe I'll wander over to the Lexus or the Ford Expedition site, a trip that is no more difficult than sitting in front of my home computer.

If Ford and Lexus marketers are smart, they will give people a good reason to come to their environment and then give them the tools to get them to stay there through dialogue. They will encourage a person to live in their environments long enough that she tells her husband, "I'm really tired of this Suburban. I think I'd like to look at the Expedition or Lexus more closely." Swoosh! There goes Suburban's opportunity.

This idea is easier to grasp if you are selling cars or computers or cameras—big-ticket items that, for most people, are considered purchases and that require service. But what if you are a packaged goods manufacturer selling your products in supermarkets or drugstores? A Provocateur will make sure that every product has a digital identity so that every single package can carry a Web address on it.

Even if you sell detergent, breakfast cereal, canned soup, or baby food, you can create an environment and engage in a dialogue with those buyers who want what you sell. (I'm sure that more people want to talk about their cars than their toothpaste, but those who *do* want to talk about pump versus tube should have a place to go.)

Tide, Cheerios, Campbell Soups, and Gerber all have Web sites, www.tide.com, www.cheerios.com, www.campbellsoup .com, www.gerber.com. These are more or less successful at encouraging a dialogue. A friend whose mouth was wired shut for two months because of an accident went to the Campbell site to ask if the company could suggest perfectly smooth soups that he could suck through his rubber bands. (Campbell's main page in fact carries the trademarked slogan "We have a soup for that.")

Before my friend signed off with his request, he had received an automated email from Campbell thanking him for his question and assuring him that someone would get back to him soon—a way to let the customer know the company had actually received the message. Two days later, a member of the Campbell Soup Web Team sent him an email, thanking him for taking the time to write, but "unfortunately at this time we can only suggest our Campbell Soup or Swanson Broths."

This customer feels, perhaps unfairly, that this response was inadequate. For one thing, other people subsequently introduced him to two perfectly smooth Campbell soups (Cheddar Cheese and Black Bean), so he wonders how well the Campbell Soup Web Team knows their product line. Also, Campbell might have suggested straining one of its cream soups or pureeing a soup in a food processor. Finally, and most radical, the team might have suggested another company's product. They might have lost a sale but built a customer's trust.

The ultimate goal should be to involve the customer in a product or a company's environment—into the culture, into the community. Marketing's task then is to make that environment richer, deeper, broader, and more exciting.

WE WANT TO BE PART OF THE PROCESS

The Provocateur's goal is to involve customers so deeply in the company's fabric they become an essential part of the company's development. Whether the firm manufactures shoes or ships or sealing wax, sells to consumers or other businesses, it can make—should make—the customer part of the company's innovation process.

C.K. Prahalad, coauthor of *Competing for the Future* and professor at the University of Michigan Business School, says that a vital source of company strength lies in the untapped power of its customers to exploit the Internet. He argues— and I agree—that the flood of product information, the ease with which customers can sort through it, and the potential they have to unite with other Internet users all combine to shift the balance of market power decisively toward the consumer. "We are saying that consumers are going to drive the firm. They are already doing that at Internet companies that started up without the baggage of traditional ways of doing business."

True, some companies have long tried to involve customers in the innovation process through surveys, questionnaires, focus groups, and other market research techniques.

The problem, however, is that these tend to be discrete events. Circulate a survey, tabulate the results, prepare a report. The Internet makes it possible to record customer reactions, comments, complaints, and suggestions continuously and endlessly—a process rather than an incident.

The mistake Generals made is that for a long time they did not foster a spirit of innovation, which is ironic since most companies started with an innovation—a better mousetrap, a better way to do something. As they grew, however, success blunted the drive to innovate. They said things like, "If it ain't broke, don't fix it," "Don't make change for the sake of change," or "Don't tinker with success."

If, because of declining sales or competitive pressures or both, the Generals decided they needed innovation, they bought some. The old school of management was to make innovation separate from the company's heart. It was not in touch with customers who can offer an endless river of suggestions.

Microsoft is an interesting case. Many industry people argue it has not been innovative, yet it is the most successful software company in the world. Bob Metcalfe, now with Polaris Venture Partners, says, "Microsoft is a fast follower, which is a respected modus operandi. They have really classy research people now, but their financial success has nothing to do with that. It is the other way around. They can afford classy people, but none of their revenue sources were produced by these classy research people. The company is just a fantastically competent company at executing, but they don't have new software ideas. They buy theirs."

The fast follower is an interesting point because one of the hallmarks of the dot-com fiasco was the talk about first-mover advantage, as if being first was in itself enough to guarantee success. "If you were a first mover, of course you would say that," agrees Metcalfe. "Now we are saying there are second-mover advantages, like scale, brand, competence, finance, business model. Microsoft has never been a first mover. Visicalc was a first mover. Then there was 1,2,3, and now it is Upsell. CPM was first, then DOS and Windows. Wang was the first word processor. Altaire or the Commodore PET was the first minicomputer. There are some first-mover advantages, but they are overrated."

With the Web, it is possible for the consumer or business customer to become part of business's development and innovation process. The Web becomes a crucial link in creating something new and better. Netscape was, to my mind, one of the first examples of this in what I call the 80 percent solution. People made fun of Netscape because they put out software that was 80 percent finished. But they wanted users to finish it. They wanted people's comments.

Look what's happening on AutoByTel, the car site. A person can link to a dealer where she will design the whole car, not just the colors. Is she part of the manufacturing process? Yes. Is she also part of the marketing process? Yes. She becomes part of the brand. And, ultimately, a Provocateur's goal is to have customers so involved in their theater, their circus, their rock group, their business, that they feel they are important to the success of the enterprise, not simply passive consumers of its products. That's the ultimate payoff: when someone feels, "I am proud to be driving this car because I was part of its creation."

Out of communication comes innovation. The General with the laboratory on the other side of the country (or world) would say at company (or industry) gatherings that the business had a genius Nobel winner who sits in the corner and has brilliant thoughts. That will still happen, and the thoughts could be the germ of a new product or service—certainly in the creation of new materials, new pharmaceuticals, new processes—but ultimately the majority of innovations will come from multiple conversations that involve both customers and companies.

For example, Honeywell's $5.2 billion air-transport business, which makes jet engines and avionics gear, uses Siebel software to track all of its interactions with customers and publishes monthly analyses so executives can spot problems and opportunities. Managers noticed airlines were frustrated with managing parts inventories, so Honeywell introduced new services to save them that headache. "Our focus used to be from the inside out. Now it's the reverse," says division general manager Lynn Brubaker. Without aggressively listening to customers, it's unlikely that Honeywell would have thought to create the service.

To attract nomadic customers to the community the company is building, the Provocateur combines the characteristics of educator, entertainer, Sherpa guide, and head concierge. So in what way is the Provocateur an educator?

4

THE EDUCATOR

*The most important thing is that leaders promote
an environment of constant learning. They make
sure the people they hire are in touch with their customers and spend the maximum amount of time
learning what the customers need.*

—Patrick McGovern,
founder and CEO,
International Data Group

The most effective leaders are more teachers than managers.
They teach by example. They tell stories from which employees, customers, suppliers, and others can learn important
lessons. Narrative is the way we help ourselves make sense of
the world.

Narrative is a teaching technique, telling stories to get
things across. The most successful companies in the communications age will have CEOs who are very good at telling
stories both for learning's sake and to clearly define and dif-
ferentiate the company. Provocateurs teach through narrative
where the company fits in the continuum of business and
why it exists. They tell customers the story of the product or
service and the history of the company to convince them that
this is a community to which they should belong. If man-

agers can tell powerful stories about the company, they can teach great lessons to associates. They build a narrative and create excitement around it much the same way one creates excitement around a theater group, a circus, or an orchestra.

Patrick McGovern at International Data Group says that he began with "International" in the name because "I started the company in 1964 with a dream of helping people throughout the world increase their quality of life by knowing how to use technology and providing the information to help them know. My dream was to reach 100 million people by the end of the century and a billion people by 2010." The combined readership of IDG's 300 magazines was well over 100 million in 85 countries by the end of 1999.

McGovern tells the story of how IDG came about. It was through the suggestion of Louis Rader, who was the head of Univac at the time. McGovern was selling advertising space for an MIT magazine, and Rader remarked, "What our industry needs is some good market information—like a good customer census—of where the computers are. I use my sales force to get the figures, the ones who complete the paperwork don't do a good job of selling, and those who sell don't fill out the paperwork. Either I have orders and no information or lots of information and no orders."

McGovern said he could put together a computer census. "At the time," he tells me, "the early 1960s, I knew there were about 10,000 computers in the U.S." Rader asked how much such a report would cost, and McGovern guessed $15,000.

Rader immediately said, "No, no, that's not acceptable."

McGovern, thinking fast, said, "Well I can probably get high school students to code the data on the weekends and keep the cost to maybe $12,500."

Rader said, "No, you don't understand, Pat. You have to charge at least $30,000, and then people will say this is serious information. They'll believe in it, in the high quality, and they'll use it. I want the information used in my company, and it's too cheap the way you're proposing it."

McGovern said, "You mean the higher the price, the more usefulness?"

Rader said, "That's right," and McGovern thought, "Boy, this is a great business."

That conversation was the origin of IDG. McGovern went home that night and wrote a computer census proposal. "Lou Rader was an inspiration because he showed me that quality information was really key. Everything you did had to be good quality, and then you could get a good value for it. Otherwise people wouldn't trust it to use it."

Through stories like McGovern's, employees learn about the character and history of the company. A company still has to build new products and develop new services, but it should tell stories about their development. It can even print the story on its product to involve customers directly in its narrative. One example: "Legend has it that in the 18th century a Spanish ship took refuge from a raging storm in the sheltered harbour of Dundee. Its cargo included Seville oranges which were purchased on speculation by a Dundee grocer called James Keiller. It was Mrs. Keiller who saw the potential of the bitter Spanish oranges. She boiled the oranges with sugar and the resulting product was the delicious preserve now known as Dundee Orange Marmalade. Although her recipe has changed a little since the 18th century, the traditions of using the finest ingredients are still used to this day. And the distinctive white pot is known world-wide as the Keiller symbol of quality."

Jeff Hawkins, the former CEO of Palm Computing and now CEO of Handspring, is a prime example of an educator telling a story. Palm's first product, the 1994 Zoomer, was a cumbersome handheld computer that bombed because it was bulky, slow, awkward, and quirky. Despite the failure, Hawkins says he knew people wanted a personal digital assistant (PDA). "Why else would they keep buying them—Apple sold 100,000 Newtons—and then, after a while, throw them in a drawer?"

To find out, he and Donna Dubinsky, Palm's cofounder, interviewed as many Newton owners as they could find. Hawkins says, "We asked users, 'Why were you disappointed, and what were you hoping it would do?' That was the real important question." He says they learned a PDA should fit into a shirt pocket, synchronize quickly and simply with a desktop computer, and be affordable—under $300.

Hawkins says they realized that people didn't want little computers as such. They wanted something to replace their address books and calendars. "Our competition was paper." Hawkins and Dubinsky measured the time it takes to look up and make an entry in a paper calendar. "I knew we had to be faster than that. Paper calendars were our benchmark."

All PDAs—Zoomer, Newton, the Sharp Wizard, Geo—shared a common challenge: entering information. For the device to be small, a keyboard had to be minuscule, which is awkward. You could use a stylus on a touch pad to enter data, but the software could not recognize different handwriting styles. Hawkins turned the question around. Rather than teach the software to recognize different handwriting styles, why not have people learn to write something the software can recognize? "People are smarter than appliances. They can learn," says Hawkins, talking like an educator. "People like learning. People can learn to work with tools. Computers are tools. People like to learn how to use things that work." Palm developed Graffiti, software that employs a simplified alphabet the program can recognize and people can learn in minutes. As one result, the Palm Pilot became one of the fastest-selling new electronic products in history.

Companies are full of stories—great sales that didn't look as though they were going to happen; the crisis when a key employee left; the decision to go in one direction rather than another. Another Jeff Hawkins story: The Handspring Visor PDA uses the Palm operating system, but it includes a slot for other gadgets, such as a modem, a cell phone, a digital camera, an MP3 player, a geosynchronous positioning device, and more on the way. A mechanical problem in the Visor's design was how to make the slot and connector low-cost and reliable. Solving those problems created a new one. The connection was so tight that when the engineers passed a Handspring prototype around a conference room only a woman who was a triathlete was strong enough to pull the add-on device out of the connector. Rather than lower the force, which would have weakened the connection, however, company lore says Hawkins told the team to design a dent in the back big enough for a user's thumb that would provide enough leverage to disconnect the device.

APPLY THE MONTESSORI METHOD

A good educator establishes the organization's mission clearly and visibly. The Provocateur/educator uses every opportunity to teach through example, word, and deed. Leaders should know that everything they do sends a message. If they are interested in learning, the people around them will see learning as a value. If they focus on educating employees, the employees will educate customers and suppliers.

The Provocateur/educator has two roles. One is teaching the organization's employees to be educators in their own right, learning and progressing and moving. The other is teaching the community that what the company is planning, doing, and producing actually benefits society. (If what the company plans, does, and produces does not benefit society, it has issues and concerns far beyond the scope of this book.) A great teacher in a classroom understands what motivates students; a great teacher in business understands what motivates customers. Moreover, a great teacher is almost automatically a great leader.

The educator challenges the individual much like a theater director who brings the most out of an actor or a coach who draws the most out of an athlete. How do you do that? How do you set up the situation to get the most out of your student? To get them to learn themselves, to motivate themselves? To achieve levels they never thought possible?

Take some real coaches. Duke University's Mike Krzyzewski is a leader who Rick Wagoner, the president of General Motors, admires (and not only because Wagoner is a Duke graduate). "Coach K has a set of principles he runs by. He brings kids into the program who understand the rules of the game and who buy into that philosophy. He's a master motivator—on a daily and long-term basis. People who know more about the sport than I do say he has the best attitude toward objectives. Obviously, he engenders great loyalty among his kids. And he engenders a lot of support from the whole university."

I mentioned John Wooden, the former basketball coach at UCLA, as another example of a great teacher and motivator. "I think most people would say he is one of the greatest college coaches of all time, with incredible principles, incredibly focused," says Wagoner. "He was able to change over the decades he coached, changing with the kids, their evolving motivations, and the gyrations in society in general. Wooden was able to stay right on top of that until the day he left."

NBA star Kareem Abdul-Jabbar, who played at UCLA, has written about Wooden's ability. "He was more a teacher than a coach. He broke basketball down to its basic elements. He always told us basketball was a simple game, but his ability to make the game simple was part of his genius."

Wooden's drills emphasized fundamentals, unselfishness, and the mental aspects of the game, says Abdul-Jabbar. "Our teams at UCLA had talent, but Coach Wooden's approach allowed that talent to be expressed. He believed that if you did things a certain way, it would lead to positive results. There was no ranting and raving, no histrionics or theatrics. To lead the way Coach Wooden led takes a tremendous amount of faith. He was almost mystical in his approach, yet that approach only strengthened our confidence. Coach Wooden enjoyed winning, but he did not put winning above everything. He was more concerned that we become successful as human beings, that we earned our degrees, that we learned to make the right choices as adults and as parents."

The best teachers are the ones who teach you how to think. Unlike Generals, they don't give you the answers. Good teachers give you the clues to help you find the answer yourself. I've always been impressed by Maria Montessori's theories that a child will learn naturally if put in an environment that contains the proper materials. A teacher-observer sets up the materials, "learning games" suited to a child's abilities and interests, and intervenes only when the child needs help. Montessori educators try to reverse the traditional system of an active teacher instructing a passive class.

The typical Montessori classroom consists of games and toys, household utensils, plants and animals the children care for, and child-sized furniture. Montessori educators also stress physical exercise, believing the child's motor abilities should be developed along with sensory and intellectual capacities.

Provocateur/educators create a business environment that is almost Montessori-like, where the leader steps back after establishing an environment of analytical thinking, of learning, of dialogue. How does one create the most passionate environment to learn not only about the customer, this company, or product but to get employees excited about that learning?

Philippe Kahn, who founded Borland International and is now the founder and CEO of LightSurf, says that in his case, "What makes it simple is that I try to always have the smartest people on the team. I like to bring in people who are smart and can learn fast, rather than experienced people who are set in their ways and won't learn as fast as the world changes. So I empower them and try to be the one making sure that everyone is communicating. I only step in to make decisions when there is not a rapid consensus reached."

I do not believe I have ever really criticized an employee in my business (I do not include those rare individuals I had to fire because they were dishonest or enthusiastically incompetent). My idea has always been to push employees so they realize their own limits and then ask for help.

When I started The Weber Group, the idea was to hire the best and the brightest people I could find and give them free rein. Who knew how far they would go? Phil Greenough is a good example. He had been at IBM in corporate communications and felt boxed in. We met for dinner, I liked him, and gave him part of The Weber Group to manage. A few people in the office came to ask, "Should he be running things?"

I said, "Yes, he should; give it to him."

"Well, he doesn't have any experience in running a PR agency."

I said, "No; but I think he's entrepreneurial enough, and I think people like him and trust him."

I just kept giving Phil more opportunity. After about three years, he came to me to ask, "Gee, where do I go next?"

I said, "Start your own PR agency."

He said, "I'm nervous."

I replied, "Just keep doing what you're doing. Leave The Weber Group. It's fine with me. How are you going to know how far you can go? You know you can always get a job. So, why don't you try it?"

He did and now heads one of the fastest-growing high-tech PR firms in the country.

No organization can (or should) keep every good person. Even in a growing business, where new and challenging opportunities open up every month, some people will out-grow the business. Bob Metcalfe, the founder and former CEO of 3Com, notes, "In a rapidly growing company, the business grows faster than the employees; in a mature company, the employees grow faster than the company."

Even with more possibilities than average, a firm simply will not meet every superstar's needs. Provocateurs understand this and do not try to keep people who are no longer challenged, no longer learning. I've always felt proud that someone left to take another bigger job if only because it made our leadership position even stronger in the industry.

Provocateurs should create an environment where people hit their own walls because it is the only way they (or anyone else) can learn how far they can go. And if that hurts the business, it's all right. It's a cost of doing business. If it's a solid business, it will thrive anyway. But it is a great practice to allow individuals to go as far as possible, and when they realize that they want to go further, they should sit with the leader and find ways to do so.

Ray Ozzie is the inventor of Lotus Notes and the founder and CEO of Groove Networks, which has developed an Internet-based program that allows close, secure, and flexible collaboration in small groups. Groove's tools permit people to do everything from team financial planning and product design to playing games. Because Groove has computers talk directly to one another—the "peer-to-peer" connection—it reflects a basic theme of this book. "Computing systems usually reflect the 'old' style of managing businesses" with hierarchies and barriers dictating rules for collaboration, says Ozzie. "But that's not the way that people or successful enterprises work today." People work best, he says when they can "self-organize," cooperating spontaneously in free-form ways.

Ozzie feels it's his job "to communicate to individuals that we want out of them as much as we can get for the best of the business. However, we realize you have a personal life, and you have to realize I am going to keep pushing you. You can't ask me to understand your absolute limits. You have to give feedback to your manager as to where your breaking points are . . . and your wife's . . . and your kids'. You have to let us know when you have a family situation, so we don't cause you to have a nervous breakdown. The company can't be fully responsible if you do, but the company must also recognize that people are people. It's up to the immediate managers to understand everyone reporting to their own circle. Sometimes they understand better than the employees themselves."

Jeff Taylor, the CEO of Monster.com, says, "I don't think you have to tell a person who has a reasonable amount of ethics and a reasonable expectation of doing something with his life, that he should actually work. I think you have to tell people—or show people—they have the resources and a rich environment so that they can do their work and take risks and make mistakes, and that they are not going to be scolded for making one. We have a fairly traditional structure here. We have managers. It's not complete mayhem. There is a business structure that has mission and vision objectives that would be, I think, probably fairly holistic and fairly direct in terms of where we are headed. And at the same time, we have a culture where people can have a good time."

A Provocateur may make a mistake and hurt the organization slightly when someone tries too much and fails. But that is far better than not trying enough. In my experience, it is healthier to overload people than to accept the ordinarily commonplace. I want my employees to feel they are achieving more than they ever thought they could—even if that means falling down now and then.

The Provocateur creates environments that are trusting, employee-empowered, creative, and that allow for failure. If a community can be flexible, it has a chance to find help in a problem situation. IDG's McGovern says, "If you expect people to do well, then they will believe they will do well. If you set people up to have a high degree of self-confidence, and you give them the resources—the learning resources and the resources of values and the resources of goals and the resources for learning—then they are going to succeed."

This means that if there is a fire, an earthquake, or a strike at the printer's— something over which the manager has no control—she can deal with it because it's a pothole in the road, not a fault in the system. Says McGovern, "By the very emphasis on keeping in touch with the market and everyone, people have a lot of names on their Rolodex to call. 'Can you help me? Can your printer take over my work?' People help each other if they are very outgoing. So we try to make the leadership be the maximum communicator and stay in touch with everybody, have lots of friends and support, so they don't sit and say, 'Oh god, what do I do now? My printer has gone on strike.'" In a secretive command-and-control organization, the drill is cover your ass and assign blame to anyone else.

At one point in the early 1990s, The Weber Group hit more than a pothole. We lost our largest account—around a third of our billings—when a new management team was brought in to the client company. Usually when an agency loses a major account it lays off employees and sometimes even the agency's viability comes into question.

We had 30-some people working on the account. I met with them and said, "It's their loss. We're going to take 90 days and do the best we can to replace it." Every senior manager and every junior account executive pulled together. We sent out dozens of new business letters and followed every lead. We quickly replaced the loss with two new clients, Legent and SAP, then a small German software company. SAP wanted us to introduce them in North America and subsequently to other major markets in the world, and it quickly grew to be our largest account. We did not lay off even one person, and within 90 days we were looking for people to continue our growth. To actually have an environment that could replace such a loss says something about creating an environment of trust, teamwork, and community.

TEACH, DON'T TRAIN

Every company has training programs, but the Provocateur focuses on learning, not training. You train a dog; you don't train people. You educate and work through experiential content to help create greater value in an employee's ability to perform well. I have seen situations where a business spent hundreds of thousands of dollars on "training" people and did not make a better company. The exercise is like high school: memorize the material before a big test, do okay on the test, and then forget everything.

Provocateurs understand the difference between that sort of training and memorization and what I call education and learning programs that stay with an employee forever. In many cases huge training budgets are a waste of money, and with certain qualifications, the training is a waste of time. Here is an example from my own company. Certain executives wanted to train everyone to be writers because public relations people need that skill. I said, "This is a waste, because if you're a good writer, you're a good writer. You might be able to make someone a little better, but you're not going to turn a nonwriter into a writer."

I believe people have certain talents, abilities, and interests. Someone who is a good writer may not also be a good salesperson. A great salesperson may not be a good bookkeeper. A fine bookkeeper may not be a good presenter. Rather than train writers to sell or salespeople to write, the company's education programs should help good writers to write better, salespeople to sell more effectively. Don't introduce a whole new concept that is a waste of time. The leader who thinks he can train anybody to do anything will construct a shoddy business. Rather than building on people's strengths, he will be papering over their weaknesses. I believe the leader should assemble a group that complements one another—not "training," more like matchmaking.

Learning is accomplished through group work, through understanding the connections between the company and its communities. Training in certain mechanical tasks is different from creating a learning culture that always looks to find new ways to apply new ideas, new technologies, and innovative methods and theories to the business. Encouraging such a culture should be the Provocateur's focus, not setting up training programs. A Provocateur wants to develop individuals so they find the books, courses, and mentors they need to develop, and are at peace with the company to which they contribute.

McGovern says that employee education accounts for 2 percent of IDG's total expenses, much higher than the typical company where it seldom is as much as 1 percent. "We gave a lot of power to the people," says McGovern. "We say, 'Here, we will give you $1,000 that you can use for any training experience you want.' They feel it's their money, and they use it responsibly to learn new technologies, new systems."

Rick Wagoner tells me that General Motors will be sending fewer executives to management programs at leading business schools but will be doing more in Detroit at GM University. The corporation had been sending executives to 58 different spring, summer, and fall programs at major universities. It was also sending another 60 people to two-year MBA or technical degree programs, so it would lose those high-potential employees for two years. Worse, some on graduation decided they wanted to go elsewhere.

To address its educational and personnel issues, the corporation has established GM University and hired Donnee Ramelli to be its president. Rather than sending managers away to school, GM is bringing high-potential people to Detroit for a three- to four-week program tailored to its needs. Harvard University professors teach about 40 percent of the material, senior GM executives (including Wagoner) teach about 40 percent, and external specialists—consultants in specific business simulations, for example—teach the other 20 percent.

"We also have consultants and outsiders with a specific

perspective on our industry," says Ramelli. "We wanted that expert in to tell us in a candid, if not brutally honest, way how we look from their perspective, how our competitors look, and what the difference is. These experts say what they think about us so that we can debate with them if necessary, and it gets us out of our seats on issues to talk about why we think we are the way we are and how can we change."

Students (the average age is around 41) come from around the world. GM brings in proportionately more students from outside North America to convey the idea that this is a global effort, not a North American project. Since GM is trying to "act as one company" and tear down the internal silos, the university also brings in students from different functions, people who've spent their working lives in one area. Says Ramelli, "This is supposed to accelerate their ability to think about the whole business. Because even if they run only a process in a specific area, they need to think about the whole business and not just that piece of it."

Ramelli points out that GM is picking managers who know they are high potential, who have a shot at becoming a corporate officer. "They are confronted by not only the best folks from Harvard, but the top leadership of General Motors. And, by the way, they are given four action learning projects they have to work on. Those are all objectives between Rick and the board. When Rick briefs them on why he wants them to work on these projects, they may listen politely to why it's good for the business, but he also says, 'By the way, I am holding myself accountable to the board to make some progress here.'" So the program may yield practical, realistic strategies.

Ramelli says, "We talk about the cultural priorities: act as one company, embrace stretch targets, move with a sense of urgency and speed, and focus on the product and the customer. If we not only say those things, but could *be* those things as a whole body, we would be a different company than we are today. It doesn't happen in one week or one year, but it's a journey, and we are picking up speed."

Ramelli says that when Wagoner talks to these rising stars, he wants to make sure they understand they are supposed to walk away with three values: "How to be strategic, how to get results, and how to build capability—and we're talking about people, not new factories." Building the capabilities of the organization's people is a Provocateur's major objective, one that another global powerhouse, General Electric, has met in innovative ways.

In its push to embrace e-commerce, GE met a serious challenge: Many of its senior executives knew very little about the Internet. CEO Jack Welch's answer: Get a mentor. Welch "ordered his top 600 or so managers to reach down into their ranks for Internet junkies and become their students. Many of the new teachers would be no older than their early 30s. Virtually all of the pupils would be established GE veterans whose ages ranged from their late 30s to nearly 60." Welch's own mentor, Pam Wickham, 37, runs the company's Web site (www.ge.com).

Through this reverse mentoring, Welch hoped the teachers would help the managers "know what competitors' sites looked like, experience the difficulties of ordering their own appliances online . . . become more savvy and get a real feel for what the best sites are doing." He also expected to introduce more youth across the organization as the corporation harnesses the Internet to launch new businesses and cut costs. "E-business knowledge is generally inversely proportional to both age and the height in the organization," said Welch. "I find this to be a wonderful tool, among many others, to change that equilibrium."

EDUCATE THE CUSTOMER

A willingness to educate is even more important today in an Internet environment because interactivity is basically about learning. In the past, business used the available tools to learn about customers—tools like surveys, focus groups, call centers, and complaint letters. These were useful and will continue to be helpful in the future since new technology seldom replaces the old; rather, it supplements. The Internet, however, offers customers a simple, cheap, and quick way to communicate with businesses. Customer email means that companies have a new way to learn about customer needs, wants, desires, and problems.

The tool also cuts the other way. The Web allows customers a new way to learn about a product or service before they buy. More people are doing extended research before they make a purchase. This means that companies have to provide customers with accurate, useful information they can use to make a decision. Call this educated marketing—where the idea is to be more teacher than salesperson.

This means that an educator in business today is less concerned about giving employees facts than with teaching them how to learn about their customers. This is important because if the relationship with the customer is at the center of an organization (as it is), and if communication is key to that relationship (as it is), then the learning process involves listening to and learning from the customer. The company that learns from its customers can build a dialogue and, ideally, a long-term relationship.

At IDG, learning is part of the company's culture. IDG calls its CEOs "chief encouragement officers"; their role is to encourage and support their people. "The most important is that they promote constant learning," says Pat McGovern,

IDG's founder. "They make sure the people they hire are in touch with their customers and spend the maximum amount of time learning what the customers need, learning the feedback on projects they are doing, and that the managers themselves set a good example by spending 40 percent or 50 percent of their time meeting and talking with customers."

If I were running a retail business, I would have my executives regularly work the sales floor, meet customers, hear their questions and complaints. If I were a stock analyst interviewing CEOs, I would want to know how much time they spend with customers (and then check with the customers to confirm their stories). A company in which the CEO hides from the customers is in trouble or will be in trouble soon. It sends a signal throughout the company that customers are not really important.

The best teachers are often the best students. They have listened and worked through a lot of what will help their students or their workers do the best job they possibly can. A friend who teaches writing in a prison says he is a better writer for having taught writing, even to semiliterate felons. He has to think about their writing and how to help them say whatever they want to say more clearly. What is the most diplomatic and effective way to ask for a parole hearing? Where should an intensifier like "only" go in a sentence? (Only I love you . . . I only love you . . . I love only you . . . I love you only . . . it makes a difference.)

Unless a teacher simply goes through rote motions every time he teaches (the terminally bored college lecturer we've all experienced), he learns something new with every student.

NEVER STOP LEARNING

Provocateurs do not actively teach people to behave the way they do (although a certain amount of behavior modification rubs off as a natural result of the contact). Provocateurs teach by building a community, establishing trust, learning, and expanding. At the same time, Provocateurs never stop learning from the community. They read not only business books; they read anthropology, history, philosophy, sociology, psychology, biology, literature, and more. A great educator has wide-ranging interests.

Pete Wakeman, who with his wife Laura founded Great Harvest Bread Company, estimates that less than a quarter of their reading is even remotely related to their work. "Favorite magazines include *The Bolivian Times* and others whose titles few would recognize. We buy books like crazy. I just noticed that Amazon is keeping track of us and has sold us more than 200 books. Even so, we are lucky to own a magic bookcase that never gets full."

One danger in learning something new is that it may cause you to change your mind, your beliefs, your behavior, or all three. Change is usually difficult, sometimes uncomfortable, and occasionally painful. As Niccolo Machiavelli pointed out in *The Prince* (1513), "There is nothing more difficult to take in hand, more perilous to conduct, or more uncertain in its success, than to take the lead in the introduction of a new order of things. Because the innovator has for enemies all those who have done well under the old conditions, and lukewarm defenders in those who may do well under the new." Rather than risk the work, the discomfort, or the pain of change, some people and organizations would rather not learn. Yet, in a world that has so much access to information, that attitude is a one-way highway to failure.

Provocateurs understand that knowledge is available everywhere at every second. If a leader can encourage employees to locate information as a team and learn from it, the result will be a company that continually redefines itself and moves ahead, and ahead, and ahead. Companies that acquire and use information continuously will advance much more rapidly than those that continue business as usual.

To gain an educator's perspective on the Provocateur as educator, I asked Dr. Charles Vest, the president of MIT, whether leadership can be taught, and if so, how. Vest says he has often been reluctant to say that leadership can be taught, believing that most leaders have learned through observation and experience. However, he immediately added, "the older I get, the more I realize that people who aren't engineers can learn and sort out characteristics and benchmark and teach a subject, so I do not have as fixed a view as I used to."

In an academic context, Vest says, leadership comes in many forms and not just in moving large groups of people in organizations. It is important to understand that a person may be an intellectual leader and not necessarily someone who can manage an activity. "Also, when one accepts a leadership position, your values have to be solidly in place," says Vest, "because you are going to be faced with making decisions and dealing with directions." The leader will not have time to ask, "What should my values be?"

An example of values? "Integrity has to be right at the top. If you are going to build a diverse organization, you have to respect and believe in diversity. In an academic context, it is extremely important to understand that what may be important in the history department or the music department is very different from what may be important in the mechanical engineering department. You have to value that difference in intellectual perspective."

By extension, I would argue that in the business context, it is extremely important to understand that what may be important to the human relations or the accounting department may be different from what is important to the marketing department.

Vest points out that in academic leadership, like business leadership, one has to make hard decisions about people. In a university these include to grant or deny tenure, pass or fail a preliminary examination, approve or reject a thesis. "You have to be very serious about what you are looking for," says Vest, "and be consistent," a position any thoughtful business leader should hold.

Vest says leaders share at least two qualities. "First of all I think it really is important to be able to get to the core of issues. Things—at least in universities—tend to come to you in pretty complex dialogue, and I think people who are good leaders in business as well as the university can see through the complexities to say, 'Look, here are the three main points.' I also think it's extremely important to see connections among people and figure out how to build those so that you get synergy into the system. It's particularly true in the university where you have to do a lot of your building by substitution and change rather than hiring and firing."

NEVER STOP TEACHING

When I finished graduate school, I became a teacher at a prep school in Pennsylvania. While teaching, I freelanced a brochure for a friend, and when I got the check for the brochure it was more than for a whole year of teaching. At that point I said to my new bride, "Let's try business for a few years; if it doesn't work, we can go back to teaching." That is when I went to Figgie International to work for Harry E. Figgie, Jr.

Harry Figgie had a degree in engineering, a degree in law, and a Harvard MBA, class of 49. He was a great General.

The executive who was head of corporate communications at the time says that once Figgie sensed you were even slightly afraid of him, he'd pounce. "He seemed to like testing you. He liked getting you right to the very edge. If you couldn't stand up to him, he knew that immediately."

Figgie had entered Booz Allen Hamilton, the management consulting company, right after Harvard. His idea was to build a conglomerate of companies that might have weak management or were having tough economic or financial times (or both), buy them, and send in a bunch of MBAs to decide what to sell, what to keep, what to add, and what to take public.

One of the first companies Figgie bought, Automatic Sprinkler Corporation of America, was not doing well financially. Automatic Sprinkler was not making a lot of money because there was no law requiring sprinkler systems in public buildings. Politicians would look at capital budgets and say, "If we build this right, are we really going to have a fire?"

The break came a short time after Figgie bought Automatic Sprinkler, when a number of government officials helped push through a federal law mandating that not only do new public buildings have to be fitted with sprinkler systems, but older buildings had to be retrofitted. Since there was only one leading company that sold sprinkler systems, Automatic Sprinkler's sales exploded. With this profit, Figgie bought American LaFrance, the Elmira, New York–based fire engine manufacturer, and eventually 40-some companies that became Figgie International.

Figgie was a difficult boss, but he also gave me opportunities to learn about business and public relations. One assignment was to celebrate the 150th birthday of American LaFrance. I said, "Who cares about fire engines?" He said, "Just go to Elmira. Spend a few days, get to know the guys who run American LaFrance, and see if it's worth having a parade. Do some research."

That experience taught me about constituencies. I learned there are people who are fascinated by fire and fire memorabilia. There are books on the greatest fires, on the greatest fire chiefs, and on fire engines. It was a complete community. New England towns still hold Fireman's Musters, a parade of fire engines and competitions between volunteer fire companies.

I also learned about the emotionality of communities and how to market to them most effectively. I was at the factory the day that the Burlington, Vermont, fire chief came to pick up his new American LaFrance truck. It was like stepping into a time warp. The chief had a handlebar mustache, his chief's hat and coat with gold buttons, and when we gave him the keys, he started crying. I was a cynical 26-year-old and thought, oh my god, he's crying about his new fire engine. But it was so touching I could not make fun.

American LaFrance ended up having a huge birthday parade in Elmira. ABC News did a 3½ minute piece for their weekend news, and CBS's Charles Kuralt did a piece. It was the perfect American story, and I was learning PR on the job. If you have a good story, especially one that is visual and emotional, you can get coverage.

The year the Cuyahoga River caught on fire in Cleveland, my wife suggested that maybe it would be interesting to live in Boston, her hometown. I was hired to run the small PR group for a Boston ad agency and learned a lot about more sophisticated public relations. Two years later, I started my own public relations firm.

The Weber Group started as a two-person high-tech public relations firm in Harvard Square in 1987. We added clients and employees and offices, and by the time Interpublic acquired us in 1996, we had just under 200 employees and offices in Cambridge, London, and Palo Alto. The Weber Group became Weber Public Relations Worldwide and was merged with Shandwick, another PR company Interpublic owned, to become Weber Shandwick with more than 3,500 employees. While running Weber Shandwick, Interpublic also asked me to run their marketing service division, consisting of public relations, research, and experiential marketing.

When I started my business, I had no idea how big it would grow or how far my talents would take me, but I knew I couldn't just stop. I had to keep learning and keep pushing and knew that if my talents and my abilities could only go so far, that would become painfully apparent.

I had no reason to go into public relations or into high technology, but what I did—which I would recommend to anybody getting into business—was assess my weaknesses and strengths. There were some things I felt I was very good at. I thought I was a good observer of situations, executives, and companies. I seemed to be a good communicator. I was interested in motivation. What motivated people to study something, to buy something, to do anything? If there is a philosophy of marketing, it is all about motivating people, influencing opinion, creating action. The story you tell, the visuals you present, the position you communicate, makes something happen. So in many ways, I never stopped being a teacher, as communication and motivation are the heart of the education process.

And just as the great teacher is often an entertainer in the classroom, so the Provocateur is often an entertainer in business.

5

THE ENTERTAINER

*I like our employee base, so my guess would be that
I would like their friends. Our parties where I'm the
DJ become a way for people who love their jobs to
be able to share with their friends. And some of
those people say, "I want to come and work here."*

—Jeff Taylor,
founder and CEO,
Monster.com

Great entertainers build a bond with their audience
through humor, talent, and charisma. Just as Patrick Stewart,
Barbra Streisand, Yo-Yo Ma, and Bruce Springsteen are their
own brands, so the successful Provocateur becomes the face
of the company.

Visitors to the Maynard, Massachusetts, offices of
Monster.com are met by a giant model of one of the company's trademark monsters and a video showing the CEO
and founder Jeff Taylor water-skiing behind a blimp—in
fact, setting a new world's record for water-skiing behind a
blimp. The stunt the video records is entertainment for a
purpose, to publicize the company's name among potential
clients and job seekers.

To promote itself, Monster.com leases two blimps from a

Virgin Atlantic subsidiary, the conglomerate Sir Richard Branson leads. At the meeting to sign the lease for the second blimp, Taylor and the subsidiary's president chatted about Monster.com's plans for the blimp. The president told Taylor, "You realize that over water we can bring the blimp right down to 50 feet above the surface, whereas over land we have to stay between 500 and 1,000 feet."

Making conversation, he added, "Richard Branson actually water-skied behind the blimp on a *Bay Watch* episode, and he holds the current record for water-skiing behind a blimp." And then he asked casually, "What would you think about seeing if you could break his record?"

Taylor asked, "How far did he ski?"

As Taylor recalls, the answer was something like, "Basically, if you can get up on the skis, you can beat his record." That sounded feasible, so, although he had only been on water skis four times in his life, Taylor agreed.

Four months later, his assistant, Kaycee Langford, called him on his cell phone, "You realize you're going waterskiing next week. Flying out Tuesday night and doing it Wednesday morning."

At that point, Taylor thought to ask, "Exactly how long *is* Branson's record?"

"I knew you were going to ask. One point five miles."

At the time, Taylor was in a New York City taxi and told the driver to mark 1.5 miles. Thirty blocks later, Taylor began to wonder if he was making a mistake.

The following week he was in Panama City, Florida, sitting in the Gulf of Mexico with three small boats. "The lead boat is going to cut my wake, and the boat on the left has three video camera crews and about four photographers. The boat on the right has a guy in full scuba gear, and I want to know who he is. He says, 'If I have to come to you in the water, let me put this thing in your mouth.' So I'm in the water, and I'm cold, and the blimp has made its third or fourth pass. A 200-foot rope comes off the blimp, with a ball at the 50-foot mark so I know when the handle is coming, but the blimp keeps going by and I can't catch the handle. And then I see this fin and think, 'Okay, somebody has a fin hooked on his back and is screwing with me.' But it turns out to be two dolphins, and everyone says that's good luck, although my heart is pounding."

On the blimp's next pass, Taylor caught the handle, rose to his feet, skied for 40 seconds, and wiped out. On the next attempt, he again caught the handle, and skied 11 minutes and 43 seconds or 3.3 miles to shatter Branson's record. "I came out of the water totally exhilarated," says Taylor, "and I'll put myself in a situation as often as someone will let me."

While this is entertaining, these are not stunts simply for the fun of it (albeit, Taylor was having fun). There is a method behind the madness.

People remember a journalistic presentation of brand much longer than a commercial representation of brand. A news story about Taylor breaking Branson's waterskiing record (with a picture of the Monster.com blimp) has greater recall than an advertising commercial.

Also, the "CEO as brand" can be a very strong marketing hook. Taylor learned well from watching Richard Branson who was one of the early CEOs as brand. Branson did not separate himself from the Virgin brand; he was always there. I have often joked that every time Virgin needed a shot in the arm, Sir Richard would take up his hot air balloon and crash it. Then he would be on the cover of every newspaper in the world, shaking off the dirt.

To be a bit of an adventurer is also to be a leader, and I think Taylor is trying to communicate to his staff and customers that he really wants to try new things and be different and to separate Monster.com from the pack of online employment sites. Monster.com needs companies to list jobs on its site (and pay it for running them), and it needs workers to search for the jobs. Without sufficient numbers of both, the company fails. But there is no simple target market. Companies seeking workers cover every industry, virtually every country, from small businesses to giant corporations. Workers seeking jobs are equally diffused. Taylor's stunts give Monster.com a personality, and having a corporate personality helps people think of you.

CONNECT TO PEOPLE THROUGH ENTERTAINMENT

Great entertainers create an environment in which people feel connected to them. The Provocateur entertains in such a way that people do not feel they are being passively amused—the difference between listening to a recording of Beethoven's Ninth Symphony and attending a performance.

The entertainer, however, does not need to be on stage, since a choreographer and a theater director are also entertainers. They create an environment in which people feel connected to the dancers, the musicians, the actors, and the players to feel part of the creative process. The greatest Provocateur/entertainers will be ones who convey a deeper feeling than superficial amusement.

Great entertainers get you to connect with them in a very personal way. The end result is both your personal satisfaction and an appropriate self-involvement that makes you want to come back for more.

Great entertainers do something that initially looks selfish. At first blush, they seem to be saying "I want to be on stage," but through some alchemy they turn that around so it's the audience that wants them on stage. Indeed, the audience wants these entertainers to be on stage for a long time because they enjoy the performance so much. (And great entertainers know they should leave an audience unsated, wanting more.)

The entertainer can touch the emotions as well as hold your attention, both of which business must do since keeping your attention is the key to a successful customer relationship. An entertainer knows when to bring in appropriate props—think of Ronald Reagan and his charts. Reagan was a master of the simple chart that transformed him from the Leader of the Free World Talking to America into The President Entertaining Americans. People watching became involved. With the charts, they could see what the deficit was doing to the economy. That his tax cuts actually increased the deficit makes his performance even more impressive.

TOUCH EMOTIONS AND INTELLECT

Great leaders—of nations, corporations, and organizations—touch people emotionally and intellectually. Peter Drucker has written that the first requirement of effective leadership "is to earn trust. Otherwise there won't be any followers." Touching people emotionally and intellectually is the first step in earning that trust.

Jeff Taylor is a Provocateur who understands how to reach out and touch his employees and prospects. Before he became a CEO, he was a disc jockey at parties and weddings, and he continues to work as a DJ at Monster.com's quarterly recruiting parties. "We invite people to bring their friends—no resumes—and come in and meet the managers and other employees. We always theme it. At one, everybody had to come packed to go to Las Vegas to be qualified for the drawing. We had 550 suitcases all piled up, and at 10:30 P.M. we did a two-minute drill to find your suitcase. You should have seen these guys flying through the suitcases trying to find their own. We drew two names of people who went straight out into limos and on to Las Vegas, right from the party."

Taylor is the DJ, the entertainer, but the party's focus is around employees bringing their friends. "I like our employee base, so my guess would be that I would like their friends. We typically get 600 to 700 people at a party—300 employees and 300 to 400 friends. We have the facility to have these parties. We do drink tickets, and we hire professional bartenders. We have drivers waiting, so if someone doesn't feel comfortable driving home, he can take one of the cars and we will pick him up in the morning and bring him back to his car. People say it sounds very old-fashioned, but it is not the beer blast of the past. It is themed and becomes a way for people who love their jobs to be able to share with their friends. And people say, 'I want to come and work here.'"

If Provocateur/entertainers create entertainment, they create an environment people want to visit. People will want to be part of the act. Taylor is "selling" his company to prospective employees and clients through entertainment.

HOLD ATTENTION WITH FUN

Fun will be more important in a world where it is increasingly difficult to hold people's attention. A business has to get its points across quickly the way good entertainers get their points across quickly and effectively.

If the leader enjoys entertaining, the employees and the other stakeholders will have a good time being part of the community. If the business's goal is to encourage prospects and customers to choose its community over others, it needs an element of entertainment to make people feel this is the place they should be. This is a place where they can, among other things, have fun.

I think many people today feel we only live once so let's make every experience count. If the company believes in making every customer's experience a good one, it will thrive. If the leader believes that every employee should have a chance to grow, be heard, and make a contribution, the firm will attract and keep good people. Entertainment makes the experience that much more attractive.

Staples is a great example of a corporation having fun about the most boring products—paper, folders, pads, envelopes. CEO Tom Stemberg has been able to create an entertaining environment with great ads. The advertising almost makes it *fun* to go back to school. In one ad, the kid looks totally bummed out because he has to go back to school, but his mother dances down the Staples' aisles, singing, "It's the most wonderful time of the year . . ." She tosses products into the shopping cart, gets up on one foot, and floats down the aisle as she sings. The ad says without bludgeoning viewers that Staples has all the supplies you will ever need, and it's a fun place to shop.

The idea of fun in marketing has been around as long as the idea of marketing, of course. A company's ads are often a doorway to an environment, and they will become more so as they become interactive. The trap (one that advertising agencies have been known to help their clients fall into) is that the advertising *only* entertains; it does not sell the company's products or services. The Provocateur/entertainer never allows the ad agency to forget the point of the entertainment—to build sales.

Provocateur/entertainers become almost evangelical. They know how to use the way they dress, the way they speak, the way they present, the props they use to draw in the audience, whether it be employees or customers or congressmen in a hearing room. Provocateur/entertainers are able to convey the feeling that what their business offers is fun, and that it is worth doing, worth buying, and worth coming back to more than once.

BRING CUSTOMERS INTO THE ACT

Provocateurs have to think about ways to stir customer senses as they create the company environment. The whole idea of creating a business environment is to make it a positive experience, a place customers and prospects enjoy visiting. Novell had a 24-hour radio station—WNOVL—and while someone waited on hold he heard music and then a disc jockey advertise about great Novell software. The station ran interviews on the future of software. Ray Norda, who was running Novell at the time, understood he had to surround the customer's senses.

I am, of course, talking about entertainment in the broadest sense as any kind of positive visual or aural stimulation. What's entertaining varies by individual. Some find a rock concert entertainment, others find it torture. Some find shopping a form of entertainment, others feel it is a necessary nuisance. Dining out can be entertainment or uninspired—although McDonald's and Burger King have encouraged franchisees to install children's playgrounds. I find the Rain Forest café to be entertainment. The shopping mall has become an entertainment center with amusement park rides, theaters, and public performances.

If a woman is happy shopping for sheets and towels on the JCPenney Web site, I argue she is being entertained as well as furnishing her home. She can, after all, buy sheets and towels from many places. She may, for example, be more entertained by Martha Stewart at Kmart. Martha shows her how sheet and towel colors and patterns can work together so the woman buys more and returns more often to the store. If a man enjoys checking his portfolio's performance twice a day at the Charles Schwab site, that's entertainment. Provocateur/entertainers need not crack jokes or croon songs to be entertaining. They say, "Come to my world; come to my channel; come to my tent; come to my stage, and you will see extraordinary things. And while you're here, maybe you'll consider my sheets, my towels, my funds."

Entertainment is not limited to consumer marketing. It is possible to entertain business customers—not with a junket to the plant or a golf game but with an email from the CEO: "On Tuesday, I am going to take you on a virtual visit to our new customer in France to show how they are using these products. Would you want to come along?" Some customers and prospects may want to see how French companies use the products. Done well, it will be entertainment with a purpose.

Not long ago I talked to a company about ways to maintain its leadership position as the Web took over its industry. "You are going to have to create an information circus where people will want to come and learn about everything from new stereo technologies to new Java applications, some of it free, some of it they pay for." The managers were not convinced. They said the approach did not sound serious enough. They seemed to feel that if they were entertaining or fun, prospects and customers would not take the company and what it offered seriously. As a consequence, people did not take them at all and they lost sales and market position.

The opposite of entertainment is not seriousness but tedium, monotony, and boredom. You can be serious about the entertainment, and serious about what is real, important, and genuine about your product or service, but still have fun and be entertaining (unless your product is something like caskets, life preservers, or fire extinguishers—something about which you probably should be fairly grim).

But if the company creates an environment of entertaining, learning can be fun. It is much like the Montessori method of teaching: I want to go to the bubble table, I want to go to the share-the-dream table, and so on. I want to go to Staples.com for school supplies. I want to go to Amazon.com for books. I want to go to eBay just to see what's being offered. People talk about auction action, and eBay is truly an entertainment commerce site. Then there's Starbucks.

SELL A COMMODITY PRODUCT WITH ENTERTAINMENT

Howard Schultz, now the chief global strategist for Starbucks but formerly the CEO who built the corporation, went into the low-margin commodity coffee business when American coffee consumption was in decline. Nevertheless, he noticed that a four-store Seattle chain was buying far more than its share of the Swedish drip coffeemakers that Schultz's then employer imported. Schultz visited Starbucks Coffee, Tea and Spice in 1981, and was so impressed by what the firm was doing that he signed on as director of retail operations and marketing a year later. In 1985, he started his own chain of Seattle coffee bars, and in 1987 raised enough venture capital to buy out Starbucks' two partners and merge the firm with his own, renaming the company Starbucks Corp. It now has over 3,800 stores in Asia, Canada, the Middle East, the United Kingdom, and the United States and annual sales of more than $2.2 billion.

"The decline in coffee drinking was due to the fact that most of the coffee that people bought was stale and they weren't enjoying it," says Schultz. "Once they tasted ours and experienced what we call 'the third place'—a gathering place between home and work where they were treated with respect—they found we were filling a need they didn't know they had. Customers today are more open than ever to new ideas. It's an incredible time to start a new business or introduce a new product because people are eager to try new things."

Simon Williams of the Sterling Group, a New York consulting firm whose category experience includes work on Kraft coffee brands, says that Starbucks "is a brand built on passion, and innately passionate relationships are much more rewarding to the human psyche than innately functional relationships." In other words, entertainment counts.

What is it about Starbucks that resonates with consumers? Schultz says that the company's own research shows that customers interact with the Starbucks brand differently from almost every other. "And I'm confident in saying that was by design. We purposefully stayed away from traditional brand building. We ran away from the Procter & Gamble model of taking a product with great packaging, broad-based distribution, and scaling up advertising with a brand manager focused on that tested formula. We turned that formula upside down by saying we'll have quite limited distribution, no advertising, and we'll build it through the retail environment and through all the things experiential branding can accomplish. As I say that, it sounds like a lot of modern marketing buzzwords, but really it's old-fashioned retail marketing—one customer at a time—and that almost sounds too trite."

Schultz decided early on that Starbucks was going to lead with the coffee bar experience first—that is, the entertainment—and the product second. "We certainly don't ignore product, but it is something we always knew we had and a lot of others didn't. There's still a lot of bad coffee out there being consumed. But we built the business through the experience, not through the product. We are definitely a product-driven company and not a marketing-driven company, but through the years we've become an experience-driven company. I think we recognized pretty early on that the key to growing the business was based on building trust and confidence with our consumers; we were already pretty confident in the product.

"Underneath all that is the underlying fact that the equity of the Starbucks brand was built internally; that's a different construct than the one practiced by most companies, or most brand managers, or most marketers. We've all read the advice of some of the great brand gurus about exceeding customer expectations. Our thought here was to originate within the company by exceeding expectations and establishing a relationship of trust with our own people." Schultz points out that retailers and restaurants live or die on customer service, but retail and restaurant pay is among the lowest in the country. Starbucks starts by calling its people "partners" not employees.

"It didn't take us long to realize that while we were selling a commodity product, our customers almost right away focused in on our process as something unique," says Schultz. "They wanted to know what we do and how we do it with almost as much interest as we have internally. When you have that level of interest in any brand, it shouldn't take any marketer too long to realize that what's really being sold is a value-added experience. In our case, it was one not solely based on the product, but on the features and benefits of the experience itself." In this case, it includes a place to read the paper, meet a friend, play a game of chess.

By offering a pleasurable, entertaining experience, Starbucks has been able to grow with relatively little traditional advertising. Schultz attributes their growth to the brand's strength and the experience it represents. "We are not only a location, but we are something that you can consume, which is unique. And the stores have become gathering places, which became an important social aspect of the brand. All that means trust, and in building a brand today, that's imperative; the rules have changed radically from 5 or 10 years ago.

"The amount of marketing noise out there is just astounding. Consumers today are in a giant wind tunnel going the wrong way. They are bombarded with advertising and marketing, yet so much of it is just noise. That's because consumers are telling corporate America, all those marketers, that they don't believe much, if any, of what they are being told. Over the years, most national products have not delivered on their promise. I think that gives us a unique advantage in the direct connection we have every day with the customer. We don't have to do traditional advertising because we are communicating every day with our heaviest users in an environment we control way beyond what we could do with any advertising. That's the basis of our bond with our consumers."

Howard Schultz believes the experience of drinking coffee should be entertainment. Folgers—aside from the quality of its product—had an audience that was not being entertained and was ready to try something else. Customers want to become part of the act, so Starbucks offered an act. People order latte, sit in the warm greens and browns, and let the soft jazz wash over them. It's a community.

The stores must serve good coffee: That's a given. But look at the way Starbucks has been able to expand geographically and extend its product line into the supermarket—coffee ice

cream, ready-to-drink bottled coffee, and whole-bean packaged coffee. Once Starbucks created an entertaining, communal environment, it was able to extend the business
because it had become an environment, one in which you
want to buy, you feel good about, and feel you are entertaining yourself.

How does a company encourage customers to be part of
its act? For starters, provide a means and stay open to customer reaction. "We're very fortunate to have customers who
are passionate enough about what we do that they let us
know quickly when they're dissatisfied," says Schultz. "We
have customer comment cards in the store, we get thousands
of phone calls in the customer relations department each
year, and we train our partners to give feedback about what
they hear." Schultz knows that its stores must not only perform well every day, they must also listen for hints that they
could do better.

Many companies find ways to engage customers. Gerber
encourages customers on its Web site by having parents talk
to each other about concerns with babies. Amazon does it by
having readers critique books. E*Trade does it by turning its
site into a "digital financial media" center, one that supplies
the stock quotes, news, and financial information that
matches the customer's interests and income.

There are intermediate stages for visual presentation and
interactive dialogue in the way a great entertainer connects
with his audience. Think of the give-and-take of a great
comedian or of a great singer. The tools available on the Web
make this give-and-take available to every business with every
constituency in an interactive way. A shareholder may not
personally hear the CEO at the annual meeting, but once the
meeting is available on a video database on the Web, the
shareholder can then participate. And if shareholders are

excited about how the CEO is presenting the company's goals and visions, and how they are going to go about accomplishing those goals through their partnerships, through their product initiatives, and their cycle of research and innovation, then they will want to be entertained by the company.

The great entertainer gets the audience so involved that they laugh, they grow misty-eyed, they gasp when Placido Domingo hits a high note. The lyrics by Andrew Lloyd Weber moves someone to the point that she wants to hear it again and again and again. Likewise, the great company gets customers so involved they buy more and tell their friends.

Provocateur/entertainers understand the environment's importance to entertainment. They know that if they induce you to visit their site, they must be effective in entertaining you and selling you or you will never return. The great entertainer, though, will know your interests and not sing opera if you want show tunes. How does a company learn the commonalities?

Go back to our original premise: The customer relationship is at the company's core. Provocateur/entertainers know how to bring individuals into the entertainment. Tom Stemberg knows people like comedy, so Staples uses comedy. AOL from the beginning has been organized by interest: sports, computers, travel, health, and now hundreds more. AOL built the company almost as infotainment. The Hard Rock Café, Dave & Busters, and The Rain Forest Café have been successful theme retailers/restaurants.

This is a whole new world. The question leaders should be asking is how do we create that stage, that environment, that place of fun, of learning, of motivating that connects our brand to the customer's heart and soul? Monster.com is good at making it easy to identify potential jobs. Starbucks is good at making a comfortable environment in which to drink a great cup of coffee. IBM is good at making their site the place to know about e-business and to work on how to obtain results.

ENTERTAIN WITH A POINT

The Web is like a big flea market. Companies are still trying to sell goods and services, but how do they induce people to come learn about their products? eBay should evolve into (and what Christie's and Sotheby's should have done) a place where someone can learn about, say, early twentieth-century American art before she enters the auction. The customer becomes smart enough to buy with some confidence.

On its digital camera site, Sony should show grandma and grandpa in Florida watching their grandson's one-year-old birthday party in Ohio. Here's the camera in actual use. Here's how you connect the camera to your PC. Here's how you edit the tape to add music and titles. Do not even mention buying the product. Sony has now created an entertaining environment.

After the person has been brought into the community, the company moves to the next level, answering questions: "Is it really that easy to use the digital camera . . . bread maker . . . personal digital assistant . . . cake mix?" Yes it is. Here's how you do it. The information becomes personalized. The customer ultimately buys, but initially came to the product from an interest in sharing an immediate video with the grandparents. That interest, sharing a family experience, is the entry point, not the camera. Nobody wants a video camera the way nobody wants an electric drill—what they really want are pictures and holes.

We are going to see more and more Internet-related performances like the famous Victoria's Secret introduction of new lingerie. As an example of how this can work, The Weber Group helped General Motors introduce e-GM with a Webcast press conference in August 1999.

e-GM, headed by Mark T. Hogan, is a cross-functional business group designed to put a wide range of products and services closer to customers. e-GM oversees GMBuyPower and OnStar and works closely with GM dealers to change the way consumers shop for and purchase vehicles. GMBuy-Power allows consumers to configure the vehicle of their choice online, search vehicle inventories, and then make a purchase through the dealer of their choice. In select markets outside the United States, GMBuyPower will allow consumers to buy cars directly online. OnStar has pioneered an in-car telematics service that allows wireless Web surfing, stock trading, and hands-free cellular calling. OnStar has millions of subscribers on the road today, creating a new multi-billion-dollar market segment.

"The Internet fundamentally changes the way business is conducted," said GM president Rick Wagoner at the press conference. "With this move, we are applying the power of our technology innovations and the strength of our human and financial resources to the Internet to enhance the way we develop customer relationships. e-GM will serve as a catalyst to enhance the customer experience, improve efficiency, and cut costs." GM already had more than 100 consumer Web sites around the world with 3.8 million unique visits in the month before it announced e-GM. GMBuyPower had more than 650,000 visitors shopping for a new vehicle.

Because e-GM reflects the corporation's commitment to Internet commerce, it was natural to Webcast the press conference. GM held the event in a new facility in the Renaissance Center in downtown Detroit. Participants saw a stage with three GM executives in casual attire sitting on stools. Behind the executives were two plasma screens with GM logos moving across them and behind that was a blue curtain. We set up chairs theater style and had video cameras at the back that panned to each individual as he spoke. On one side of the room we had set up multiple machines that could demonstrate all the GM online technology that was being included in the new offering. We also had video monitors so that everyone in the audience could see the video that was being streamed to the Webcast.

Reporters around the world—more than 120—were able to watch the press conference live and call in their own questions, so that an automotive writer in, say, Brazil or Germany or Japan had virtually the same access to Wagoner and Hogan in Detroit as a reporter in the room. Ordinary people, of course, could also watch the press conference (although they could not ask questions), and more than 4,200 did so, dramatically more than the 90 that was the average for previous Webcasts. Television stations could receive a video feed from the event, which we sent out via satellite, or if time was not an issue, we'd send a tape in the mail.

How did the event go over? e-GM generated more than 70 million media impressions in August. Some 43 U.S. TV stations aired e-GM launch news, including outlets in Boston, Chicago, Detroit, Miami, and San Francisco. "Satellite Media Tour" interviews with e-GM President Mark Hogan appeared on CNBC, PBS's "Nightly Business Report," FOX News, and Bloomberg TV. More than 30 newspapers, Web sites, and trade magazines covered the announcement, including *The Wall Street Journal, The New York Times, USA Today, CNNfn, C/Net, Red Herring, Computerworld,* and *InfoWorld.*

A September 1999 corporate online image and reputation study by Hass Associates found that GM "enjoyed the auto industry's most positive presence on the Internet, largely because of its well-publicized launch of an Internet-oriented business unit." GM received the highest level of positive attention during August on more than 80 Web sites and newsgroups that are frequented by investors and others interested in news and information about the auto industry. In other words, the Webcast did well.

As of the writing of this book, my company Weber Shandwick Worldwide is averaging two or three Webcasts a week as the cost has come down and we can produce them quickly. We are seeing a rapid move toward an entertainment platform that is visual, interactive, and multifaceted. This is where Provocateur/entertainers can rise to great heights, because they can start bringing in other employees, satisfied customers, music from the ad campaign, colors from the logo subtly in the background to entertain with a point more effectively than ever.

ENTERTAIN 24 HOURS A DAY

The media has combined news and entertainment. We are living in a world in which information must be presented in an entertaining way to be heard at all. In a culture where news has become entertainment, business as entertainment cannot be far off. It is going to be a fact of life that business leaders need to be prepared to present their companies and their visions in an entertaining way.

Ultimately, the company will have to offer 24 hours of entertainment by constituency—prospects who want information about products and services; customers who want to buy; reporters who want information; stock analysts who want financial data and the business outlook.

In time (and sooner rather than later), I believe a company will offer 24 hours of entertainment by constituency. Customers are clamoring to hear what IBM's Lou Gerstner has to say about the new storage device to see if IBM is really going to beat up EMC, its major competitor in storage devices. Customers will be entertained by the product or service. Employees will be entertained by the mission, vision, and compensation. Shareholders will be entertained by the financial returns. A great leader will have to know how to keep a 24-hour entertainment running, one that has highest levels of sincerity.

We will ultimately have 24/7/365 business channels that companies will refresh continuously to keep people coming back. The same will be true for business-to-business as for business-to-consumer sites. As the Web becomes filled with what, for lack of a better description, we will call 24/7 interactive visual destinations, they are going to become environments. My Yahoo! is a good example of a destination site that keeps growing with its visitors, and it keeps surprising them. Business leaders should understand that they have an amazing theater or, if you want a sports metaphor, an immense stadium available to them on the Web.

Leaders have to start thinking like entertainers. That is the big point. They have to ask, Once I get prospects into my theater, what do I do with them? Sell them things, yes, but what else? How do I keep them coming back for more? Some ideas: Make detailed instruction sheets (or manuals) available for every model of every product the company has ever produced. Announce new products, features, benefits, and prices. Establish bulletin boards where customers can talk to each other about their experiences with your product or service. Provide recipes if you're a food company, drug interactions and contraindications if you're a pharmaceutical company, simple maintenance instructions if you're a car company.

Coming up with entertaining ideas to keep people returning is something leaders have to get their employees to think about. It will be constituency-based entertainment. On the business-to-business side, some prospects will want new ideas on the use of this software or buying paper in bulk. It might sound boring, but some customers will want to know more about it, how other people do it. It takes the chat room idea to a new domain.

The goal is to tap into their ideas, and it will be huge. The Provocateur/entertainer will say, "How do I keep this thing alive? How do I have my *Seinfeld?* How do I have my 24-hour news program?" Employing audio, video, and colorful graphics, the entertainment will be so engaging that people—prospects, customers, employees, suppliers, reporters, everyone—will routinely return to see what's new.

In that way, continuing this whole community of entertainment, of education, and of moving is so cool because companies can do so many different things; they can appeal to myriad diverse interests. Amazon.com can have chat rooms with popular authors. L.L. Bean can have chat rooms with hikers and fishermen. Nike can have chat rooms with basketball players. Schwab can have chat rooms with financial advisers. IBM could have Internet gurus on e-commerce that someone could replay as many times as necessary. The company can offer the kind of entertainment online connected with the company's business. (Back to the principle that an educated consumer is your best customer.)

ADD TO YOUR REPERTOIRE

Just as great entertainers continue to add things to their repertoire, so do Provocateur/entertainers. Jeff Bezos, the founder of Amazon.com, started with books, added CDs, then DVD and videos, then just about everything else: art and collectibles, auctions, kitchen tools and equipment, lawn and patio furniture, tools and hardware, electronics, software, toys and video games, health and beauty aids, and furniture, lighting, and rugs. Plus, Amazon.com's zShops "offer hundreds of thousands of new, used, and hard-to-find products from specialty retailers, small businesses, and individuals—things like buffalo steaks, office furniture, used books, maternity clothes, golf clubs, second-hand CDs and videos, car parts, and time-share accommodations at resorts."

All this creates an entertaining environment in which people want to browse, shop, and buy, returning to my point that entertainment is an environment that keeps you attentive. For example, I went to Amazon because I was frustrated at not being able to find a real store or Web site that sold software for kids. The kids wanted new software for Christmas. At Amazon, I found the programs I wanted, but the company had made the presentation so enticing—by age group, by subject area—that I started to feel entertained. I went to Clifford the Big Red Dog, and it was connected to something I thought my son would like. I looked deeper into what that kind of software teaches and—click!—put it into my electronic shopping cart.

Bezos adapted the "Attention Kmart shoppers! Come to aisle five before all the snow shovels are gone. They are only $9.95." When everybody runs to buy the snow shovels, that's entertainment.

Oprah Winfrey, who is the ultimate Provocateur/entertainer, has recently established a magazine, *O,* that adds to her environment of the television show, production company, book club, and more. Now she will sell products through the magazine. A great leader will be like Oprah, who has been able to extend her interests into many related areas and create that environment of entertainment, buying, learning, and guiding.

The Provocateur/entertainer's challenge will be to orchestrate an authentic and entertaining presentation of what the company is doing to keep viewers returning to that channel. Lou Gerstner wants his constituencies returning to IBM.com time and time again. Jeff Bezos wants his constituencies returning to Amazon.com. Scott McNealy wants his constituencies returning to Sun.com. Provocateur/entertainers almost need the freshness of a nonstop Hollywood mentality.

One reason that *Seinfeld* obtained massive audiences was its innovation; the content needed to be fresh for every episode to get people to sit and be part of the show. Creating the show was exhausting but exhilarating, and was worth the record-setting money NBC gave to Jerry Seinfeld and his colleagues. The greatest CEOs of the next 5 to 10 to 20 years will be the ones who can sustain that kind of creative process.

Provocateur/entertainers are able to induce customers, shareholders, and reporters to come back for another act and another act and another. The tools exist to create entertaining environments to affect that loyalty. Which is why Pepsi-Cola is spending around $1.2 million (3 percent) of its advertising budget on the Internet. "This medium is here to stay, and we buy that," says John Vail, director of digital media and marketing for Pepsi-Cola.

What, one might ask, is a soft drink company doing on the Internet? Selling Pepsi? Well . . . yes.

The Web is the medium of choice for Pepsi's prime demographic audience—people under 25. While it is almost impossible to measure online advertising performance—to connect a banner to a sale, for example—Pepsi has made deals that do show tangible results. Example: In the summer of 2000, Pepsi made a barter arrangement with Web portal

Yahoo!. Pepsi printed the Yahoo! logo on 1.5 billion cans. In return, Yahoo! took over Pepsi's established loyalty program, PepsiStuff.

PepsiStuff.com let customers collect points from bottle caps: open an account at the site, enter the unique 10-digit number from a bottle cap, and receive points. Customers could redeem the points for merchandise on the Web site; prizes included CDs, concert tickets, electronic goods, and more. To make the site even more entertaining, it included an auction so that customers could bid their points on prizes.

Something like 3 million customers logged on and registered at the PepsiStuff site during the promotion (it ended December 31, 2000), giving Pepsi detailed consumer data that normally it must pay for in market research or glean from focus groups. Information that once took months to collect could now be had in days. What's more, Vail was able to tweak the program while it was in progress, maintaining the right inventory of the most popular prizes. "Instead of lag-time data, we had real-time, and we could react to it," says Vail. Sales of Pepsi and sister brand Mountain Dew rose 5 percent during the six-month online promotion, and it cost about one-fifth what it had been as a mail-in project.

PERFORM BEHIND THE SCENES

It is important to note that the leader does not have to appear personally on stage, and good Provocateur/entertainers also know they are not the entire show. Everyone can stand up and perform his or her own solo like a clarinet player in a good jazz band. In a great sports team, everybody has his or her part and the audience knows that this player is a great passer and that one is a great slam-dunker.

Meg Whitman does not have to personally entertain the

people who come to the eBay site. eBay could add a tour by a world expert on seventeenth-century American furniture before an auction; the tour may be both entertaining and informative, but Whitman does not have to give it.

The media and the public relations industry incessantly cite the need for today's CEOs to be business "rock stars." Public relations agencies even have practices dedicated to creating "CEO brands." I believe the CEO as brand is not interchangeable or synonymous with the company. John Chambers is not Cisco. Jack Welch is not GE. And even Michael Dell is not—or should not be—Dell. Cisco has its own developed brand and personality and environment, and John Chambers is the conductor or the Provocateur. He develops his own John Chambers brand, which is the smart salesman, driver, and visionary of the Internet world.

General Electric has its own corporate brands and sub-brands. Jack Welch is a brand himself. (Think not? How many people would buy a book with his name on it? We'll see when his book is published.) Welch complements the corporation—to make a serious understatement—but he has done a very good job of not being GE. The corporation would continue to thrive if Welch were hit by a bus. Indeed, part of a Provocateur's success is in creating an organization that continues to prosper after he or she is gone. Seiji Ozawa can leave the Boston Symphony, and it will continue to be a great orchestra. The Boston Symphony can have any number of guest conductors who will make great music with it. At some point, Provocateurs should think of themselves as brands. Being an entertainer is just one piece of becoming a deep, moving brand that can motivate customers, employees, and others.

Provocateur/entertainers have a special attitude toward

the world. They understand that life is grim, life is serious, life is real, but they also say let's have some fun while we're living it.

Too many executives seem to have the idea that if top management is seen as having fun, the world will perceive the company as not serious. That's obviously false. Quality entertainers have fun but know they are good. They know the fundamentals of what they do. They have practiced hard to act, to play the piano, to sing, to dance. The same is true for great Provocateur/entertainers.

George Conrades is the CEO of Akamai, a company that provides a global Internet delivery service for data, including streaming media, and applications that improve Web-site reliability while reducing complexity and cost of IT infrastructure. It has a network of more than 12,000 servers in 62 countries, continuously analyzing Internet traffic and delivering data and applications over the most efficient route from servers located as close as possible to the requesting user.

I asked Conrades, who had been a senior executive at IBM, what's been the biggest surprise of leading the start-up. He tells me, "How much total fun it is to be surrounded by people who are such high caliber. Because the intelligence and energy level are so high and because they interact well, I've never seen such incredible progress. I've never seen individuals contribute so much on their own initiative and have everybody else celebrate their achievements. I drive home at night and I don't worry. There are at least 15 very bright, very motivated people working on any given problem."

ENTERTAIN DURING THE BAD TIMES

It is easier to feel like entertaining when the company is growing. There are opportunities, bonuses, and good feelings. But the economy does not always expand, and industries do not always grow. How do you have fun when customers don't buy, the stock tanks, and employees start taking extra-long lunch hours?

One can always promote innovation, even within a business that is not growing. We have been using the metaphor of the community, but I would like to shift to a metaphor of the garden. A vegetable garden still provides enjoyment when it is the same size every year. You watch things grow in a limited space; similarly you can still do that in a limited marketplace company. The challenge is to continue being innovative in thinking about additional services, about creative things the company can do around the product.

Maybe this year we'll plant pumpkins. Let's inject a little innovation into this process to see if something does take off. In that way the company can start the growth or change or innovative cycles that are so important to keeping an environment fun, interesting, and motivating to employees and customers. When the economy does turn around, the company is well positioned to take advantage of the opportunities that appear.

I know that some mature industries will find it hard to figure out a way to grow. It is one thing when your technology is evolving every week, another thing entirely when the last major advance was in 1950. Nevertheless, I believe a business in the most moribund industry can grow through innovation, creativity, and Provocative leadership.

And to lead the company into new, more profitable paths is the task of a Sherpa guide.

6

THE SHERPA GUIDE

Now we're thinking, how can we make customers happier? What opportunities are there to advance that experience with us? It's a way for us to both address an ever extending relationship with the customer and, frankly, a chance to grow our revenues and profits.

—Rick Wagoner,
president and CEO,
General Motors

The Sherpa guide is a Provocateur who is able to conduct others—customers, employees, suppliers, even entire companies—along an uncertain path, developing individual skills and strengthening commitment at every step.

A Sherpa guide is not the same as an educator, and the well-rounded Provocateur is both. The educator listens to prospects and customers before the company develops a product or service. Once the product is available, the Sherpa guide helps customers use it. Stated differently, the educator sets up the tour, arranges the travel, reserves the hotels, and chooses the sights the group will visit. The guide takes over once the traveler is on the move. Once the customer has bought the product or the service, once she is standing before the temple, the guide helps her get the most out of it.

The educator tends to function best in a classroom (which may be a conference room, a cubical, or a shopping mall). The classroom is the place to learn what people want and to help people learn. The educator helps people answer questions like: Why is this Ford Explorer better for me than that Chevy Suburban? Why is this Dell laptop better for me than the IBM Thinkpad? Why is Canon's video camera better than Sony's?

The Sherpa guide functions best at the customer's, employee's, or business's side (which may be a computer screen, a printed manual, or a DVD disc). Here's how to get the most out of your new car, laptop, or video camera. Guides think about how to make the customer's experience so rewarding, so interesting, so comfortable they want to return for the next adventure.

PROVOCATEUR/GUIDES LEAD CUSTOMERS

Doug Burgum, CEO of Great Plains Software, is a Sherpa guide. The Fargo, North Dakota, company develops and manufactures business-management software for the midsize market. In 2000 the company had sales of almost $200 million, more than 1,500 employees, and offices around the world.

Burgum grew up in Arthur, North Dakota, (population 40) where his family operated a farm and grain-elevator business. He went to North Dakota State University, then to graduate school at Stanford. He joined McKinsey & Co. in the early 1980s and left after two years to become vice president of marketing at Great Plains Software (GPS). In 1984, he mortgaged the family farmland, convinced his mother and siblings to do the same, and bought the company, becoming president. At the time, GPS had about 15 employees.

A year earlier, Burgum had gone to his first Comdex, the computer industry show, to promote Great Plains Software. He felt, based on the traffic at the GPS booth, that the show was going well until he checked the program to see which other companies producing accounting software for small business were also exhibiting. He is still sobered by what he found. "There were 63 companies listed," he says.

How do you stand out from 63 competitors? Great Plains sold its products through retailers, and Burgum did not want to hurt their margins (or his own) by cutting prices. Nor did he want to gussy up the products by adding bells and whistles that, while giving GPS something to talk about, did not add real functionality.

Burgum, however, thinks like a Sherpa guide. He looks to Marco Polo, James Cook, and Meriwether Lewis and William Clark for lessons in risk taking, teamwork, and having the courage to do what has never been done before. Burgum likes to remind himself and his employees, "Life is a journey—and a good traveler has no fixed plans and is not intent upon arriving." He believes that openness to the unexpected, combined with a refusal to give up dreams no matter how outlandish they appear to others, is what leads to great discoveries and accomplishments.

So in 1983, rather than cut prices or add features, Burgum addressed the biggest problem with accounting software at the time: "Nobody was answering the phone," he says. Customers with problems could not get answers. But answering customer questions raised its own problem: If Great Plains gave every call the attention it required, it would go out of business paying its support reps.

Burgum's solution? Charge for customer service. It was not a brand-new idea; software developers had always bundled the cost of support into the program's purchase price. But no developer had dared to force customers to pay for the right to call the company for help. Great Plains thought it could do so because "accountants charge their customers for their time," says Jodi Uecker-Rust, a group vice president at Great Plains. "Sure, theirs is a professional service, but so is ours. We're not telling people how to plug in their keyboard. We're helping them set up general ledgers and their chart of accounts."

Great Plains introduced service plans that allowed each customer to pay a fixed amount for an unlimited number of support calls, or they could pay on a per-call basis, but nothing would be free. Fortunately for Great Plains Software, accountants accepted the concept, and sales continued to grow.

With the policy an apparent success, Burgum asked more questions: Can we guarantee that the more customers pay, the quicker an expert on their problem will call them back? If customers could talk to the same reps every time they called, could they develop relationships with people who know their needs? The answer to both turns out to be yes. Today, Great Plains calls customers back within half an hour. As an example of the relationships that can develop between reps and customers: One accountant sent a rep and his wife plane tickets to Chicago and took them to a Bears game.

Burgum ignored people who said he would never be able to recruit the talent he needed to move to Fargo. He says he was inspired by the Lewis and Clark expedition of 1804. Lewis, a quiet intellectual, found in Clark "a partner who was as outgoing as he was introverted and as skilled in the outdoors as he was competent at book learning," says Burgum. They deliberately chose expedition members from very different backgrounds who shared a dream of exploring the West. Burgum asks his employees, "Do you see this as an adventure? Do you want to be part of this group moving forward?"

George Conrades, the CEO of Akamai, is another Provocateur who, like Burgum, exhibits Sherpa guide characteristics, reflected in how the company deals with customer calls. Akamai's customer care people are responsible for solving any technical problems that arise. They field the day-to-day phone calls whenever a customer has a question or needs help.

"There are two things that are distinctive in the way we manage customer care," says Conrades. "First is that even though customer care resides within our sales and support unit, it's tightly wedded to our research and development unit. In fact, we often rotate R&D people through customer care. That creates two big benefits. It brings deep technical knowledge into customer care, which enables us to answer our customers' questions quickly and confidently. And it exposes our R&D people directly to customers, so they can draw on that customer knowledge to refine our technology."

Conrades says that Akamai receives hundreds of requests per quarter for service improvement of some kind. These may be in Akamai's base business or something that suggests a new offer. If a customer says to a customer care rep, "I like what you're doing, but could you do this with it?" Akamai tracks those suggestions for possible innovations.

Which leads to the second distinction about its customer care: "We treat every call as a high priority. Most customer call centers employ a form of triage an escalation process," says Conrades. "A call comes in, and it's answered by a fairly low-level employee who has minimal expertise. If it's a simple question, that employee may be able to answer it. If it's more complicated, the caller gets bumped up to a second level to an employee who has a slightly higher level of knowledge. If that person can't answer the question, the caller gets bumped up to the top level, where he finally gets to speak to a real expert."

If the company's goal is to minimize costs, that kind of system makes sense. It's cheaper to hire novices than experts. "But from the customer's point of view, it just makes it harder and more time-consuming to get the information you need. You have to wait for a callback, or you have to make another call yourself when you realize the information you received was incorrect or insufficient."

Akamai's policy is to take all questions on the first call and to address all inquiries upfront. "We don't refuse to respond to any question," says Conrades. "Eighty-five percent of the time it is not even in our network, but we want to know because we may learn something. We have Ph.D.'s in customer care, and they are commissioned to listen for things that don't affect us, or aren't our problem, or aren't our fault, but could be a new service if you hear it often enough. Maybe there is a way we could have precluded a given problem."

The policy offers Akamai another benefit, says Conrades. "Our customer care people write tools to automate themselves, which they love to do because really smart people hate repetitive tasks. They are thinking, 'I don't want to hear that question again,' so they write some kind of tool that can be accessed by customers through an online portal, and go on to the next one. With the level one, level two, level three system, the people on the first two levels don't care if they keep hearing the same question."

CUSTOMERS NEED GUIDES

Business is a journey, not a destination, so it requires guides. The relationships a company establishes are not static; they grow and change. Some become incredibly fruitful, while some wither and die. As the contemporary economy becomes more and more experiential—as people grow more interested in experiences than in products per se—they will need guides to help them find the best experiences. The Sherpa guide says to customers, "Take my hand; we're going on a journey. I know what's ahead. I've been there, and I'm going to show you wonderful things."

The great Sherpa guide has listened to people, analyzed the information, and knows what is—and is not—important to customers. Such a guide knows what a person can and cannot do (can walk 10 miles a day, cannot climb a rock face), and what interests, engages, and delights her. The Sherpa guide shapes an experience that makes customers feel so pleasantly surprised they want to go again, go deeper. The customers of Provocateur/guides say, "I want the next experience from Saturn," or "I want the next experience from Panasonic," or "I want the next experience from Norwegian Cruise Lines."

The Sherpa guide embodies the idea of exploration. Provocateur/guides instill in employees and customers the idea that business is a pilgrimage, one based on vision and one that has no final destination. In this situation, "vision" is a verb, not a noun, and the vision is constantly evolving.

The Generals would lay out a vision that was very noun-like. By that I mean it did not move. It was not an ongoing experience. It was not about discovering what's around the next bend. It was: "We are going to build a car (or a washing machine, or a clock, or whatever), and that's it." Generals gave little or no thought to the process or the experience of those involved in both the product's creation and the customer's encounter with the final product.

Sherpa guides learn as they go. If they turn down a different path, or they see a new tree or flower, that becomes part of the overall plan. Few companies build a dialogue with the customer as conscientiously as Great Plains or Akamai. Some companies are attentive and sensitive, and after receiving one input from customers they make a change to the product. But few companies return to customers continually, building a conversational loop to understand what is happening and how to continually improve a product.

Since business is an endless journey, goals need to be experiences and not end results. A goal should not be to reach the mountaintop as fast as possible, but to savor the experience. As Robert Louis Stevenson wrote in 1881, "To travel hopefully is a better thing than to arrive." Everest may be a destination, but reaching Everest's summit is like watching a product finally roll off the assembly line. It is the experience of driving that is the value, not the car. It is watching a grandchild's first steps, not the video camera. Producing the product is a destination, but we have destinations only so we may undergo the experience of reaching them.

Occasionally, like an Everest expedition, you have one chance to make the dash to the summit. Most businesses do not have many chances to connect with prospects and make them want to come back. If a customer enjoyed her first experience buying books at Amazon.com or sheets at Bloomingdale's, she may come back, a sign the retailer kept her involved. Perhaps she does not buy every time, but she still enjoys visiting, seeing what's new, being in the environment, being guided to potential purchases, or all of the above.

HELP PEOPLE WITH EXPERIENCES

In today's experience economy, people need a Sherpa guide to help them along the road of experience. Business is not as either/or as it once was. In the past, either the company sold a product or it didn't, and once it made a sale it often had as little to do with the customer as possible. Today, the important thing is not the sale itself but the relationship before, during, and after the sale.

The great Sherpa guide has listened to customers carefully and knows that it's not important to this particular person to find a fancy restaurant but it is important to see birds and flowers. With enough information, the company can suggest, "You should go to Wyoming for at least 10 days because you will see extraordinary birds and flowers, and this is how much it will cost because you should hire a guide who specializes in wildflowers."

A friend works as a tour guide in Japan, leading groups of Americans. He sees it as his job to infect the people he guides with the enthusiasm he feels for Japanese culture. In Kyoto, on the way to the sixth temple garden in four days, the tour passes a dozen model homes a Japanese developer offers. Some groups want to see the Zen garden; others want to give it a quick look and spend an hour going through the houses to see how the Japanese live. My friend listens to the group and adjusts the tour accordingly.

Provocateur/guides bring sensitivity to listening and then shaping an experience that makes customers feel it is remarkable and enjoyable. The experience is so great they want to go again and go deeper. That's what business leaders should want in customers. Rick Wagoner, the president and CEO of General Motors, should want his customers to say, "I want the next experience from Chevrolet, from Buick, from Cadillac." Jeff Taylor, the CEO of Monster.com, should want people to say, "I want to find my next job through Monster.com."

True, General-led companies stuffed products—software, answering machines, or cars—with functionality, but they would not always help customers fully understand the functionality. (How many people can program their VCRs? Use the microwave for heating more than leftovers?) Instruction guides were poorly written and often covered several similar product models to save the marketer's printing budget. Customers often ignored the guides when the product was new and had lost them by the time they wanted help.

The Web makes it possible for a manufacturer to post a separate instruction guide for every single model—including products from the past—and to show with words, pictures, and motion how exactly to use the product. In the future, successful companies will help customers to effortlessly explore and learn about a product or a service in depth. Customers will be able to learn what they want at their own pace and on their own schedule.

Provocateur/guides are leaders who have listened, learned, and personalized the customer's experience with their companies and their products. These companies can return a year later to offer an even richer experience because they now know that someone really liked the flower walks and were not interested in the birds or did not care as much about Zen Buddhism but loved the Oriental art.

Sherpa guides also understand what is needed for the trek. Pack a poncho in case it rains, bring extra water, and don't forget the matches. Provocateurs show both employees and the other communities what they will need for the best experience. They are capturing more and more individual data to fashion environments people want to visit and to develop products and services they want to buy.

The best Provocateur/guides learn about individual interests through evolving technology that I'll talk about in Chapter 8. They build the data sets to profile business or consumer customers so they can continue to customize their communication to build a better relationship, sell more products or services, or both.

Manufacturing companies are looking at Dell, Gateway, and Cannondale Bicycle as models for how to build-to-order for individual customers. That can mean no finished goods inventory, fewer returns, and loyal, happy, satisfied customers.

In a sense, it does not matter that Michael Dell began his business by selling personal computers. Because Dell today knows so much about its customers, it should be able to effectively sell them a wide variety of related goods and services, including financing, extended service contracts, Internet access, and more. If someone is a good guide, he knows a great deal about the people he is leading and knows that even though the group has never been to, say, the Sonora Desert, they will, based on past experience, enjoy it.

INNOVATE FROM THE COMPANY'S CENTER

Returning to an earlier point that a company must endlessly innovate, it should cultivate a culture of innovation based on customer relationships. I know that's easy to say, and I have visited dozens of companies where executives say they do exactly that. But we are not that far away from the Generals' world in which innovation in R&D labs was about as far removed from headquarters as they could put it. Top management seems to feel that if sales or marketing or finance or manufacturing or operations hears about developments in the lab, they will stop focusing on current products and instead start worrying about products that do not yet, and may never, exist.

Marketing has to become the common denominator in all business functions. Finance has to understand its part in communicating to the customer, too, when it sends out an invoice. Sales has to maintain a constant dialogue to make sure the customer is content. Manufacturing has to encour-

age a constant dialogue that brings the customer into designing new versions and correcting quality bugs.

If a customer has a problem, there is a system to deal with
it, no matter who the customer contacts—the salesperson, a
customer service rep, or a friend on the board of directors. In
a business relationship, most customers go directly to their
salesperson with a service, delivery, finance, or other problem. Often the salesperson doesn't care or doesn't know how
to solve—or have the authority to solve—the problem. Too
often all he can do is pass the customer off to a clerk, who
also doesn't care and isn't getting a commission on the business, either. The Provocateur-run company will find a way to
keep everything in a dialogue loop to maintain the relationship and reward employees for their contributions.

Rick Wagoner, the president and CEO of General Motors,
points out that only a handful of companies have survived the
past hundred years, survived because they successfully adapted
themselves. Some survivors changed what they do, and some,
like GM, are in a business that changes slowly. "We are in a
business that has changed a lot over 100 years, but nobody has
changed the way you transport people. But it is sobering to
look back at companies that were huge from 1900 to 1950 that
aren't around or take a significantly different role."

Wagoner says the companies that can dynamically reinvent themselves and live many, many years are truly interesting. "Part of our job is preservation of the enterprise. So
besides all the day-to-day pressures and the building-
shareholder-value pressures and innovative-product pressures, and leading-an-e-business pressures, behind you is this:
You want this company to be successful for another 50 years.
Are we doing the right stuff for that?"

To answer his own question, Wagoner tells me that GM
is trying to change the way it looks at the market. In the past,

for example, it began selling parts because that was a way to sell cars. Now, "we are trying to think more broadly. Let's keep our eyes out and look what else we can do to enhance our relationship with our customer. Can we be more proactive? A great example is cell phones. In the mid-1980s when they first came in, we basically said, 'Shoot, to get somebody to buy a car, I guess we have to put a cell phone in it.' So we reluctantly did, rather than saying, 'Hey, there are five million people talking on the phone. What's the business opportunity we have? How can we make it easy for them?' Rather than offering a great service that will help keep selling new cars and trucks, now we're thinking: We have customers . . . how can we make them happier? What opportunities are there to advance that experience with us? How can we integrate it for our customer in a safe, cost-effective way? It's a way for us to both address an ever extending relationship with the customer and, frankly, a chance to grow our revenues and profits, too."

If I ran a company that manufactured products, I would hold monthly how-could-this-product-possibly-be-better sessions. What do we know about the way customers use our product? What would they like to see more of? Less of? What new technology or material could we use to cut costs? Raise quality? Allow a whole new approach? Whether it be an automobile or a piece of software, a machine tool or a bottle of salad dressing, I would have representatives from all parts of the company say whatever they think. Set no limits to how this could be more innovative.

It is amazing that with immediate communications available, many CEOs are out of touch with the actual business realities of the day. And that is why, over the history of business, most great movements and directions came from the bottom up and not the top down. Pat McGovern told me that virtually all of IDG's successful businesses have come from customer suggestions or employee customer contacts; relatively few of the product ideas management originated were major successes.

Generals tend to frustrate innovation through meetings and memos. Provocateur/guides understand that even though meetings will always be with us (indeed, I suggested a monthly meeting just a moment ago), they can create a culture to get things done. In today's communications economy, we should be able to evolve a community through a conversation rather than a memo, a meeting if necessary, then a decision.

The whole process of decision making in General-led companies was bizarre at best, and thoroughly political at worst. The Provocateur/guide's process of decision making should follow a whole different path, if possible. Here is an example: The leader sends an email to all employees, outlining a possible restructuring. The email is not an edict, and it is not final. It is the beginning of a dialogue. It suggests reasons for a change, some ways the company should be structured, and asks people what they think. It starts a conversation, and leads it. "Change" carries the connotation that the company will lose things that actually work well. There may in fact be many things that do not need to change, but businesses do require constant innovation in which employees, customers, and suppliers feel comfortable.

A person may have a favorite hotel or restaurant or Web site, and over the years, although the changes barely register, management renovates the rooms, adds new dishes to the menu, and introduces new functionality to the site. The hotel/restaurant/site experience remains the same but different; it continues to keep the customer's interest and maintains her comfort so she does not go elsewhere.

A great Provocateur/guide-run company maintains an element of consistency. The Royal Shakespeare Company is for me the epitome of great theater. But it surprises me every time I see a play; the company brings in a different actor or actress I did not know was going to perform or has put a different twist to familiar scenery. Nevertheless, as a member of the audience I feel safe within the community I originally joined, confident that the play will be stimulating and rewarding.

Another example: Automakers would be foolish to change the way a car's steering or brake pedals work; it would be dangerous. (Americans who have rented a car in England or Japan understand the distractions of adapting to a right-hand drive.) Automakers do, however, regularly introduce enhancements—all-wheel-drive, antilock brakes, air bags—that improve the product. If the company is able to create a community of value that will exist and build on itself, the payoff should be immense.

Innovation best occurs in real time, which I feel will be easier with the Web. By real time, consider the example of my friend's Suburban. Chevrolet is not going to visit her house to modify her Suburban, but it might have said, "This is the first year of a radically new design, and we would like your comments on these five things that we changed." She would have told them about the two things she does not like and why. That is real-time innovation because the company is collecting data on a regular basis so they don't repeat the same mistake in future models. With it, Chevrolet has built a relationship because it can now say, "Here, Mrs. X, we apologize for the two things you hated. We have heard from many others that that innovation was not quite right, so we are going to adjust it in the future. We know that doesn't do a lot for you, but here is a free . . ." ski rack or concert tickets or something else the customer values.

Apply the example to a company's marketing questions: Should we go into this product area? Add this service? Does this move make sense? Tapping involved communities that will give management instant feedback to make decisions is the next level of innovation. It is hard to find examples of companies doing this today because I don't think many actually do it. But it is an idea whose time is coming.

The constant circle of innovation and technology is going to allow us to gather information, organize it, and apply it for better products and service. Stewart Alsop at New Enterprise Associates notes that part of the ethics of operating in this new economy is how companies treat an individual's private information. "That's perhaps the highest-order objective in all this technology to make life simpler. We want to deal with those things we want to deal with and do it with the least amount of hassle. But the only way you can accomplish that is by having your preferences recorded and distributed so that vendors can supply based on your preference. You have to adopt an attitude that you want people to know who you are and what you want to get the services you want. I absolutely firmly believe that, and I think that people do. I think consumers want the benefits—but they don't want companies to abuse that information."

GENERATE A SENSE OF TRUST

Provocateur/guides understand that business in the Internet age has to do with first creating an environment and then leading a journey through that environment. They are skilled and experienced and have been to these places (or similar ones) before. They are available to point out the cool and interesting things along the way. Once we know what we want in great communities and companies, then we want somebody who knows the territory to help us explore it.

Provocateur/guides generate a sense of trust. People trust them for help in this new environment.

Companies, if they are not dying, are changing, innovating. That is the environment that businesses want to create, and Sherpa guides, by the nature of what they do, help people understand what is new, changed, and innovative. The company keeps the environment fresh and unexpected, while maintaining a sense of security, reliability, trust, and fun.

One way (of many) to do this is to constantly talk about merger and acquisition activity. Would that be a good company to approach? Such inquiries should not take the focus off what the firm is doing, but will create an environment that entertains possibilities. What would life be like if we were twice as big? What if we had that complement of an offering? What if we were bought? Generals, by the way, used to hide this kind of speculation, feeling perhaps that any merger talk weakened the company's bargaining position.

Another way to keep a company vital is to set new research directions. Try to come up with new products, new services, new directions, and new partnerships.

Ray Ozzie, the CEO of Groove Networks, notes that establishing a level of trust between the top people is absolutely critical. Also, "everyone should be acting and building their organizations, their suborganizations, as though they are completely replaceable. There shouldn't be any problem just dropping things and walking away for two weeks. Obviously, you have appointments and you have external commitments, but the organization should know so well what is expected of it that it is fault tolerant." If someone needs something and the immediate supervisor is not available, there should be a mechanism to deal with the issue. "That is extremely important when you get into phases of the business where you have to go more on the road," says Ozzie.

"or an emergency happens. A crisis. Or you're doing a merger and suddenly you're not available."

While the software industry has always been filled with independent mavericks and has therefore tended to have managers who allow more freedom than many industries, the attitude is spreading to other areas. "Software has always been managing at the edge," says Ozzie. "It is managing chaos. Everybody asks, is software an art, or is it a science, or is it engineering, or what is it? That's tough to say because it's not so fixed as to be engineering, and there is a right-brain side of it, and people tend not to be easily managed. They can't necessarily predict themselves what they are like and what they are going to run into, so the environment is fairly chaotic."

The Provocateur/guide creates an environment in which it is productive to have the unexpected. Much like the guide in Japan who will say, "I know this isn't on the itinerary, but I really know this great papercraft shop. It might not be your taste, but I really think based on what you've said you might want to look at it." A great Provocateur/guide knows when to suggest something.

Ultimately the great Provocateur/guide wants to disappear. The tour guide, after introducing his group to the Japanese temple and talking about its history and significance, lets the group experience the building and the garden and create their own memories. A great company does the same thing. It wants the customers to get so turned on by the place where it has led them that they are going to buy. Ideally, that experience is so good they come back for more.

SHOW THE WAY TO RICHER POSSIBILITIES

I was always fascinated by a phenomenon in the software business. We would introduce a product for, say, Lotus

Development and then research the ways customers were using the new functionality the product provided. We inevitably found that people were not using the new functions very much; they took advantage of only about 20 percent of the software's capability. So even though Lotus pumped the new product full of features and benefits, customers ended up using pretty much the same old product.

I realized that even though a lot of the new functionality was very good, no one at Lotus was asking customers whether they were thinking of the usefulness of specific features. It held focus groups to explore improvements customers would like to see in the software and then incorporated improvements they suggested. Every time Lotus gave the program more graphics—bubble charts in addition to bar charts, for example—customers seldom used them. Until Lotus established a usability lab, it never followed up to ensure that customers actually understood and used the new features.

A Provocateur will figure out how to help customers use features and be comfortable with them before giving them more. You don't want to end up with 10 features piled one atop another that customers never use—and, in fact, start to alienate customers.

A friend says he owned his Handspring Visor—not a difficult product to use—for six months before he realized what the four buttons on the front do. Why wouldn't Handspring, which is a very creative company, have a Web site that immediately sends everyone who registers their new Visor an email and walks the customer through the basic features? One reason could be because Americans don't like to read manuals. But a Web site with streaming video is interactive and visual; a human being shows you how easy it is to use the device.

I have an Olympus D490 Zoom digital camera, which the box says is "highest quality, versatile, easy to use." I have not used it, however. I opened the package, but the manual is so intimidating I put everything back in the box and it sits on a shelf. And I'm someone who has grown up in technology.

I bought Sprint phone equipment for the house in Florida, including a message service—but no one explained how it works. I assumed it was like other systems: pick up the receiver and if there is no dial tone you have messages. In Florida, I picked up the receiver and heard an electronic *beep, beep, beep, beep* . . . My first thought: The phone is broken and I just bought this stuff.

I used my cell phone to call Sprint and report the problem only to learn it's not a problem. You dial a special number through the beeps to obtain your messages. I felt dumb and irritated. Somebody could have said, "Mr. Weber, you've bought the call answering capability. When you have messages, you will pick up the phone and hear a beep. All you have to do is dial through that."

Sprint needs a Provocateur/guide to say, "Here's a customer who just bought sophisticated phone and fax equipment. How do we help him use them to be more productive, to make his life easier?" Sprint could have made a follow-up phone call. They could have sent email. They could have directed me to a Web site that told me how to set up the equipment. They didn't, and instead of one isolated, irritated customer, Sprint now has thousands of people reading about its inadequacies.

To be fair, of course Sprint is not alone. Tell friends a product horror story, and they will tell you theirs about cars and computers, airlines and appliances, insurance and Internet service.

Provocateur/guides look for new tools to help people understand and enjoy their products on a consistent basis. To enjoy the video or digital camera, to suggest new ideas about how to use it. A company cannot make too much information available, ideally in a place customers can easily find and in a format they can easily understand.

I am on my fifth BMW because they excite me with something a little different every time I go to look for a new BMW. BMW has done a very good job explaining its car, which has more integrated circuits than a computer. A new BMW has an awesome array of control buttons and indicators, but to ease the new owner through the array, the car also comes with a CD that talks the driver through the features while driving. During the first few days I had my car, I put on the CD and would learn a few things each day. If I had questions the CD did not address, I could call a toll free number. The BMW Web site has more answers. BMW is a good example of how to help customers use and appreciate the product.

Generals did not see themselves as guides (leaders, yes, in the form of "Follow me!" as they charged up the hill). Generals saw the company's job as to make the best product possible and push it out the factory door. The things that got businesses in trouble often resulted because they did not go the extra mile on the actual use of the product or the company's relationship.

Moreover, in time good Sherpa guides will train people to be their own guides. When that happens, customers know their own destinations. They know where they want to go. They know how to learn something new and buy something new. Venture capitalists have traveled across the territory before and know how to help a new company. Eventually, management will not need the VC's help.

At the same time, you want to make sure that the Sherpa guide has the right experience. Generals who were very good and had lots of experience were often unable to apply that experience to building customer relationships. They used their experience to make decisions on the business battle-field, and they often made the right decisions for that time or their companies could not have survived. Today's leaders need to use their knowledge to help make the customer's experience over time better, richer, and deeper.

PROVOCATEUR/GUIDES AS NEW LEADERS

When Provocateur/guides are hired for or promoted to a new position, they, like every human, carry mental, emotional, and experiential baggage. They need analytical time (or self-research time) before they make major decisions about what to do or where to go, unless the situation is so dire it demands immediate action. When leaders come into an existing situation, they have to approach it differently from how they would a start-up. Certainly a Provocateur could come into an existing company and wreck it by considering it a clean slate with no history, no traditions, no culture. Even a Provocateur who has spent a career within a corporation can stumble upon being promoted to the top position and make a similar mistake.

One recent example is Durk I. Jager, by all published accounts a Provocateur on the right track to make the neces-sary changes, who resigned in June 2000 as CEO of Procter & Gamble after 17 months on the job. It appears that the culture was stronger than Jager and that P&G's board would not give him enough time for his changes to show strong posi-tive results. "We undertook too much change too fast," said John E. Pepper, a retired P&G chief executive who was reinstalled as the corporation's chairman. "We clearly took on more than we were able to execute."

One of Jager's most controversial decisions was to allow marketing money for one brand to be shifted to promote another, thus repealing a time-honored P&G practice. As one result, core brands such as Bounty paper towels, Always feminine-protection pads, Charmin toilet tissue, Downy fabric softener, Pampers disposable diapers, Pantene hair care products, and Pringles potato crisps lost sales and market share. P&G lost control of some costs as it compensated certain managers for their success at rolling out brands without having to worry about profits. "We moved people into new jobs with new systems. We lost some of our instinctive feel for the business," says the new president and CEO, Alan G. Lafley. Bounty had four brand managers in 18 months.

Jager changed P&G's lengthy budget process, replacing it with "stretch" goals, which meant a business could spend based on targeted sales. When P&G's board saw that projected sales had grown just 1 to 2 percent and per-share earnings projected to be flat—not up the 15 to 17 percent announced earlier—Jager had no choice but to resign.

At the same time, reported *The Wall Street Journal,* P&G "is struggling with brutal price competition around the world, a stodgy 163-year-old corporate culture, and a stock market that doesn't favor Old Economy makers of soap and diapers." But if Jager's reforms were not the way to increase P&G's sales and earnings, what is?

Lafley, who has been with the company since 1977, said P&G will "return to our conservative" budget planning and abandon Jager's "stretch" forecasting. "Stretch and speed are means to an end. . . . They're not ends in themselves and never a substitute for good business sense," said Lafley.

Provocateur/guides can use past and current events to work in their favor to shape an environment best suited to motivate the employees. It is critically important to know how the business got to its present situation before the Sherpa guide tries to lead it out of that situation.

GUIDE WITHOUT CONSULTANTS

On the surface, it would seem that management consultants act as Sherpa guides for corporate executives. The problem I see is that management consultants do not actually go on the journey with the company.

The big consulting firms tend to hire absolutely top-notch MBA graduates who have had two years of experience between their undergraduate and graduate degrees. As a result, they do not have much hands-on, practical experience. They're like people who have read books about skiing—indeed, they know the history, economics, theory, and physics of skiing—but have never actually skied down a mountain. Also, I find that consultants often come into the company and listen to the management, not the customers.

Their recommendations are not based on an intuitive management style, as opposed to the Provocateur's leadership style. Consultants know the rules, but the world is becoming more intuitive-based, more experiential-based, and tools like the Web, which are increasingly experiential, are going to be extremely important to management.

Provocateurs are more in touch with the entire company than with one specific area. The great leaders of the future will be those who have a core competency like finance, marketing, operations, or human resources, but are flexible enough and intelligent enough to learn and broaden what they do. Rick Wagoner presents an example.

Wagoner has discussed with me what General Motors has been learning about running a global business. He points out that speechwriters coined the phrase, "GM was global before global was cool," but global today differs greatly from what it was just 10 years ago. At that point, a company with an operation in Germany and Brazil was global. Those businesses more or less ran themselves, and, to oversimplify the relationship slightly, headquarters sent a telex once a week.

Now, says Wagoner, global is very different. "The lessons we learned about what works or not is what I call operating on the ground, which I think a lot of new companies don't do very well. They assume they are global if they fly a couple of people in and start selling their software. But you are global when you have Germans and Belgians running the operation in Germany, Brazilians running Brazil, Chinese running China, and they are thinking the same way you are, talking about the business in the same way, applying the principles the same way."

Because all business is global but all sales are local, says Wagoner, management's challenge is to use the global resources to help sell locally. "Customers aren't the same—maybe luxury buyers are similar—but customers are very different because the market circumstances are very different. So you have got to be able to do what works locally. With a few exceptions, we are so much better in the market where we've got manufacturing firms and engineering presence. I think we have better talent, more robust careers for Brazilians because we don't just have salespeople. We have engineers, manufacturing people, and we build a richer talent base and attract better people."

Wagoner feels that one key is to build a common mind-set among leadership—ideally a global mind-set as opposed to an American mind-set. Another key is sustainability, the strength and flexibility to ride out the economic ups and downs, which is where the time will tell if the business has the right strategy. "But going into a country, starting up, leaving if it's not working, coming back when the economy is hot is not being global. That's being an opportunist. You can't build a business—at least the kind we're in—by doing that. But on the other hand, you can't, particularly when the pressure is on the third-quarter earnings, offset losses somewhere else. You have to set up a business that can operate with a mix of businesses that can be sustainable. There are going to be some rough roads. We probably have better returns on our investments in Brazil than any place in the world. There have been some years when it was off, so you have got to know the business's overall position to be able to ride out the ups and downs. Communication helps a lot. It's not difficult to be local; it's difficult to be global. And today we have to do that with technology and efficiency."

As an exercise, take the characteristics of the Sherpa guide and think about your company's customers. How would you plan a formal tour of the company and its products or services or both? How would you make the appeal so compelling they buy? What are they looking for? What excites them? What do you think they would pay for? What are they worried about? What kinds of ways do they like to have fun? This exercise can quickly move a culture of marketing and communication and relationship management to the company's core, which is what you have to do.

Provocateur/guides allow their people to have their experiences and make their mistakes, as long as it is not a mistake that is going to destroy the business. A mistake may cost money, and it may be embarrassing, but it is often the best way—or the only way—to learn. Doug Burgum at Great

Plains Software has tried to acknowledge and learn from his mistakes, just as his hero-explorers did. Several years ago, he approved the release of some software that had glitches and caused customers numerous problems. As a way to show his humility, he stood in front of a group of sales partners, smashed three eggs on his head, and apologized. He also asked his customers to compute how much time they had lost because of the problem. "We couldn't send them checks for the time they had lost, but we wanted them to know we understood that our problem was costing them time and money," he says. "Nine out of 10 of those affected said they still wanted to work with us."

7

THE HEAD CONCIERGE

The CEO should be in charge of the experience to please the investors and the clientele—all constituencies. And cleanliness in the office, whether you take care of it or not, whether you are truthful or not—that is the experience of the company.

—George Colony, CEO,
Forrester Research

A great concierge is the ultimate purveyor of service, and we have moved into an era in business in which marketing is at one with service. I said earlier that marketing—the relationship with the customer—should be the core of everything a senior executive does. Part of marketing is service; and the best metaphor for great service is the head concierge at a great hotel.

The more you stay at a fine hotel, the more you work with the concierge, the more he is able to help make your stay enjoyable. The great concierge knows your preferences in wine, food, flowers, art, theater, and sports. Moreover, the great concierge knows where to find what you prefer. The great concierge is selfless and involved in the guest's complete experience.

(One reason why Japanese service is extraordinary: The word for "guest" is the same as the word for "customer." The friend who visits your home is *okyakusan,* and the person who buys from your business is *okyakusan.* Their idea that a customer is an honored presence is evident in their language.)

The concierge knows the guest who likes flowers and makes sure there are flowers in her room. He knows the guest who likes contemporary art and suggests a gallery opening. He watches to see who will be checking in and leaves a message for their arrival: "Please call Jerome if you would like to go to an exciting new Vietnamese restaurant."

I love the Four Seasons Hotel chain, but after staying 40-plus times at the New York Four Seasons, and after asking 40-plus times for allergy-free pillows, I thought it was time for the company to wake up. So, apparently, did the Four Seasons. Recently I checked in and said, somewhat irritably, to the front-desk clerk, "Again, I have to ask, like I do every time, can I have—" She put up her hand to stop me. "Mr. Weber, we've already put allergy-free pillows in your room." I was impressed because I'd never taken the time to complain or suggest they add that information to the data they maintain about me.

This equation has two sides: Know your customers and know the resources. It is not enough to know a guest loves German black bread in the morning; you must also know where to obtain German black bread.

Furthermore, Provocateur/concierges think beyond customers to the employees, suppliers, partners—the entire expanding circle of those involved in the enterprise in some way. They provide the tools, contacts, and resources so that employees can work effectively.

Because most of us come into contact with a concierge when we stay at a hotel, many believe that a concierge is a servant or a gofer. No. If you accept my premise that the customer relationship must be at the company's center, then it is important to analyze the great concierge to see why he is effective and try to pattern oneself on how he works. It starts with a service mentality.

I asked George Colony, the CEO and founder of Forrester Research, Cambridge, Massachusetts, about the connection between leadership and service, and he says it is all about the experience customers, employees, visitors, suppliers—everyone—has with the company. The experience is either favorable or unfavorable, and he wants the former.

"I always check the bathroom at the office," says Colony, "because that is part of the everyday Forrester experience. It reflects the service of Forrester. If there are paper towels on the floor, I clean them up. It's the same with a Web experience; if your home page is slow, it suggests you're a slow company. If the Web page is hard to work with, it suggests you are hard to work with as a company. If the Web page is devoid of content, you're the wrong company. That is highly, highly relevant. So the word for me is 'experience,' and the CEO should be in charge of the experience to please the investors and the clientele—all constituencies. And cleanliness in the office, whether you take care of it or not, whether you are truthful or not—that is the experience of the company."

The head-concierge attributes in a leader are very different from the attributes of the educator, who teaches customers; from the entertainer, who amuses or delights; and from the Sherpa guide, who shows the way. The concierge serves.

This is different from the typical General, who usually felt a service mentality was irrelevant (except when he was the beneficiary of the coddling). Generals feel people should be satisfied with a quality product at a reasonable price. But to be great in the foreseeable future, leaders must sustain a service mentality. This attitude positions the company as the faithful and honest servant of the customer.

HIRE FOR A SERVICE MENTALITY

When I started my business in the 1980s, everybody in public relations hired journalists because clients wanted good writers. I obviously did not have the knowledge I do now, but I intuitively knew there was something wrong with that idea. I suspected that journalists as a group probably were not that skilled at service, and I was starting a service business, not a writing business. Writing was a skill they needed, but not the only one, so I hired the most eclectic people.

One of my first hires graduated top in her class from Cornell in psychology, one was an engineer from MIT, another an engineer from Rensselaer Polytechnic. We started having more success in high-tech PR than the companies that hired journalists. After about 20 hires, we finally took on a journalist. This person was frustrated very quickly, and so were we. Journalists are used to having immediate access to high levels at a company and to getting quick answers. Our man now did not have that and felt something was wrong. Also, he only knew how to write. There are many other elements to a service business besides writing, but he did not understand the service mentality.

An executive who has been a master at inculcating a service mentality is Herb Kelleher, one of the founders and now chairman of Southwest Airlines. Kelleher is a concierge who creates a culture in which people want to do their best. He says, "I've tried to create a culture of caring for people in the totality of their lives, not just work." Southwest has chili cook-offs, lavish Halloween productions, and Christmas parties in July, and when mechanics working the graveyard shift pointed out they could not make it to the parties, Kelleher and some pilots held a special barbecue at 2:00 A.M. Kelleher or Colleen Barrett, president and COO, sends personal notes acknowledging births, deaths, weddings, and promotions.

In 1997, when Southwest won an award for the fifth consecutive year for the best on-time performance, best baggage handling, and fewest customer complaints—suggesting that Southwest's service extends beyond the employees—Kelleher had the name of every one of Southwest's 24,000 employees engraved on the overhead bins of a special Boeing 737-300. Says Kelleher, "There's no magic formula. The intangibles are more important than the tangibles. Someone can go out and buy airplanes from Boeing and ticket counters, but they can't buy our culture, our esprit de corps."

How does Southwest instill such esprit? It starts with a policy of "hire for attitude, train for skill." Ann Bruce, a manager at Southwest Airlines University, says that "the company deliberately looks for applicants with a positive attitude who will promote fun in the workplace and have the desire to 'color outside the lines.'" Southwest tries to inculcate the feeling that the employees own the company. "A great value is placed on taking initiative, thinking for yourself, even if that means going against something in the policy manual," says Kelleher. "For instance, employees have been known to take stranded passengers back to their own homes in emergencies."

Kelleher adds, "We structure training exercises so that everyone has to contribute to complete it successfully. Then we point out how each contributed in their own way. The quiet guy came up with the solution; the noisy one helped execute it."

A Provocateur's employees feel empowered to create and innovate and think about problems wherever they work. Ultimately you should create your own environment and solve your problems in creating it. *Harold and the Purple Crayon* by Crockett Johnson is a delightful book about the power of creating your environment, making your own problems, and thinking your way out of them. Harold is a little boy who decides to go for a walk in the moonlight with his purple crayon, but because there isn't any moon, Harold draws one. And he draws a path . . . and a one-tree forest . . . that turns out to be an apple tree. To guard the tree, Harold draws a dragon that frightens him so much his hand holding the crayon shakes and draws waves that Harold falls into. But he draws a boat and is saved. At the book's end, Harold draws his window, his bed, and the covers over himself. Provocateurs are able to give their people the purple crayon with which to solve the business's problems.

Ray Ozzie, the CEO of Groove Networks, understands like Kelleher that creating an atmosphere in which everyone perceives his or her contribution is a value. Ozzie tells me that the firm has biweekly sessions in which someone from the organization gives a presentation of what he or she does or what is happening in that part of the business. "Right now we have the luxury of including the whole company, but even when it's not the whole company, this is very useful because marketing people have this attitude toward development people; development people have this attitude toward marketing people; and nobody knows what the consulting people do. Getting people to recognize that others actually have a valid job function creates dialogue. We have a Q&A session afterward, and we encourage people to ask stupid questions because it's obvious that nobody knows what the hell anybody else does, so it's a learning experience for everybody."

PUT CUSTOMERS FIRST

Provocateur/concierges manifest a special attitude toward customers, employees, and the wide world. They truly want the customer's experience of the company to be positive, the employee's to be rewarding, and the world's to be well-disposed. Concierges are self-effacing because—within reason—customer wants and needs come first.

Bob Metcalfe, who now holds the title "venture partner" at Polaris Venture Partners, a Waltham, Massachusetts, venture capital firm, tells me that when he worked at IDG and was organizing technical conferences he once called Lou Gerstner at IBM. The call went something like this: "Mr. Gerstner, would you like to speak at my conference? John Chambers will be speaking . . . Larry Ellison . . . Bill Gates. Would you like to join them?"

Gerstner: "Will any customers be there?"

"No. This is an industry gathering."

Gerstner: "I'd rather not. I like to spend my time with clientele."

Gerstner, who might have been perceived as a General, shows many concierge traits. Gerstner's credentials were those of a turnaround specialist, not a creative or an innovative leader. IBM was a company in desperate need to be fixed, so a lot of observers (including myself) said, "He's going to go through with his axe swinging."

IBM got into trouble in the 1980s by, among other things, changing its business model. It had been leasing its machines almost exclusively and then it began selling them outright, including the installed base, which broke an ongoing bond with the customer. The internal political culture supported the mainframe, but anybody else—including other divisions within the corporation as well as other companies—was an enemy. As George Conrades, who was a senior IBM executive at the time, says, "They were as much afraid of the PC division and the AS400 as they were of Hitachi. We also decided that the greatest external enemy was the Japanese computer manufacturers and that the only way to beat them was to be the low-cost producer." IBM built plant capacity, which meant the sales force came under increasing pressure to sell the machines rolling off the assembly lines and that necessity turned the corporation into a command-and-control organization, managed as much by the finance department as anything else.

Customers were saying, "I'm awash in these damn boxes. I need help." By that time, says Conrades, the IBM salesperson's response was something like, "If you think two boxes at this price is great, wait till you see what a deal you get when you buy three."

When Gerstner came to IBM, he was astute enough to understand that one of the greatest and most powerful sales forces in the world had lost sight of serving customers to concentrate only on selling to customers. IBM had developed a culture of selling to keep the plants running, to maintain sales, and to keep Wall Street happy (at least in the short run). Management did not value personal service to customers, and, worse, in its effort to cut manufacturing costs, IBM had also inadvertently cut quality. This was a simple formula for disaster.

Gerstner surprised us by listening to the customers and looking at how the market was evolving. Using the Web, he focused on applications that help executives run their businesses better. For example, Gerstner saw the need for a service model that would help corporations and individual entrepreneurs run more effective and better businesses. It wasn't about the technology. He got back to what IBM was good at—holding the customer's hand, walking her through solutions, and doing it better than almost anyone else. In 2000, IBM Global Services hired more than 19,000 people, invested $400 million in professional development and knowledge tools, and spent $50 million in e-business training.

Gerstner says, "We provide consulting, implementation services, outsourcing, and now e-sourcing, aimed at the heart of the hosting and service provider opportunity. After years of hard work, we've got the most capable services business in the world. In fact, IBM is now the largest business and technology consultancy. We have 50,000 consultants who billed more than $10 billion in revenue in 2000. We have created a network of business innovation centers, offering customers everything from front-end Web design to the heavy lifting at the back end. And just as important, we have built a field force that includes thousands of experienced industry specialists—many of them former professionals in their respective domains, from manufacturing to consumer products, from health care to government."

As an example of how this can work, Farmers Group insurance company implemented IBM's DecisionEdge for Relationship Marketing. DecisionEdge applies algorithms from IBM Research to company data to allow a comprehensive view of customers so management can see how the company can maintain and enhance individual customer relationships. DecisionEdge includes hardware, software, consulting, and services.

By analyzing large volumes of claims information, the program helps Farmers to determine the claims risk of its customers more accurately. Insurers typically know relatively little about their customers as individuals, according to Professor Merlin Stone of the United Kingdom's Surrey European Management School, University of Surrey. "This explains why customers generally do not buy more than one product from insurers," Professor Stone says. "When they do buy more than one product, the customer's decision is usually based on features and price, rather than successful targeting. In addition, the second purchase most often is made through a different channel of distribution than the first."

"DecisionEdge helps actuaries, underwriters, and marketing managers develop a customer-centric view of their business," says Virginia M. Rometty, general manager of IBM Global Insurance Solutions. "It allows them to see which customers are most profitable, discover unique sales opportunities that might otherwise be missed, and identify new opportunities for cross-selling. Customers also benefit because insurers can provide more customized service, reduce premiums in some cases, and offer insurance products that are more likely to suit customers' needs. Like a great concierge, IBM is trying to anticipate customer needs through communication and analysis of weaknesses and strengths.

The Provocateur/concierge has the ability to proactively anticipate customer needs and to embed that anticipation in the company's culture on a day-to-day basis. How do we consistently obtain useful information from customers without violating their privacy or sense of propriety? How do we stay one step ahead of customers, build increased dialogue, and create an environment in which they want to buy?

An example: A woman buys a new Saab, replacing a three-year-old model. The dealer (because he's read about customer relationship management and has built a database) knows the customer skis and points out the value of Saab's special winter package and the ski rack that fits the new car. If the salesperson introduces the subject properly, customers do not feel they are being sold; they feel they are being helped, and, in fact, they are.

This is very different from an auto salesperson who sells an undercarriage treatment, upholstery preservative, window VIN etching, extra-dark window tinting, and an extended warranty. In a real sense, Provocateur/concierges do not *sell* anything; ideally, they create an environment customers find so comfortable and rewarding they return to buy again and again. We are rapidly moving into a time when no company will be successful unless it has quality service at its heart. In the global village, word of shoddy work spreads quickly.

Great concierges live for quality service and offer unexpected things that add to the relationship. I know you like the theater; we have two tickets available. I know you like Indian cuisine; a restaurant has recently opened featuring southern Indian cooking. I know you like photography; there's an Ansel Adams exhibit in town. If human beings may be considered data sets—they have certain interests, antipathies, likes, dislikes, hobbies, cares, and wants—concierges may be regarded as data collectors—they learn what individuals like and dislike. Over time, like Amazon they should know more and more about the customer. Because they store the data, a replacement or another person in the company (even, as with Amazon, a software program) can provide the same service level. It boils down to the idea that the success of an organization is based on its ability to listen and serve, to anticipate and surprise customers and prospects in good ways.

Ray Ozzie says he learned a lot about serving customers the hard way while solving Lotus Notes support problems. "It always came with CEO calls. Some partner of Arthur Andersen calls Lou Gerstner—since IBM at that point owned Notes—who says, 'The whole organization worldwide is down! How many minutes is it going to take you to solve this problem? We paid you tens of millions of dollars for your software—fix it!'"

A hidden bug in the first round of Lotus Notes software brought down the whole system when it was exposed. Once the user tripped the bug, it ran through an entire network like a virus. Andersen and other companies had spent millions of dollars on this software, which was becoming the internal communications standard, so the bug was eating right at the heart of the business.

"How do you respond to that kind of a crisis?" says Ozzie. "You get on a plane and go to the source of the trouble. At the time, I made a lot of mistakes. This is all pre-Internet; it takes magnetic tapes, and suitcases, and airplanes, and mea culpa. But that's what it all comes down to from my perspective: how you respond, and what the customer thinks of you after the whole experience."

Ozzie had to put together a service team and send the engineers to client offices where they rewrote the program to correct the bug in the system. Many early software developers did not understand they could not simply write a program and put it out in the market. Software, as Ozzie was among the first to understand, is actually more of an ongoing service than something on a disc. Ozzie realized he would need teams of developers who understand the idea that software never ends; it is an ongoing commitment.

If developers wear the software on their sleeve because they have created it, it is relatively easy to convert them into a service organization because they feel it is their child. They want to make sure they are there to keep it functioning and growing. How the organization responds to a crisis, says Ozzie, "is a testament to how the company is managed, how empowered the individual employees feel they are. Not just empowered, but how responsible they feel to solve problems versus the idea that 'Well, it hasn't escalated to my level yet.'"

SEEK TO UNDERSTAND

The successful service organization takes customers by the hand and brings them into a world that lets them be in charge of how much they want to learn, to buy, or to reveal about themselves. Lands' End offers many different ways to shop—by mail, by phone, or online. The Web site (www.landsend .com), in addition to offering customers the ability to talk to a real human being while online, allows customers to see how various garments would look on themselves. A visitor fills out a MyVirtualModel questionnaire (height, weight, hair style, hair color, skin tone, etc.), and an image appears on the screen that resembles the respondent. She can then click on a garment to see what it might look like given her (or his) hair, body shape, and skin tone. The site lets prospects know if a product is in stock before they order. (Too many sites accept an order and only after the fact—and sometimes after a day—email the customer with the news that the product is out of stock.)

Generals focused their attention on sales and profits—transactions—and one has to respect that since without sales and profits there is no business, but those metrics do not extend service or build a relationship. If customers feel a company exists only to squeeze as much out of their purses as possible, the business environment will become one of lost sales and lost customers as they migrate to a company that understands the relationship and the environment. But when the relationship is strong, price becomes less important to a buying decision (although price almost always remains relevant).

Executives often mistakenly assume that price outweighs all other considerations. That may be true for some customers in some industries, but it's not true for everybody, and, depending on the product, it's not even true for the majority. Every pricing study I've ever seen shows that while 15 to 30 percent of the customers in a given industry are very price sensitive, 70 to 85 percent are not. Moreover, when a study asks salespeople and their customers to rank various items—price, quality, company reputation, service, and so on—on their importance, the salespeople almost invariably rank price as the most important factor affecting a sale. Customers almost invariably rank something else—and often two or three things—as more significant than price. If you have not done such research, it could be a valuable exercise.

With business products, price must be put into a context. The brightest people I know who study pricing say that business-to-business marketers must show prospects that buying the product or service will save money, make money, or (best of all) do both. If a B-to-B company cannot make that case and put convincing figures on the savings or the profits, it has a critical problem. "Because of our quality, the machine will go for 6,000 hours before you have to perform preventative maintenance; buy our hardware/software system, and you can double direct sales return while cutting mailing costs in half." Once the firm *can* show savings or profits, then its service, quality, salesperson's personality, and all other intangibles come into play.

The General has a product mentality whereas a Provocateur/concierge has a service mentality. The Provocateur will instill the service point of view throughout an organization, even in a heavily product-driven industry. I once chatted with the head of marketing for a polypropylene manufacturer. He was worried because the industry had been consolidating; polypropylene was becoming a pure commodity with customers interested only in price. "What can we do to get out of the price/commodity spiral? We can't run the plant any faster or make the stuff any cheaper."

The answer is to start finding new uses for polypropylene and to provide design and manufacturing support to prospects and customers. Develop a creative staff that other manufacturers cannot duplicate. Intel has been brilliant at this. Intel does not just manufacture computer chips; it shows prospects and customers how to use Intel chips in new and creative ways. GE Plastics was exceptional at finding innovative uses for its Lexan polycarbonate: panels for lightweight armored trucks, for example, and unbreakable street lamps.

Vernon W. Hill II, the CEO of Commerce Bancorp of Cherry Hill, New Jersey, is a concierge in an industry that has been cutting services and adding fees—banking. Commerce offers free savings accounts, checking, and money orders. It has teller service, including drive-in service, from 7:30 in the morning to 8:00 at night on weekdays, branch service with tellers on weekends and holidays, including Sundays, and 24/7 call-center service with live representatives available. There are free coin-counting machines for customers and noncustomers and bathrooms in each branch.

As one result, Commerce ended 2000 with $8.3 billion in assets, up 25 percent from the previous year. Net income was $21.4 million, up 21 percent. It has 150 branches in the greater Philadelphia market and throughout New Jersey. Deposits in at least three New Jersey counties exceed two area big-bank competitors—and all this growth has come with rates that do not lead the market.

To grow their assets, most banks loosen their credit practices or lower their loan prices. They fund growth with whatever deposits they have and, says Hill, if that's inadequate, they borrow in the wholesale market. "Our model is the com-

plete reverse of that. We gather deposits. We make all the great
loans we can, but it's deposit-gathering first. We have a 49 percent loan-to-deposit ratio when the industry's is about 90 percent." To gather deposits, Commerce offers great service.

Many large banks have been pushing low-end customers
out—or providing the least service possible to them—citing
the "80/20 rule" after an industry study found that 20 percent of retail-bank customers account for 80 percent of bank
profits. Many banks have tried to make the unprofitable 80
percent profitable by cutting services and adding fees.

"We are diametrically opposed to the 80/20 rule," says
Hill. "It has destroyed more banks in this country than any
other theory." If followed to its logical conclusion, Hill says
he could never "take a deposit from a 21-year-old because by
definition he would be a loser. I would only take accounts
from older people with high balances. In five years, that
client base could be dead. The rule says you've got a portion
of your client base that's great and should be treated won-
derfully, and you've got another portion that's awful and
should be run out. Then there's this middle portion which
you should give average service to and charge as many fees as
you can." Hill finds this morally repulsive. "It means I would
be teaching my young hires to treat some people great, abuse
others, and overcharge everyone else."

Rather than teach young hires to abuse customers,
Commerce encourages employees to go out of their way to
"wow" the customer. A "wow team" randomly shows up at
branches to reward rank-and-file personnel with cash, bal-
loons, and company paraphernalia. Commerce goes out of
its way to hire highly motivated people and gives them perks,
including sales incentives and stock options. Employees get
$50 for each stupid rule they find that gets eliminated, and
branch employees split $5,000 whenever a nearby competing

branch closes. Like a great concierge, Hill likes to visit branches and talk to the staff and customers.

BE AUTHENTIC

Provocateur/concierges create an environment in which people are not afraid to ask for anything. They are not afraid to ask for advice or to expect certain levels of service, response, courtesy, and knowledge. This was true, of course, even before the Web. I remember my mother calling L.L. Bean, which was one of the last to adopt 800 numbers so she even paid for the phone call from Cleveland, Ohio, to Freeport, Maine. But such lovely service. They would talk about the weather in Maine, and the clerk would describe how the product was made, and did my mother know it was actually manufactured by people just up the road? My mother would stay on the phone for 10 minutes, pay for the call, and be happy about it. That's an involved customer.

Think of the Web's ability to create an environment of interest, comfort, expectation, and fulfillment of expectations that makes it easier for people to buy. It uses technology to facilitate the environment. Provocateurs understand that they can create a productive environment with what's available at their fingertips.

Verbind markets services that companies can use to track customer behavior, and former president and CEO John Kish believes that to some extent we accept that marketing is part of the ecosystem in which we live and breath. Nonetheless, it's easy to identify cases where marketing is annoying or distasteful while it's difficult to point out cases where marketing is truly loved.

"One of the other things we spend a lot of time talking to people about is the ideal relationship with a company,"

Kish tells me. "The word that comes up most commonly is 'comfortable,' not a word you typically associate with business. But if you really get down to it, what people look for is comfort in the relationship they are maintaining. The relationship some people have with technology is comfortable. That's fine where the technology becomes so much a part of the way we live we don't even think about it as technology anymore. The refrigerator is a great example. Seventy-five years ago, the idea we could use an electric motor to compress a gas that cooled on expansion was remarkable. Today, it's just a part of the way we live, and we don't think about the refrigerator as representing anything technological."

Verbind started with the financial services sector, and those customers really want a deep comfort level with the company that has their money. The relationship is built on trust, so the technology must be such that customers continue to trust the company. Today we are shifting from a world of customer satisfaction questionnaires—"Are you happy with our service?"—to a more subtle evaluation based on customer behavior. I suggested to Kish that creating a comfort within your constituency—one of the marks of a concierge—makes buying decisions easy.

Kish says, "I think that as you find comfortable relationships—whether they are retail relationships, banking relationships, communications relationships—you no longer think about them. Of course I go to the local market because I know where everything is. I always know where to look for Coke when I am walking down an aisle of soft drinks, always on the middle shelf, always in the middle of the aisle. Banking relationships are the same way. My bank treats me well; they are there when I need them, like the fire department. I want to know they're there, but I don't want them there all the time. I don't want them coming to my door to give us money. Technology is going to be designed with an understanding of the psychology of the people using it, as opposed to the way it's been done up to now, which is sort of a blunt instrument. We throw it at you, and you either learn it or you don't."

Comfortable relationships, of course, extend to the office, and I was interested in Jeff Taylor's attitude toward the employees at Monster.com. I said, "It's great to let somebody play foosball in the office, but how do you know they're doing their job? Isn't there anarchy?"

In response, he says he takes the opposite approach from most executives. "Most people say, 'Go get the business then hire the employees.' I always hired the employees and then went and got the business. Now, I also worked very closely with the employees once I hired them, and made sure that they understood the company's mission. We have a big training facility here, and everybody is in training at least three, four times a year. Everybody goes through a week to two weeks of full orientation, and that's when they start to learn about this extremely high expectation—work harder, think harder, than you have ever thought before. But at the same time you do have flexibility to play foosball or hang out. There are lots of team spaces here. Every one of the office clusters has teaming spaces. There are a lot of open spaces for meetings."

One key to a productive environment and an ongoing customer relationship is authenticity. Authenticity—truth told, genuine feelings expressed, weaknesses/failures/mistakes acknowledged—is at the heart of any solid relationship. Authenticity, of course, involves everything the Provocateur does, whether educating, entertaining, guiding, or acting as a concierge. Without it, the leader is a confidence man and will eventually crash. In a communications era in which the

strength of a brand is the strength of the customer relationship, authenticity resides at the core of everything. If you and
your organization are not true and good at what you do, why
would anyone want to work with you or be your customer?

More than once I've been forced to put my money where
my mouth is when a client wants to do something deceptive.
At one point, Digital Equipment wanted to introduce a
product that management thought would replace the personal computer. The idea was that businesspeople don't need
a smart desktop computer if it just connects to a server somewhere, all they need is a "dumb" terminal, the Multia. With
one on her desk, a secretary would only have access to certain correspondence files. Executives would have access to
financial data and more. Digital Equipment wanted to push
this as the ultimate revolution of computing. I kept saying,
"It does a couple of things very well, but it's not a revolu-
tionary product, and it would be wrong to try to position it
that way." Ultimately Digital took over and tried to market
it, but the Multia failed because it was not what Digital tried
to make it out to be.

If I sense a company is trying to make a quick hit, or is
trying to dump something that might not be the best for its
customers, I say we can't help. The communications will be
unacceptable to a discerning public, and the damage will be
tremendous when people learn that there is no authenticity
at the company's heart. Who would buy a Firestone tire
knowing it has covered up potentially fatal product defects?
Who would buy a Mitsubishi car after learning that it has
refused to make product recalls for design failures?

Inauthentic companies always run into trouble eventually, but the speed of today's communications makes eventually sooner than ever. One widely publicized example is
DrKoop.com, which established its Web site in 1998. When

it went public in June of that year, the stock briefly reached over $40 a share. Because the site is associated with former Surgeon General Dr. C. Everett Koop, the chairman of the company, it became one of the most popular health sites on the Web. Unfortunately, the line between information and promotion has not been clear. Dr. Joshua Hauser, a medical ethicist at the University of Chicago, said that when he visited DrKoop.com in July 1999, he found a list of hospitals and health centers described as "the most innovative and advanced health care institutions across the country."

In fact, "the list was an advertisement for 14 hospitals, each of which had paid a fee of about $40,000 to be included. The bad publicity may have wounded DrKoop.com fatally, as it has suffered through staff cuts, failed merger talks, and management shakeups. In August 2000, the company reported it had received $27.5 million in equity financing and claimed it had enough cash to last 18 months. By February 2001, the stock was trading for less than 25 cents a share and DrKoop.com was fighting delisting by NASDAQ. Since the site's strength was based largely on Dr. Koop's reputation, however, it is hard to see how DrKoop.com will recover once it has been so tainted.

As we all know, life is not fair, but being authentic about feelings in business and counsel and direction wins more than it loses. Trying to beat the system, grabbing as many clients as possible, would often put the company in the wrong place.

The Web is making it more difficult to beat the system. As in the past, companies have to gain trust, one person at a time, but the Web permits unhappy customers to broadcast their complaints as never before. The Web will be the shoddy manufacturer's nightmare. Just as Amazon posts reader comments about books (and, in a further wrinkle, reader ratings of the comments), a growing number of sites encourage customer evaluations of cruise lines, cars, and a variety of consumer products. If you haven't looked at one, you might check out BizRate.com, Epinions.com, ConsumerReview.com, or ConsumerWorld.com. The Web is creating a giant *Consumer Reports*. And if companies don't try to facilitate that *Consumer Reports* mentality—welcoming objective, third-party evaluations—someone else will.

Well-rounded Provocateurs have characteristics of the educator, entertainer, Sherpa guide, and head concierge. Today's Provocateurs also have access to technology that can make them and their companies much more effective in dealing with customers, employees, suppliers, and all other stakeholders.

8

ENOUGH TECHNOLOGY
TO BE DANGEROUS

I think customer relationship management is a matter of using technology to reinforce tried-and-true values.

—George Conrades,
CEO, Akamai

To thrive in a world of nomadic consumers, you need to know enough about technology to build a community. You do not, however, have to be a computer scientist to use technology effectively any more than it is necessary to be a certified public accountant to read a balance sheet and P&L statement.

Provocateurs understand that the Internet is to the communications economy as the assembly line was to the manufacturing economy. As the industrial age focused on the physical process of manufacturing parts and assembling products, the Internet age focuses on the electronic process of capturing data and marketing the product. The end result is—or can be—a stronger relationship with the customer.

For a long time, companies employed management information systems (MIS) or information technology (IT) to do things they had done since the invention of double-entry bookkeeping. The punch cards, computer tapes, and mainframes just did it faster and—as long as there was no garbage in—did it more accurately than clerks in eye shades and sleeve garters.

In 1980, Harry Figgie, the CEO of Figgie International, complained to me, "Where did this MIS line come from on the P&L? It came from nowhere and now it's my second major expense." The situation must have been similar at other *Fortune* 500 companies. Figgie said, "When I came into business, this wasn't even a line item on the balance sheet." He was buying technology for inventory control, personnel records, and finance accounts, but he wasn't happy about it.

Generals did not like technology because it was infrastructure; it was capital expenditures. Most only grudgingly acknowledged the company needed it to play the game. Generals thrived at a time when the back-end technology to record, store, and manipulate data was developing rapidly. For 20 years, IT churned out computer reports. IT created processes, although these did not necessarily change customer relationships.

Provocateurs realize there is a level of technology that, if used properly, can give a competitive advantage by communicating with customers more directly, more frequently, and more conveniently to dramatically better effect. Technology can help access data and information, making it flow to help strategic decision making.

A problem for traditional companies has been that the IT department and the marketing department were physically, intellectually, and emotionally far apart. Actually, it is even worse in high-tech companies. The IT people look different from other employees, they are usually the furthest away in the headquarters, and they even dress differently. But, if marketing and innovation drive the company, then the IT department and the marketing department must work together to develop programs that help find and keep customers. Provocateurs understand that, in the future, IT will not be a separate department down the hall that just tries to keep the servers humming.

We are already starting to see the shift. A Forrester Research study of who was making most of the purchase decisions in the company for marketing technology applications found in the middle of 1998 it was 80 to 90 percent IT decision makers. A year later the figure had dropped to 50 percent IT, drastically shifting the decision-making power for front-end or electronic consumer relationship management applications—eCRM—to marketing people (or at least marketing department kinds of functions). My guess is that if they did a third-year cycle, IT would be down to 25 percent, and marketing-related and management titles would be at 75 percent, as top managers realize marketing's need for the technology.

With the advent of the Web, companies started to focus less on functions like accounting and purchasing and more on the technology's communications functions, connecting with employees, customers, suppliers, and other stakeholders. Leaders have to understand that the machines in the back room—the servers, the switchers, and the software to connect everything—are pretty good. We can integrate large financial systems and inventory control systems globally. Businesses in general are not good at the front end, which are the applications that go on top of or complement the backroom applications—the sales, communications, and groupware applications.

The Internet, with its speed, ubiquity, and experiential qualities, is the engine driving communications today. It is important to remember that the Internet is still in its infancy, and this telephone on steroids will evolve into an even more powerful medium. "Webcasting," "commerce-casting," and "chatterbots" will become household words. Most important, the Internet allows for one-to-one communication, which is why email and its evolution is *the* killer app.

WHY EMAIL IS THE KILLER APP

According to Jupiter Communications, 93 million Americans sent a total of 335 million email messages per day in 1999. Personal email has grown 50 percent per year, outstripping even the Web, whose users have grown just 21 percent per year, says Jupiter. A year ago, 23 million Americans used email to order goods from corporate Web sites, accounting for much of the $20 billion consumers spent online. That figure will be more than $140 billion by 2003, according to Forrester Research, while business-to-business online sales grow from $109 billion to $1.3 trillion.

Thanks to the communications revolution, technology-enabled marketing allows organizations to build strong relationships with their customers and, at the same time, improve their operational efficiency. Say (to invent only slightly) that 10-year-old Joey Smith in Evanston, Illinois, sends an email to Nike. He is upset because his new shoes have fallen apart. With today's technology, a company can sort and respond to email almost instantly. Within a day, Nike can send Joey a personalized message from a famous athlete who endorses Nike footwear: "Dear Joey: We're really bummed out that you've had trouble with our shoes. We do our best to make sure this kind of thing doesn't happen, but when it does we want to make sure you're not hurt by it. If you print out the coupon at the bottom of this letter and take it to The Foot Locker at the Skokie Mall, they'll give you a new pair of shoes. Thanks for letting us know about the problem, and sorry for the trouble we've caused you. If there's anything else, just drop me a note."

The note and coupon go a long way toward repairing the relationship the boy has with the company. Equally important, the company can capture Joey's information on the product's failure to forward internally to Nike's product development, manufacturing, and quality-control departments. Within a week, Nike has tracked the bad shipment, withdrawn defective shoes from store inventories, and where possible contacted everyone who has bought them to proactively offer replacement shoes.

While this scenario was somewhat hypothetical as I wrote this book, I expect it to be real by the time you read these words. After all, two or three years ago Nike was simply deleting most of the email it received because it did not know what to do with it. At some point, someone realized (and convinced management) that the people taking their good time to write the company were a potential asset. So Nike and other companies evolved from deleting the email to "We should answer it." That evolved to realizing that email contains useful information: "My shoes are falling apart" or "I'm going to start playing tennis, something I haven't done for years. Do you have any ideas?" Now you start getting into the realm of unobtrusive or participant marketing, marketing so subtle that the customer does not even know it is marketing and collaborates in the process.

The challenge obviously is to find some cost-efficient means to extract the grains of gold from the tons of gravel. Someone who writes Nike, for example, might start by complaining about the way their sneakers fit, segue into a Nike's girls' soccer club, and conclude by asking about the company's labor policy. Nevertheless, V.A. Shiva, the founder of EchoMail, Inc., a Cambridge, Massachusetts, software firm, says, "Human communication is not as diverse as we think it is." EchoMail, which handles Nike's customer email, scans messages and applies a dictionary of key words and word relationships known as a "semantic network." For instance, if the program finds the word 'Web site' and 'problem' in close proximity, it might conclude that the email's issue is an online ordering problem. Depending on how an email gets classified, EchoMail can choose either to reply from a selection of prewritten responses (companies maintain 10 to 50 canned replies to common requests and complaints) or forward the email to one or more departments for humans to address.

Many managers originally thought customer email was a nuisance and a distraction, and no one worked through the messages because no one wore the title Email Reader. A lot of companies have thrown the function into the call center, which is probably not appropriate because email is far more strategic. A Provocateur has to understand all entry points of communication a customer might use to reach the company and how to manage them. One day the customer might use the 800 number, one day send an email, one day a letter or a postcard packed with the product. The company must consider all these communications for data point collections. The process of email and digital communications will be the primary application for obtaining data and building on it.

MAKE EMAIL VALUABLE TO RECIPIENTS

Junk mail is not junk if you want it, and this is true of email as well as the stuff the U.S. Postal Service brings to your house. A brochure from the British Travel Agency is a valuable planning tool if you are going to the United Kingdom; it is wastepaper if you never leave town. An email from Nordstrom's announcing fall suit specials can be helpful if you are in the market for new clothes; it's clutter if you work at home in shorts and T-shirt. A company's challenge is to send email and snail mail only to those prospects and customers most likely to be interested in what the company has to say.

With the Internet, people will tell you if they're interested or not. Many sites allow visitors to opt out of future contact. Some shortsightedly make it difficult to make the choice. They are like insecure entertainers who bully the audience, afraid that if they give the power to opt out, they won't have any business.

Provocateurs have enough confidence in company products and services to believe a market exists. A company does not have to force people to look at stuff they don't want to look at. It does not have to waste money sending out direct-mail packages that people throw away. The leader who does not have confidence in the company's products (and who does not invest in improving them) and who is a graduate of the Barnum School of Marketing (motto: "There's a sucker born every minute") will find the pool of prospects drying up. As information grows and spreads, it becomes more and more difficult to disguise poor products and poor service— sort of a reverse Gresham's law with the good products driving out the bad.

Email is the firm's "ears around the world," and it can be its voice back to the world. Email can generate high-response rates, but just sending email is not enough. The effort must be made internally to back up the brand message. My Yahoo! is a great example of personalization by listening. They are creating products that seem very specific to you but are not.

At My Yahoo! Directions, for example, you can ask for a recommended route and save it for the future. Yahoo! is per-
sonalizing, then getting visitors to personalize within their
personalization.

Apparently MSNBC noticed I regularly click on a number of technology stocks, because suddenly, every afternoon,
an analyst pops up on the screen of my computer that is connected to MSNBC to air his views on technology stocks. So
without sending me a message or invading my privacy, the
site is saying, "This guy is looking at a lot of tech stocks, let's
make sure he tunes into our program." Personalization is
mandatory, with each customer and business partner, even
each employee, requiring attention.

With the rapidly evolving filtering technologies come the
opportunity to create comfort zones of interest as an opportunity for companies and CEOs. The organization has the
ability to communicate with itself, not just externally, and
the ability to really be on top with instant messaging and the
technologies available. I worked at a *Fortune* 500 company
where we were still driven by the *memo* that someone worked
on for an hour or two (or much more), which was primarily
faxed. It was designed to cover your ass or to bulldoze your
way to some answer. The ability to communicate on an
ongoing basis with email is an advantage internally. It also
sets a tone.

This is an important point. An email is a dialogue. It is
not like a memo. It isn't "Here's my version," then wait to see
if somebody writes another version in response. Email is an
opportunity to go back and forth quickly to solve a problem.

Unfortunately, this is not always the case. Recently I ran
into a problem with one of my employees. We were talking
about days to complete a project: He said it would take 14
days; I wanted it done in 10. We traded emails back and

forth that grew more and more testy. I finally picked up the phone to discover he was talking calendar days; I was talking business days. So email is not the final answer (but then, what is?).

Technology also allows a business to understand customer usage patterns so the company can continue to build a relationship: "We know you had trouble with our messaging system. Do you feel comfortable with it now? Have you tried this?" Today, this is relatively easy to do, but it requires a new way of thinking. The company has to be part guide. With the advent of the Web and interactive communication and the focus on communication, we finally started to see the development of applications that are more able to affect a business than report a business.

KNOW THY CUSTOMER THROUGH TECHNOLOGY

In some ways, we are trying to return to the time (which was probably a figment of Hollywood and popular imagination) when you could drop into the bookstore on Main Street and the proprietor knew you and your tastes. She would say, "I've set aside a copy of the new Sinclair Lewis novel for you." When you went into the corner drugstore with your prescription, the pharmacist knew your drug history and could warn you—or even call old Doc Holley to alert him—of a potential drug interaction. When you visited the local banker (who looked a lot like Jimmy Stewart in *It's a Wonderful Life*), he knew you were having trouble with your old truck and knew you were good for a loan on a new one.

These values—interest, concern, service—don't change, but the economy sure has. It's infinitely more complex for one thing. The bookstore on Main Street with 2,000 books and, perhaps, 200 regular customers, is now a Barnes &

Noble/Borders with 50,000 books and 1,500 regular customers. The corner drugstore is a mini-supermarket/convenience store with hundreds of new pharmaceuticals. The bank now offers insurance, brokerage, online bill-paying, home equity loans, and more. The sheer number and variety of products and services has increased dramatically.

Second, there has been business consolidation and the rise of chains. One would not expect the CVS or Walgreen pharmacist to know your medical history the way the entrepreneurial corner druggist knew it. You wouldn't expect the Fleet Bank or Bank of America manager who has been advanced from one branch to another to know you the way the manager who grew up in town knew you.

Through technology, however, the Internet bookstore, chain pharmacist, bank manager, or travel agent *can* know you. Call the concierge at a good hotel, and he will respond to your name; technology tells him what room is calling and who is registered in that room. Amazon.com knows my taste in books and music and routinely recommends new titles.

Even if the technology is not perfect, Provocateurs need to be aware that there are many tools available to facilitate and make it easier for their companies to be personal, individualized, dialogue-based, and service-oriented. The technology may not be more efficient than older systems (although it probably is), and may not be cheaper (although it might be), but it can provide personalized individual contact, which makes all the difference.

One current problem seems to be that companies are using the technology for their convenience, not their customers'. Call your HMO about a claim and you go through seven recorded menus before you reach a human being who may or may not be able to help. The technology, which ought to assist customers, becomes a barrier.

Michael Dertouzos at MIT's Laboratory for Computer Science points out that many companies today are using technology that purports to offer service, but really does not. "It is really torturing you with the obstacles that people put in your way. I marvel every day. I could check you through your airline and have you going in a matter of seconds. The ticket should go into a slot and then come out. It should have a seat on it, whatever your preference, and you should not have to spend any time standing at a counter."

In contrast, I was impressed with Media One, now called AT&T Broadband, our Internet email service. My wife's email wasn't working, and she couldn't fix it. I called and went through several prompts to reach the right human being. Curious, I asked, "Where are you?"

He said, "Physically? Tampa, Florida."

"I'm in Massachusetts."

"That's nice. What seems to be the problem? Let's go step by step." He walked me through the process, and in 15 minutes the email was working. "Anything else, Mr. Weber?" I thought it was a textbook example of how to use technology to automate the screening process and help learn what needed to be done.

Akamai is another company that understands the importance of the customer relationship and leverages technology to improve it. CEO George Conrades tells me, "I think it is a matter of using technology to reinforce tried-and-true values. We had the luxury of starting from scratch with no legacy in systems, so I didn't have to reengineer anything." Rather, Conrades told Akamai's IT manager, "You've got 10 million dollars for new applications. Put in the most advanced customer relationship management system you can because customer service is going to be critical to us."

Akamai's customer care system attempts to resolve every customer inquiry on the first call. Says Conrades, "The first objective was: Don't abuse the customer. If you're going to answer the question on the first call, you need information about the customer immediately—one common database. We have multiple functions within Akamai that touch customers. All receive the same database. All update the database. Any email, trouble ticket, billing information, customer statistics are all in one place."

MANAGE CUSTOMER RELATIONSHIPS ELECTRONICALLY

The goal is customization, building a database of knowledge about the customer. If the company has the process and the data, it will stay ahead of competitors. Who, after all, would you rather deal with? A company that knows your name and your purchasing history (your sizes, tastes, interests, address, service record) or one that, no matter how many times you return, has never heard of you?

At this writing we are experiencing a land grab of technology applications, all staking claims to be a program of choice. This new world is the Web as the communications vehicle for managing relationships, gathering data, and working to make things easier for the customer. Inevitably these will integrate and combine as the leader for electronic customer relationship management (eCRM).

The earlier a company embraces eCRM and understands it, the deeper the relationship it will be able to build with its customers because it will have more data. Just as a marriage should grow better over time as the spouses learn more about each other, a company's relationship with customers should grow better if it learns more and more about them—and uses the information wisely and prudently. Even today there is a ton of automation programs that can help companies capture data.

The key point is that people are data sets. As discussed throughout this book, a company can collect valuable data about its customers through the process of dialogue data. Through ongoing dialogues across a variety of communications media such as online, phone, mail, and surveys, an organization can gather information that goes beyond simple facts and figures to habits and behaviors that can then determine how best to reach the customer. These "conversations" not only build a relationship, they provide valuable insight into the needs, wants, and desires of a business or a specific customer so that the company can satisfy those needs effectively.

Every person, every business is a data set within a community and can be managed to a certain level automatically. We will continually evolve very sophisticated eCRM applications to streamline the automation of that relationship, and we as audiences, as a business or a consumer on the other side of that automation, will continually evolve in accepting new levels of automation. We accept an impersonal email from Amazon.com that says, "Your books have been shipped." That is better than nothing because it tells me Amazon got my order and now I can start looking for my books.

That is significant because unless there is a massive recession, erasing demand and putting workers on the street, the American economy in the near future will have fewer people coming into it. Businesses will have to figure out a way to have machines do more kinds of work. We will automate, and have automation accepted on a personal level.

At the same time, we are going to continuously improve personalization, or what I call e-personalization, where you want direct service, not from a machine, and even though it is in e-form, you will get a person assigned to your account. Robert Reich, the former Secretary of Labor under Clinton, told me not long ago that one of his big concerns in the job market was the digital divide. Where are jobs going to be for the rank-and-file Americans who have only a high school diploma? I said I thought there would be a lot of opportunities in the Web-centric world. He asked, "Are you sure?" He thought the whole idea of the software business is to eliminate jobs.

It is, to a point, but I see an opportunity in the levels of automation. At some point, customers are going to need a personalization agent. As companies grow their e-environments, they will need individuals to be responsive to customers so that when they need help—with a product (their printer won't print), with a bill, with a warranty, with anything—they have someone with whom they can talk. These representatives may have a hundred customers or several thousand; that will depend on the level of personalization the customers require. But through the use of eCRM, the reps will also have a complete record of the customer's contacts with the company on their computer screens.

The end of customer relationship management is dressing it up and creating the environment that makes it easier for customers to buy. That is where the creative people come in. They might, for example, create a visual annual report where the CEO talks about the year the company has had. Creative is integrated at the point of dissemination to either

the individual or the group with which the company is trying to communicate and thereby build a dialogue.

There are many new developments in technology available to help companies with sales management, content
management, personalization, campaign analysis, email
management, even live collaboration. Today a leader has to
understand there are many ways to automate, to have the
company move faster and build and cement relationships
more efficiently. And they have to have the talent for their
organizations.

9

FINDING TALENT: IT'S NOT ABOUT RESUMES

If each of us hires people who are smaller than we are, we shall become a company of dwarfs. But if each of us hires people who are bigger than we are, we shall become a company of giants.

—David Ogilvy, founder,
Ogilvy & Mather

Provocateurs are obsessed with finding great talent. They don't want competent ambitious people; they want superstar performers. Good is not good enough. So what else is new?

Jeff Taylor, the CEO of Monster.com, argues convincingly that we are in the beginning stages of what may be a decade-long period when power shifts from employer to employee. "We are going to move from an environment where, when somebody leaves, you think 'Ah, that person wasn't very good anyway' and hire a new person. There won't be a new person. There won't be enough workers." Taylor tells me there are four factors involved.

One is baby boomer exit. By 2003 there will be more boomers leaving the workforce than new workers coming in. Thanks to a 20-year bull market, boomers are going to retire earlier. They are going to leave the 1980s and 1990s-type job and become philanthropists or work for nonprofit organizations. They are going to do something to have fun . . . become artists . . . walk around the world. They are going to do things that are meaningful in their lives, which for most will not be the jobs they've had.

The second factor is "tenure." Between 1950 and 1970, the average tenure of a worker in a job was 23.5 years. The average tenure reported in 1996 was 3.5 years and was heading down toward 2.5 years. Taylor says the average tenure for an engineer in the United States right now is 13 months.

"Look at the fallout from that," says Taylor. "My grandfather worked for Bell Telephone for 37 years. He was a Depression survivor. After 19 years, Bell Telephone Personnel went to him and asked, 'Would you like a different job?' He said, 'If you show me where I sit, I'll take the job.' It wasn't about the job; it was about *having* a job. My father will retire on his sixth job. I'm already on my sixth job. My son takes his Walkman apart and is trying to move the chips around, and he is trying to program tick-tack-toe and chess and stuff on his PC, and I think my son will end up as a self-described entrepreneur, individual proprietor, micro-business owner, free agent."

The third factor is the global village. "Everybody understands there are not enough skilled workers," says Taylor, "but what they don't understand is what the Internet has done to create a global village where you can get a programmer in India who is going to stay in India to do your programming. You never could have met that person 10 years ago. You wouldn't have had the faculties to find the person. But as a consequence of the technology, you don't necessarily have to have somebody sitting in the next office to do the work now. They can be sitting in a third-world country."

The fourth factor is somebody selling something on the Web that you will enjoy. "What I call e-business is having your logo turned upside down and shaken physically, having smaller profit margins, and having to reorganize your business. You have to retool your whole business around the interactive nature of business. You are going to have to retrain your current employees, so you have decision makers at the bottom and lots of consultants at the top rather than a few decision makers at the top and lots of administrators at the bottom."

SYMPTOMS OF TROUBLE

The social contract has changed. Just as many Americans were permanently scarred by the Great Depression of the 1930s, so were many traumatized by the corporate downsizing of the late 1980s and early 1990s. The old social contract—the idea that if you worked hard and were honest, the company would take care of you—was broken. In the General era, the employee had a job, a paycheck, and if he (it was usually a man) didn't get caught with his hand in the till, he'd have a job for 40 years. He might not go as far as he wanted, but he'd be working at General Motors, General Foods, General Mills, General Re, General Electric, or General Signal until he retired.

But with downsizing, all employees realized that corporations have no loyalty to individuals (blue-collar workers had always been more cynical). One can work hard, be reliable, dedicated, and loyal, but the job can evaporate tomorrow through no fault of your own.

Today, most employees realize that while their jobs can vanish, even the company disappear, their skills and experience remain. They can take them to another job, another company. Employees have no—or little—loyalty to the company. People should be loyal first to themselves. At the same time, most want to believe in a job, and they will respond to a leader who says, "I have faith that you're honest and good at what you do, and we'd like you to be part of what we're trying to accomplish."

Provocateurs attract and retain people only by understanding that the former game is over and prospective employees know it. The business has to become open, hip, forward-thinking, and skill-based, where it's (usually) fun to work, where it's innovative to work, and where the leaders think about the needs of the workforce. The leader will have to be loyal to the employees (even when they, the ungrateful wretches, leave for other jobs). To recruit and retain loyal people, the leader has to truly believe in a mission and a vision, one the employees also think is an authentic, winning formula.

A number of Generals adopted the pose that they knew virtually everything and therefore didn't have to consider the needs of the workforce. Generals tended to think, "I could be the head of human resources." "I could be the head of marketing." "I could be the head of manufacturing." They felt that any sign of weakness or unfamiliarity diminished their authority. They were, of course, kidding themselves if they truly believed their employees accepted that pose. As Dr. Charles Vest at MIT says, "Eventually you have to learn that you really can't do everything yourself. You have to surround yourself with really good people and give them free rein. I foster an environment that allows all questions to be answered, but not necessarily by the leader. There is just no other way of operating."

As David Ogilvy, who built advertising agency Ogilvy & Mather into one of the best in the world, wrote, "If each of us hires people who are smaller than we are, we shall become a company of dwarfs. But if each of us hires people who are bigger than we are, we shall become a company of giants." Joel Raphaelson, an Ogilvy & Mather creative director, joined the company shortly after David Ogilvy founded it. We were once talking about the agency and how it grew, and Raphaelson said, "In my experience, David Ogilvy was almost unique among corporate executives in knowing what he could do, what he liked to do, and what he was no good at—and he hired people to do those things he either didn't like to do or was no good at. More to the point—and what made him unique—he left them alone to do their jobs."

So how does the Provocateur find, recruit, and keep good people?

START WITH A TRUE VISION

The Generals' style of recruiting was a sham—"we want the best and the brightest and are going to pay the most money. You are going to work for a hip, cool company." But it really wasn't hip and cool, so the offer was a form of bait and switch.

Whether a General or a Provocateur, one has to start with a focused vision. A corporate vision is not: "We want to sell more products, make a lot of money, and get the stock price up." A true vision describes what the company stands for and where it wants to go. It should be aspirational, inspirational, and easily understood by a wide variety of stakeholders—employees, customers, investors, and opinion leaders. It should not be just a snappy slogan or a corporate catchphrase. Rather, it should embody and explain the corporation's strategic intent.

Ford's vision, says Jason Vines, head of public relations, is "to become the world's leading consumer company for automotive products and services. The company spent months examining what it would take to be successful and grow its business in the twenty-first century. It determined that, for its first 100 years, it viewed itself primarily as a manufacturing company that pushed products out the door and let someone else interact with the customer."

Ford's management realized that because customers had changed, competition had changed, and business economics had changed, the strategy of pushing was not going to work anymore. Vines says that Ford "began to rebuild its business around the customer, restructuring its entire global operations to be more flexible, nimble, and perceptive in giving customers exactly what they wanted and more." Sixty percent of the revenue related to automobiles comes after the sale—finance, insurance, parts, service, even recycling. "Ford wants to be a bigger part of these businesses both as a way to grow revenue and as a way to better understand the needs of its customers. That means becoming a consumer company, not just a manufacturing company. The vision Ford settled on emerged from this process of strategic evaluation, it wasn't just tacked on as an afterthought."

Having a common, inspirational vision can only help a firm's recruitment efforts. Recruitment is a big issue in the world where unemployment has been in the low single digits for a long time. In addition to its vision, a community's attractive elements include sharing equity, a place where skills are valued and shared, where one actually can learn and achieve more (versus simply climbing a corporate ladder), and the excitement of innovation, of participating in something new.

FINDING

In looking for talent, many large companies say they look first to the top 20 or so colleges around the country, predictable names with supposedly predictable quality among graduates. Yet, the story of the uninspired student who goes on to succeed in the world is practically a cliché. Winston Churchill was a poor test-taker. Martin Luther King Jr. scored below average on every section of the graduate school boards, including verbal aptitude. Richard Branson of the Virgin Group had trouble with standardized admission tests. Educators know that test scores often predict applicants' academic performance in college but they are unreliable guides to career success.

Finding the best people is going to be increasingly the single most difficult challenge for leaders to grow their companies. They can have all the ideas, and they can create the innovative, stimulating, successful environments we have talked about. They can be part educator, entertainer, Sherpa guide, and concierge, but if they can't recruit and keep good people they will not be able to grow their businesses. We have looked for too long at resumes based on narrow and focused accomplishments that line up for narrow and focused jobs.

Bob Metcalfe at Polaris Venture Partners makes the distinction between hiring and recruiting. "Hiring is the wrong mind-set. Hiring connotes running an ad, collecting resumes, interviewing people, sorting through a huge heap of wannabes, and choosing somebody. Recruiting connotes finding the world's best people, who are already working somewhere else and have no interest in joining your company and somehow getting them to take a job that is smaller than the one they currently have, but persuading them that very soon the job will be bigger than the one they now hold. My maxim is that B people hire C people, and A people recruit A people."

Like Jeff Taylor at Monster.com, David Hayden at Critical Path has applied the Friends and Family Hiring

Theory to his business. Says Hayden, "You can accelerate the vetting of new hires much more quickly if they are friends or associates of your friends. You are just continually expanding a spiral of people who know each other, who want to come and work for something because it's cool and because they like the people and they like working with their friends. You still have to apply a filter, but you can short-circuit the whole process of long interviews. In two years we grew from nothing to about 175 people, 80 percent hired on the friends and family strategy."

A leader should distinguish between entry, middle management, and top management jobs but should also eliminate those labels. A leader needs to attract very bright young people who bring a passion, energy, and healthy naiveté to the organization. This may be their first real job, but they should be considered intellectual peers within the organization. Every idea should be a peer-to-peer idea, every contribution a peer-to-peer contribution. Try to maintain this employee environment and you will get more innovation, creativity, and market dominance than from an organization having many levels.

When I started my company, I swore we would only have three titles—account executive, vice president, and president. By the time we grew to 50 people, we had 11 titles. I find the need for titles amazing, and it has grown worse in the new economy where *Fast Company* runs examples of what it calls "Job Titles of the Future": Chief Zookeeper (Elias Shames, telezoo.com), C3PO (Kyle Shannon, Agency.com Ltd.), Chief Acceleration Officer (Lloyd Walker, Human Code Inc.), Chief Detonator (Chris Holten-Hempel, SparkPR), Chief Reality Officer (Jeff Pundyk, Zwirl.com).

These companies haven't reduced the swarm of titles; they've actually worsened it. A prospective employee should not be thinking: "What is my title going to be?" She should be thinking: "What is my role going to be? And how am I going to achieve the company's goals through achieving my personal goals?" Titles in general seem diversionary and problematic annoyances that take the focus away from the true job.

HIRING

Ray Ozzie believes with Bob Metcalfe and David Ogilvy that you should "hire people better than you by design. Otherwise, why are you hiring them? They are experts. They are better in the thing they do and so you have to hire with that and err on the side of trust. My optimal thing is to build a relationship with the people who are essentially my peers and direct reports that is as close to a marriage as I can get. I know what they're good at; they know their domain of authority and control and independence. I know what they care about, their sensitivities, their hot buttons, and where they ought to be involved in a decision. They know the same things about me, so we can operate largely independently, except we know when we should involve the other person. It's not perfect; it's like a marriage. If you've got kids, you have to support each other or you're going to have real trouble. And there are some decisions that each one knows you generally make independently. In some marriages, people buy cars independently, in some they would never; in some, it's okay to make a major purchase on your own, and in some it's not. But if the marriage is going to work, you have to find the zone of understanding."

My friend Jim Mullen founded and built Mullen Advertising, headquartered in Beverly, Massachusetts. I like his criteria for increasing the odds that you will fill your company with good people:

- Hire people who are smart.
- Hire people who are simplifiers.
- Hire people who are really willing to commit themselves.
- Hire people who are different.
- Hire people who show signs of entrepreneurship.

Speaking to this last point, Jim says, "You need to institutionalize entrepreneurship, but you can't do it with people who are born bureaucrats. Look for signs of independence, even troublemaking in your interviewee's history. In an entrepreneurial organization, a major portion of every person's job is inventing her future by thinking about the ways evolving business challenges will affect her responsibilities. Remember that no one has a better grasp of the operational realities of any job than the individual who's doing it. Therefore, no one is in a better position to make the progress more effective and, since the person is an emerging entrepreneur, no one has more motivation to do so."

The Container Store, a $214 million retail chain headquartered in Dallas with stores in eight states, has been named the best company to work for in America in a *Fortune* survey. "In an age where every company seems to offer harried employees a salve of on-site services, pet-friendly policies, and stock options, the Container Store promises only that it will treat its workers like humans. Grade-school-type maxims—treat people as you want to be treated, help others—are granted policy status. Employees undergo constant training. And instead of tightly guarding financial information, the Container Store opens its ledger to all employees. The outcome: a company whose turnover is a fraction of the industry's, losing just 28 percent of its full-time salespeople a year, versus the industry average of 73.6 percent, and just 5.3

percent of its store managers, compared with the industry's 33.6 percent."

Leonard Berry, director of Texas A&M's retail-studies center, says that Container Store employees are honestly happy and attributes that in part to the homework the company does on its salespeople. "One of their keys to success is that they hire very well," says Berry. "It's such a generous place, such a high-trust place, that employees love it. They hire people with the same values as the leaders. That's the cornerstone."

Provocateurs guide their organizations on what to look for in a potential hire, how to assess whether the person has "star" potential, and whether the person has the makings of a Provocateur. When interviewing, the Provocateur doesn't focus on candidate job history or what they have done, but rather on who they are and *how* they have approached challenging situations.

The Provocateur focuses on determining whether a candidate offers qualities such as common sense, diverse interests with expertise in specifics, good analytical skills, and the confidence to act on his or her own beliefs. Who this person is, both at work and at home, is crucial. After all, the candidate is joining a community and will likely take a place in the community similar to the role he or she is used to playing at home.

A Provocateur leader says, in effect, "Here is the play we're doing, the symphony we're performing. Now, what players must we have and what kind of parts are there going to be?" Even a small part is critical. If the orchestra is to play Bartok's *Music for Strings, Percussion, and Celesta,* the conductor needs a celesta player. If it is playing Tchaikovsky's *1812 Overture,* the conductor needs cannon shots and church bells. They are only one part, but the piece requires them and the audience expects them.

Good employees today want to learn through an association with the company. They want to research and accomplish mergers and acquisitions. They want to learn how to work with three new software packages. Again, we need to develop and understand a skill-based learning culture. During the period from roughly 1985 to 1995, resumes tried to include a *Fortune* 500 corporation and very few skills. Today some resumes say, "I know all these software packages, have learned communications skills, selling strategy, writing a business plan. I want to move to learn more skills." While it is important for anyone hiring new talent to understand a department's needs and the qualities necessary for the job being filled, it is also important to understand the applicant's goals.

Provocateurs need the analytical ability to see strengths and weaknesses in the team and then know how to complement them to get a job done. Skill sets, analytical thinking, creativity, humor, thoughtfulness, intellectual intensity when appropriate, and the ability to collaborate in an energetic and spirited way are more meaningful than a polished resume.

People have core competencies. Do you need to have a solid marketing sense to be a great marketing person? Yes. Do you need experience? Yes. Do you need to be a software engineer to develop great software? Probably. A friend, who hires programmers, says that what distinguishes pedestrian programmers from the good ones is their ability to read code; if they can't read code, they can't develop software.

Does the candidate know the basic language of the job? If so, that's the key to how you put the team together. The person you involve in marketing might not know how to read code, but complements the programmer so that he pushes the developer to new creative heights. Conversely, the person who writes the code may say to the marketing person, "What you're asking for can't be done by the machines we have today," and suggest a workable alternative. What skills does a candidate possess? Is she a great writer? A good analytical thinker? Does he have the basic education in the specific area in which he needs to work? Too many employers use their gut feeling instead of analyzing skills, which gets a lot of people in trouble.

I look for people who understand what they are good at and what they are not good at, and are honest about both, because it is easier to build a team with people who are honest about their abilities and weaknesses than it is with somebody who thinks (or says) he can do everything. I look for basic, well-rounded, educated individuals. I often ask, "What book are you reading now?" If a person says, "I'm not reading a book," that tells me something. You can tell from a conversation whether someone is intellectually inquisitive, analytical, has interests outside the job, and is personable enough. I think that there is an underlying drive—some people call it a Type A personality. A star has healthy self-esteem, not to the point of arrogance, but to the point of "I feel so comfortable with my abilities that I'm going to try and I'm going to succeed. If I make a mistake, I'll learn from it, but I will continue."

I am not a big fan of the overly positive. It is important to have a positive attitude and to think broadly and effectively, but it is also important to be realistic. I have seen people, because they have an overly positive attitude, think they are achieving superior results when they are actually mediocre. Leaders should rate analytical abilities grounded in reality and the underlying drive to achieve more highly than a positive attitude.

Finally, don't just check references. Have as detailed a discussion with the sources as with the applicants. Would their former employers hire them again, for the kind of position

you have open? (But know the state and federal laws govern-
ing reference checks—and they change. In most states, it's
illegal to ask direct or indirect questions about a candidate's
age, sex, religion, race, marital status, sexual orientation, dis-
abilities, politics, pregnancy, drug use, medical history, or
arrest records.)

KEEPING

Mukesh Chatter, the founder of Nexabit Networks, says
that Ray Stata advised him from the day he started the company, "Take good care of the people, and good things will
happen." When Nexabit's senior managers considered for-
going employee life insurance, Stata, the chairman and
founder of Analog Devices, said, "When people are working
long hours, spouses and kids are participating in building
the company; it's our moral obligation to provide life insurance." Chatter said that Nexabit spent two and a half times
its annual payroll on life insurance and the investment has
paid off in employee loyalty.

We have a better-educated workforce than has ever
existed. These are people who are saying, "Wait a minute, I'm
not just going to bow to the company anymore. I'm a smart
person. I'm an individual. I'm going to take control." The
Web is about taking control of one's career, so there's been a
psychological shift from "I need a job. I want to be loyal" to
"I don't need this particular job. I'm loyal to myself." A short-
age of skilled workers has put companies on the defensive.
They fight to recruit people. The power has shifted in a very
short time from the company to the individual. It is analo-
gous to the shift in power from the company to the customer.

Provocateurs lead best in this world in which the power
has shifted. They provide the organization with a valuable
goal. They tell employees and customers, "We're not going to

rape the planet. We're not going to exploit women and children. We're going to make life better for our customers. We're going to offer our employees an opportunity to grow professionally." Work in a provocative organization is not just a paycheck. It's not just a pension at the end of 30 or 40 years.

Even as the evening news and business papers are announcing layoffs and consolidations, the American workplace is evolving to a kinder, gentler place. Managers have realized that they must do more than pay good salaries and lavish perks on their star employees if they want to keep them. They must also—maybe you should sit down for this—be nice to them.

A Gallup study shows that "most workers rate having a caring boss even higher than they value money or fringe benefits. In interviews with 2 million employees at 700 companies, Gallup found that how long an employee stays at a company and how productive she is there, is determined by her relationship with her immediate supervisor. 'People join companies and leave managers,' said Marcus Buckingham, a senior managing consultant at Gallup and the primary analyst for the study."

Randy Hodson, a sociologist at Ohio State University, says, "There's been a big push to have employees work harder and smarter, but not a lot of attention is being paid to what managers should contribute to the new workplace. The nature of the new bargain"—that is, the new social contract, supplanting the old—"entails greater mental and physical effort on the part of workers in exchange for benefits that are often left vague and undefined."

Hodson, who studies corporate responsibility, says that about 60 percent of the employees in the companies he studied "displayed good worker citizenship, even at a level above and beyond what might be reasonably expected. What jumps out of these studies is that workers get really irritated by the absence of management citizenship. They'll put up with over-work or limited pay, but not incompetence or abuse. Workers don't like chaos. They don't want to come to work in a place where the situation is unreliable, uncertain, supplies aren't there, machinery doesn't work, or where one supervisor says one thing and another supervisor says another." So a major part of the Provocateur's task is to make it possible for employees to do the jobs for which they were hired.

Provocateurs know that human skills, expertise, and rela-tionships are an organization's most precious resources. Often, however, they are hidden in the company's cubicles. Most businesses are filled with talented employees whose skills are either underused or misused entirely. When a new challenge crops up, the wrong manager steps forward and the company's real expert never hears about the opportunity.

Employees complain that while they are working harder than ever, managers rarely seek their contributions or thoughts on anything beyond their immediate jobs. Managers do not ask what career step they might want to take next. Or, if they ask, they do not offer any follow-up advice about what the employee must do to achieve it.

One employee at a communications company who, for obviously good reason, did not want to be identified told *The Wall Street Journal,* "I have lots of ideas for how this company could move onto the Internet, but I'm not one of the inner circle of people making those decisions and don't know how to approach them. They all sit in adjacent offices and seem to talk more to each other than anyone else. There's little reach-ing out to a broad array of employees for ideas and input."

Part of this problem is simply time. It is difficult to make time for unscheduled conversations with coworkers about ideas, asking for input on projects, helping to identify skills needed to advance, and finding what positions a staff member may aspire to achieve. (A Dilbert coffee mug tells the world: "Let me drop everything and work on your problem.")

John Kish, former Verbind CEO, worked for Larry Ellison, the founder of Oracle, for six years. I asked Kish, who started Oracle's Desktop Group, what one can learn from Ellison's leadership. He says that "Larry surrounded himself with exceptionally bright people, and while it's not popular to believe this, Larry actually did want people to disagree with him. There was a forum in which you did that, and ideas evolved as a function of the disagreement. At the end of the day there was never a doubt over who was in charge, and if Larry said, 'March left,' you marched left. But the fact is he was very good at getting exceptionally bright people in a room, trying to focus them on a question, inviting discussion about it, and ultimately making a very quick decision as to which way to go."

Some managers don't ask their employees for ideas because they don't want to share power. Or they hang on to workers who deserve to be promoted because they don't want to replace them. Yet in my experience, reluctance to help employees express their talents invariably backfires. People who feel underutilized or ignored become demoralized and unproductive, and the best ones find jobs elsewhere. In time the leader who does not want to share power or promote good people ends up leading an organization of plodding drones.

More than once, I have been surprised by the people who end up being the most productive in a company, the ones who feel most at ease in the environment. They tend to be those who feel they are supported, that this is a place in which they can create, and that there is a common larger goal and vision to be the best at something. They feel there are opportunities they can take to learn things they don't know. They can learn new software; they can learn something about finance; they can learn sales.

To help them learn, we are only beginning to tap the computer's capabilities as a teaching tool. It can introduce material at the student's pace, offer the information in several ways—text, pictures, with audio, with movies or animation—and will repeat the same lesson as often as the student wants. Language CDs, for example, introduce the vocabulary, show scenes with the words in use, and with a microphone attached to your computer will visually compare your pronunciation with a native's. The computer—and the Web—offer a variety of ways to reinforce the information, to review, and to test yourself, all at your own pace.

MANAGING

How does one manage in a world in which you have more creativity, more innovation? It is hard, but you have to keep focused on the company's vision and goal, its core competencies, and how people's skills complement one another. It should be natural and comfortable to ask Bill for the financial analysis and Tim for the marketing analysis. In the Provocateur's environment, one is driven by the next accomplishment and the next contribution to the working community, not the next job title.

Then what? Once I have moved through the chairs to become first violinist in the New York Philharmonic, is that the end? No, it is just the beginning because you should be at a level now that allows you to give creative input that helps change the whole tenor of the orchestra. Help choose new pieces to play. Help interpret a Mozart passage differently. Help rehearse the orchestra when the music director is not available.

More to the point of this book: Once I've become CEO of a successful company, is that the end of my life? No, it is the beginning because you can help build an environment that will be the best in a category. Jeff Taylor came up with the concept of Monster Board, and everybody thought he was crazy. Then he sold the company and could have walked away. But he stayed and is changing the way business recruits by building dialogues with thousands of people. He is setting the agenda for e-recruiting, which is becoming the dominant way to find workers. Taylor sees Monster.com as a place where he can make his vision become reality.

Too many people in the General era looked to achieving one position and then staying in that chair until they retired or died—a behavior the Generals encouraged. Provocateurs say to new hires, "This is just the beginning," and surprise the employee with the job. They push people's limits, forcing them to try things they didn't know they could do. I believe management should load people (most people) with more than they can easily handle. I believe this about myself, and I believe it about managing people. Give them as much as possible. No one knows his limit until he has stared it in the face. Even then, it may be a paper wall and—surprise!— he can tear right through it.

Of course there is always the Peter Principle problem— promoting someone beyond his level of competency. The best talent adjusts and performs after some difficulty. Provocateurs know—or promote an atmosphere in which the employee can air her distress—when they have put someone in an environment a little ahead of her ability. They make an extra effort with supporting or complementary staff to help her settle into a more effective role.

Nevertheless, it can be a mistake to promote a great writer to a position as editor, a great salesman to be a sales manager, or a great programmer to be a project director. You can lose great talent and gain a mediocre editor, sales manager, or project director. The leader should understand the qualitative difference between skill at a craft and ability to manage other people.

As John Kish, the former president and CEO of Verbind, explains, "I think we are starting to get to the point where we realize that the unfortunate consequence of something most businesses do—take perfectly great individual thinkers and pound them into being perfectly horrible managers," says Kish. "They turn out to be absolutely the worst senior managers, and yet, that is the way we get funding cycles going. The interesting thing is that the venture capitalists are now seeing themselves as keepers of the vision, and I think we have to be very, very careful as we enter an environment where the bankers think they understand what is coming next."

A lot of leaders don't look clearly at the strengths and weaknesses of certain excelling employees. They often take someone who is a great engineer or a great marketer and try to get her to do things outside that core competency that maybe she doesn't like, doesn't have the ability to add to her core competency, or just doesn't want to do. This positive and productive urge to promote then really harms her true value to the company as a great engineer or a great marketer.

Bob Metcalfe, who is now a venture partner at Polaris Venture Partners, points out that people have operating ranges. When he was starting 3Com in the early 1980s and he was running the sales operation, he took the company's sales from $0 to $1 million a month, "mostly through personal selling. After that, sales became too technical for that approach to work," and another executive took over. Sales of more than $1 million a month were, according to Metcalfe, out of his operating range.

"How do you know when it's time for a change?" he asks. "How can you tell when the person who did such a great job six months ago has hit the upper limit of his or her operating range? The first sign is a decline in performance—salespeople missing quotas, engineers slipping schedules. At first it looks like the plans were too ambitious; then it's everybody else's fault. At some point, unless things start improving, sometimes even before the proof is conclusive, changes must be made. You have to be able to say, 'If you can't do it, we'll just have to find someone who can.' If you wait too long for the person to learn what they need to know or for conclusive proof of whose fault it is, you may bring the whole enterprise down. Better to risk the lawsuit for wrongful discharge and save the venture."

Provocateurs are willing to spend money on the mistakes creative, enthusiastic people inevitably make. Mistakes are good; they indicate that people are trying new things. Leaders have to allow for mistakes. Leaders have to support their employees; they create an environment in which mistakes are an opportunity to learn.

Obviously leaders can't tolerate the same mistake repeated over and over. ("The wise man makes the same mistake only once," says the proverb.) But if you pick the right person, an occasional mistake only makes her better and stronger over time. Provocateurs want an environment in which mistakes are not punished as such. The company looks at them, analyzes them, and uses the experience to make the company stronger.

Some might disagree, but I believe that the value of the paycheck drops somewhat as employees understand the company's vision, have more control over their part of realizing that vision, and are able to increase their skills and opportunities. When employees truly understand the value of building a positive experience for the customer, they also understand they will ultimately make more money and get more responsibility for themselves.

Generals focused on the reward before the process, salary and perks before customer wants and needs. Provocateurs focus on the process—finding, satisfying, and keeping customers—and the reward will come. "One thing you can't do," says David Hayden at Critical Path. "You can't buy loyalty or allegiance. There is a huge misconception about that in the world right now. The golden handcuff idea is a myth. It's a fallacy. This is a human nature issue. People will go when they want to go, and they should. No matter what the money is. Keeping people in place because of money is the wrong motivation."

Hayden agrees that building a community should be the leader's primary task. "You build a community around work, which includes nice amenities, but they don't have to be some of the silly things you see now—refrigerators stocked with cookies and ice cream or women roaming the halls giving massages 24 hours a day. That is a silly manifestation of our attempt to create better working environments than we've had in the past, but it's largely about space and architecture. It is largely about the kind of ambient environment that you have in a place that makes people like to come and work."

In every community, there will be weaknesses every now and then. If in our town, children's test scores are significantly lower than in comparable communities, let's pull together to fix them. We may realize that we haven't been paying enough attention to the teachers we're hiring, the superintendent, the school board, the curriculum, the town's growth. Get the community involved in making a decision, or at least understand the direction in which the school system should be moving.

Business is the same. Build a community of employees, customers, suppliers, and partners, but understand that when one part falters, we all pull together to bring it up to what it should be. It is not just HR's problem, or marketing's, or manufacturing's. According to Jeff Taylor, if an employee plays foosball to avoid work at Monster.com his peers on his team will step in to bring him back into line. Usually before the manager tells someone to stop playing, the community takes the responsibility.

Ray Ozzie draws the analogy between a business and a central nervous system with lots and lots of independent operations going around it. "You have to have groups of people who work effectively with one another. That's easy to say, but you have a dysfunctional organization if groups aren't self-forming. If somebody hears of a customer problem, you need an organization where (a) people can get the information they need—and that is part of the central nervous system—about the customer and the problem, and (b) already know who to call or make it very easy to understand who to call to form an ad hoc group to solve the problem, or take advantage of the opportunity, or work on the design feature, or whatever."

A business, says Ozzie, must have people who are willing and who are empowered to create those groups. They must know how to solve a problem among themselves and how to put information back into the systems so it becomes part of the record. "If you have people or an organization where people are largely sitting in their cubes doing their jobs and don't feel like interaction with others is part of their job, it's going to be a dysfunctional organization. It's going to not work in the kind of way I'm talking about."

Groups have to be self-forming and spontaneous, responding to a situation as it arises. Management can't usually appoint committees to solve problems as they come up because by the time management has identified the problem, appointed the committee, and the committee has acted, the problem has become a crisis. What you want are people who know where to go for help and the authority to do something.

Ozzie notes that in some ways this is an environment stacked against the introvert. It is stacked against the person who isn't a real producer. "That doesn't mean that introverts don't have a place. There are individual contributor roles of many types throughout organizations. But I would do what it takes to create an organization that encourages self-forming groups."

At the same time, Tom McMakin, the former COO at Great Harvest Bread Company, cautions that overconnectivity—everyone connected to everyone else all the time—can be a detriment. He says that there are maximal points of connection; if there are more points, the system becomes inefficient. At Great Harvest, it's very clear to McMakin that the individual bakery is one point of connection. "It makes sense for one or two representatives from each bakery to mix it up in the national community" rather than have everybody in every bakery be connected to everybody else. The bakery representatives then create "their own live, non-computer-based, face-to-face learning community in their own bakeries, and they mix it up there. That's maximal efficiency."

Great Harvest has found that "in this Internet age, we can be overconnected. We found that there's a natural level of connectedness in our system. People have three to seven friends in the system. They're the people that they talk with online. They're the ones that they trade phone calls with. You don't need to be connected to everyone."

McMakin says, "It's possible for a highly networked organization to bind up with too much trading of information. We actually teach our owners to block out a lot of what's going on in the system as a whole and concentrate on their five or six or seven different friends, knowing that if there's a hot recipe or a hot promotion, the network will feed them the information over time through those three or five or seven friends." Otherwise, managers can spend all their time reading and responding to communications, most of which are irrelevant to their lives and jobs.

ARCHITECTURE, DRESS CODES, AND COMMUNICATION

The physical environment is also important. Hayden says, "I have an architecture background, and it's a pet thing with me. Our first building was a big, cool, open space we made cooler by some of the little things we did in it, but at one point we had like 50 engineers working in one big space. Elbow to elbow. Lots of talking. Lots of collaborating. It saved money, but it also, I think, accelerated the building process. We had a lot of work cut out for us to build the service. I have to have a private office because I'm the CEO and sometimes need to have a private conversation. Today, a lot of the better offices have private conference areas for that even if everything else is fairly open."

Architecture is important, not from a metaphoric point of view—the architecture of a business plan—but to actually encourage engagement in the vision and with other people in the firm. A Provocateur will look at how the offices are arranged. If they are isolating and unchangeable, see if the firm can get out of the lease to go to a building that promotes community. Jeff Taylor at Monster.com has organized the office to be almost like a student union, with many places where people can meet formally and informally, but with private spaces to which they can still retreat for quiet work.

Over the years, people have tried different physical approaches to make business run more efficiently. Cabletron, a New Hampshire company, put no chairs in its conference room to send the message that it did not want employees spending a lot of time in meetings. I think it was a good creative attempt, but probably the wrong message because Cabletron still had to hold some meetings. It was like saying we will never need a meeting, which, alas, is impossible. So why not create a more comfortable environment for those times when the firm absolutely, positively must have a meeting?

I believe there should be no dress code. Of course, people should not come to the office naked and certain jobs traditionally require costumes—uniforms for nurses and prison guards, shirts and ties for conservative bankers, gold-trimmed jackets for airline pilots. But if the job's nature does not require a uniform, the company should not require one. If it does, the company should pay for it, the way Cirque du Soleil pays for the costumes its performers wear or how the U.S. Army, Navy, Air Force, and Marines provide uniforms. There should not be an expectation of what I call surface matters—a white shirt and conservative tie, a perfectly clean desk, rigid work hours. The expectations should be at a deeper intellectual level.

Anything that moves communications to the next level with employees is important, getting them to think together, to not compete against one another. The Provocateur's attitude, stated and implied, should be: Our purpose is to create a community with all our constituencies to create better products and services to attract and retain customers.

Jason Vines at Ford says that the first priority for communications should be the business's own employees. "A lot of companies, in their eagerness to run out and tell the world, ignore their own employees, or make a minimum effort to explain things to them. That's a big mistake. The troops need to know what hill you're charging up, and why. If they don't, when you yell 'Charge!' they're going to scatter in all directions. Or, more likely, nobody will move. People are resistant to change. They prefer to stay right where they are."

The leader's job is to explain why remaining in place is unacceptable, and why the alternative—the corporate vision—is so much better. What's important, says Vines, "is that you don't overestimate the effectiveness of your efforts, and that you not be afraid to repeat yourself. Over and over and over. George Bernard Shaw once said, 'The greatest problem in communication is the illusion that it has been accomplished.'" Ford considers employee communication a top strategic priority. Not just for the big-ticket items—vision, mission, values—but for anything that impacts employees and the business—even breaking news items. Ford's policy is to let employees know first, unless logistics or the law won't permit it.

One should also be realistic enough to recognize that bad things happen to good companies. The economy can drop, a competitor can introduce breakthrough technology, a natural disaster can destroy the factory. If the business has the financial strength and employee loyalty, however, it will make adjustments, survive, and thrive.

If the Provocateur creates an environment where people can earn good money and be recognized, that's just the cost of entry. The leader wants to excite people about a common goal—creating the fastest search engine on the Web, manufacturing the most reliable cars, or developing a new asthma medication. If you create a business environment with that excitement, you will attract and keep the best people.

The employees' goal should be to find an organization that gives them opportunities to grow in ways they would not otherwise have, to explore their limits, and to see how far they can go—not "up the career ladder" but "with your abilities to achieve." Perhaps into the company's inner circle.

10

THE NEW INNER CIRCLE

*There are always different perspectives, and it is bet-
ter to surround yourself with people who think differently than you. Better yet, people who are smarter
than you! You can see the problem on some boards
where they're all cronies. That's a huge mistake.*

—George Conrades,
CEO, Akamai

When there are no more organizational fiefdoms—finance,
legal, manufacturing (as there should not be, because every
person in the company is working directly or indirectly to
improve the customer relationship)—who and what should
comprise a Provocateur's inner circle? Certainly not an "old
boy" network.

Today's leaders need official and unofficial advisers who
challenge their thinking, provide unusual perspectives on
strategy, and offer new types of support and inspiration. A
formal board of directors is necessary for a corporation, but
a Provocateur can often improve a board's contribution. The
board should complement company management, rather
than simply mirror skills already in place.

Leaders also need informal inner circles of associates—
insiders and outsiders including company employees and

suppliers—for advice, suggestions, and criticism. I also believe more companies need an inner circle of customers who can advise the company on service, new products, and other innovations.

THREE MISTAKES ENTREPRENEURS MAKE

Bob Metcalfe, who is now a venture capitalist with Polaris Venture Partners, tells the story of hiring his bosses when in 1981 he founded 3Com (from COMputer COMmunication COMpatibility) to manufacture and sell networking equipment such as interface cards and high-speed modems for the consumer, commercial, and telecommunications markets. Before starting the company, Metcalfe spent two years meeting every venture capitalist who would see him. He asked for advice, not money. Since he was planning a new company, he wanted to know what killed young companies.

When Metcalfe then returned to ask for money, "foremost in my pitch were the three mistakes I was not going to make: One, uncontrolled ego of the founder, in this case moi. Two, lack of focus, although I had a lot of product plans. And three, lack of capital. You want to raise lots of money, even money you don't expect to need, because you'll probably need it anyway. A lot of entrepreneurs try to raise money as late as possible so they can retain their equity, but they end up flying too close to the sun and crash and burn."

In the process of raising money for 3Com, Metcalfe found—an early indication that they lacked confidence in his ability—many venture capitalists wanted a seat on his board as a condition of their investment. Metcalfe refused. "I said I wanted to build a really good board, but I didn't want to contractually agree to having a company representative. 'But,' I said, 'if I invited you to be on the board, would you serve personally?' Dick Kramlick, who was the leader of New Enterprise Associates, said yes. I think he said yes knowing I had just refused to let anyone be on the board against my wishes. That scene played out two more times, and once the deal was done, I invited all three VCs onto my board."

3Com did not have a venture capitalist associate or junior partner or recent MBAs on its board. "I got three of the top capitalists of the day on my terms," says Metcalfe. "They weren't coming because they had demanded it as a condition of their investment. They came because I invited them." And to watch their investments.

Metcalfe tells me he invited them as his way to fight the uncontrolled ego of the founder problem—to have a board actually in charge of running the company. He did it, he says, because he had decided that 3Com's success was more important to him than running the company. It was so important, he would risk getting thrown out by his board.

"Which meant that, a year later when they all decided I shouldn't be CEO any longer, I had no ground to stand on," says Metcalfe. "I had chosen these people for this very decision, and they were making it right in front of me. When I was informed that I would no longer be CEO for good reason—although it did not feel that way at the time—I couldn't storm out in a huff, like so many other founders do when they lose the CEO title. I felt, because I had chosen these guys for this duty, who am I to say they are wrong?"

The board offered Metcalfe the job of vice president of sales and marketing, "which was a measure of our desperation. And then I lucked out and succeeded wildly at that job in the next two years, before it outgrew me. So I just kept working on this list: My company is not going to fail because of the uncontrolled ego of the founder. It is not going to fail because of the lack of focus. And it is not going to fail because of the lack of money."

I asked Bob Metcalfe what he would look for in a board member if he were installed as a CEO with the option of replacing board members who don't attend meetings, or who fall asleep during meetings, or who can't remember the general condition of the company from one meeting to the next, or all of the above.

"It's clear they have to be replaced, much less clear who to replace them with," says Metcalfe. "You want to replace them with people least likely to want to be on the board. People who are intelligent, energetic, and hardworking, and still in the game, and why would they want to be on your board? If I have a company to run, that's a full-time job. Why should I take my company's time, or my personal time to worry about your company?"

Fortunately, he says, that question has several good answers. One is that boards "frequently want their chief executive to be on other boards for his edification. Learn things about other markets, how things are done elsewhere, pick up tips from leaders. Another reason goes back to co-op-petition"—the idea that companies often must both compete and cooperate. "Boards are where I have seen the co-op-petition go on. Members of boards are the modern version of the interlocking directorate, and venture capitalists frequently play this role for small companies, but the same thing goes on with big companies. The deeply set co-op-petition relationships are established at the board level, so being on another board is a way of uncovering opportunities for co-op-petition. Then there is the money, which is generally not the strongest reason."

I asked about member expertise. Many companies never put marketing—even sales—people on their boards. What should they look for?

"Not lawyers," says Metcalfe. "Some of the companies I'm involved with feel obligated to have their lawyer on the board. I think that's a horrible mistake. You want legal advice, but you don't want lawyers telling you what to do. The lawyer's job is to tell you what the risks are, not to make a decision for you."

TROUBLE ON BOARD

The Rite Aid Corporation, with headquarters in Camp Hill, Pennsylvania, is the poster child for bad boards. *Business Week*'s 2000 annual survey of corporate governance rated it the second worst board in the country (Disney's was the worst). At Rite Aid, "which has restated its financial results for the previous three years, the audit committee met only twice in fiscal 1999. Four of the company's nine directors were insiders and five board members are 70 or older." As Richard H. Koppes, a consulting professor of law at Stanford University, said, "It's a corporate governance nightmare." And the rot at the top apparently shows up in Rite Aid's financial performance. Although revenues were up almost 12 percent in fiscal 1999 (to $12.7 billion), profits were down almost 55 percent (to $143.7 million). In other words, profits as a percent of revenues were 1.1 percent; they were 1.4 as a percent of assets. The drugstore business is tough, but not that tough. In contrast, CVS's 1999 profits as a percent of revenues were 3.5 percent, 8.7 as a percent of assets.

Symptoms that a board of directors is not what it should be include:

- *The company regularly misses market opportunities.* Examples include Microsoft and the Internet, Barnes & Noble and online bookselling, and Kmart (and Zayre, Bradlees, and Caldor, to mention only three defunct mass merchandisers) missing the mass-marketing success that Wal-Mart has found. The inability to conquer a category is a board problem, because it has the authority to set a new strategic direction—or at least strongly suggest that management explore new possibilities. In the Microsoft case, no one seemed to be advising from an inner circle, pointing Bill Gates to a different way of looking and thinking. Until late 1995, Microsoft's executive suite seemed clueless about the Internet's implications. Indeed, management seemed to regard it as just another piece of software. A company statement in February 1995 said that "tens of millions of personal computers around the world that now use Microsoft software will be connected to a network that both embraces the global Internet and rivals it in size. Although online information competitors like America Online, CompuServe, and Prodigy have taken nearly a decade to amass an estimated total of 6 million subscribers, Microsoft hopes to overtake them all within a year of its scheduled launch [of The Microsoft Network] in August." Only after Netscape went public and Internet growth exploded did Gates begin talking about the Internet.
- *Customers wander, become more nomadic.* The company has not put the customer relationship at the center of the organization. Customers do not feel part of a community and have no loyalty.
- *The company is not communicating well* with itself or its customers, and probably doesn't communicate well

with its board, and therefore the board is not achieving what it could. It is like any dysfunctional family. The idea is simple: A company that doesn't communicate well with its employees, doesn't get those messages down, doesn't have the appropriate learning programs, and doesn't construct the proper communications with the outside world is not going to succeed. Therefore its board will not do well, because they are not going to understand exactly the company's objectives or where its future innovations will come from. Customers complain or make suggestions to somebody, but it stops there. Employees can't do anything to change policy, so they don't report their ideas and valuable suggestions vanish into the ozone.

• *Sales fall, costs get out of control, and innovation suffers.* To use the Gates example again, where is the innovation at Microsoft? They buy it or copy it. If the board focused on innovation, it would have forced CEO Gates to create an environment of innovation instead of an environment that acquires innovation as a last resort.

Cisco buys innovation, but Cisco also maintains a culture of innovation, or so it seems from an outsider's perspective. Cisco's management understands what customers are going to want, so it recognizes strategic holes that have to be filled. It then can make acquisitions thoughtfully. Microsoft has made a lot of acquisitions out of fear of being overtaken in certain categories. They wait until they are threatened, and they let a little start-up get to the point where they are actually a major competitor, and then they try to acquire them or squash them.

That goes back to setting a culture of innovation with an

inner circle, which Microsoft has gone away from. They watched Lotus 1,2,3, take off and created Excel. They watched Notes take off and created Exchange. They watched Netscape take off and created Explorer. True, as I said earlier, a company can be a fast follower and still be a leader. But the leader needs to understand the necessity for innovation, rather than just observing innovation.

Provocateurs have to work at not thinking they are the only brain on the job. The inner circles and the board are a group brain. How you get the complementary thought leadership together is more of a challenge than thinking you are smart. As simple as it sounds, it is tough to learn. You have to admit you don't have all the answers.

In fact, I don't have most of the answers, but I have analyzed the market, and I have looked closely at our customers. I have scrutinized our product and product development. I know where we are weak and where we are strong. I need to validate that and then add creative minds and superior thought leadership that will strengthen the weak parts and make the strong parts even stronger.

A General typically said, "I have all the answers. I have the strategy right here," while he tapped his head. And, at a particular moment in time, the General may in fact have all the answers. But markets, the world, competition, and people change, and today's correct answer does not keep. The organization must constantly evolve and grow, to find the second correct answer, the new correct answer. You have to get to what works quickly and then move in such a way that the new answer builds on itself. The example I often use is that customer relationship management is one of the core elements of success. The longer you wait to start a process of automating and building the customer relationship management program, the further away you will be from your competitors who have already started because the program builds on itself, growing richer, deeper, and broader.

Provocateurs can achieve phenomenal results by creating and encouraging an innovative environment. The loyalty and passion of the inner circle is important. I suspect that many CEOs complain privately that their boards have no passion. There is no real interest in the business. There is more of a checklist mentality—have you done this? Have you done that?

BOARDS SHOULD PUSH MANAGEMENT

A company always needs to be innovative. There must be centers of innovation and moving forward; these centers need to be the firm's lifeblood. Nonetheless, passion has to come from both sides in a Provocateur-run institution. Not just from the bottom up, which everybody seems to accept, but the board and the CEO must have the passion to push down into the organization. Ideally, the leader ends up with a company that becomes more homogeneous in its approach to its customer relationships, product development, and its sales process.

The board has to push for the systems, the processes, the culture, and the attitude that permeate the company, while ideas may come from anywhere. It may be rare for a director to walk into a board meeting to announce, "I have a product idea for you," but it should not be rare for a good board member to say something like, "Have you thought about looking into digital photography?" If the leader forges a circle of advisers who become the innovative center from a vision and an incentive, a cheerleading, an intellectual point of view, that will make the job of innovation within the company much easier.

People argue it is not the job of a board of directors to be creative or innovative. I argue it is. If they are not creative, how do they stay fresh? How do they promote innovation at the company?

Jack Welch invited Scott McNealy, CEO of Sun Microsystems, to join General Electric's board of directors. Welch says, "Scott brings GE a whole irreverence. He's an enormous pain in the ass sometimes, yelling and screaming. He makes our guys know it's okay to be informal. We pride ourselves in being direct and informal, but he's much more informal than we are. He talks about speed in ways we don't usually think about. He brings urgency, a view of where things are going with IT. I wanted all the brains and enthusiasm of another generation and an industry that's changing the world. I think getting Scott was a big deal for our company. And having Scott as a role model for the young managers in our company is fantastic. So for us, it's a real coup. He's young enough to relate to our young people in a totally simpatico way."

But the arrangement works for McNealy who said, "Actually, I think we've gotten way more out of Jack than they've gotten out of us. We're becoming a more competitive company by learning how to take advantage of after-the-sale revenue opportunities through services; we're learning about the boundaryless way to operate inside a company."

As George Conrades at Akamai points out, "There are always different perspectives, and it is better to surround yourself with people who think differently than you. Better yet, people who are smarter than you! You can see the problem on some boards where they're all cronies. That's a huge mistake."

We seem to have had an American tradition through the General era of picking friends and business leaders, and relying heavily on financial expertise when creating a board of directors. These members tended to be executives who knew how to analyze the books, manipulate the finances, or had access to capital. Starting around the 1960s, companies began to add the tokens: the academic, the African-American, the woman. A company that enlisted an African-American academic woman filled three board seats right there.

Esther Dyson is a technologist and a marketing thinker, but she is also a social anthropologist and author. Martin Sorrell, the CEO of WPP Group plc, invited her to join the board of that marketing communications conglomerate. In the old days, under a General's leadership, she would have been named because she was a woman. Today, her knowledge of emerging markets and technology, as well as her diverse interests, which range from Eastern European cultures to the digital economy, provide solid strategic value.

Constructing a board in the old days was a very different exercise. Board members guarded stockholder investments, voted on the CEO's compensation, and replaced him for egregious incompetence. Often they were almost a rubber stamp. The original objective may have been to keep the CEO honest—they, after all, represent the stockholders' interests—but at many corporations the board seemed to become a small, exclusive, and highly compensated club.

With some Internet companies—I sit on the boards of eight—board members work with different company departments. I believe that a board member who has full exposure to the company's nitty-gritty operations adds immense value to the business. To make a sweeping (and probably unfair) generalization, many big company board members who came out of the General era wouldn't know who runs marketing or manufacturing or human resources if they saw them in the executive dining room.

Bob Metcalfe sees his job as a board member as to "stand up to the CEO. Make it a point to argue with him, because very few other people will and it's for his own good. It's amazing how easy it is to be valuable, because a lot of people don't know the first thing about running a company." He gives as a simple example (one he says is true, but condensed) the firm that had its development operation in Boston, its marketing operation in Pittsburgh, and its factory in Puerto Rico. Metcalfe said to the CEO, "You're spread all over the map. That is stupid. You should really consolidate in one place."

The CEO said, "Be in one place? You mean . . . so we don't have to travel . . . so we don't have misunderstandings and diverse cultures that war with each other?"

Metcalfe said, "Yes. It helps a lot if you're in the same building."

The CEO said, "But we couldn't get the head of engineering to move here, because he really likes living in Boston."

Metcalfe said, "It doesn't sound to me like his commitment to the company is all that strong. Maybe you need a new head of engineering."

Great plays do not come alive if the director does not cast the correct actors or actresses to create the tension, the emotion, and the inner life that takes a performance from the ordinary to the extraordinary. Management is the same.

Before a board makes recommendations or decisions about leadership, members should spend time looking at the company's strategy. Where is it today? Where does it want to be two years from now? What is its mission? I recently talked to a CEO who told me, "I'm not quite sure what our mission is anymore."

I said, "What does the board think the strategy is for the next three to five years?"

He jumped on me: "Nobody thinks about five years out!"

I said, "Well, okay. Sorry I asked."

"The board doesn't know anything. They don't know what our strategy is."

The company may be a web of connections, but somebody has to be in charge. From a communications point of view, you need to have the best talent that is most effective to communicate on the basis of constituency. Who would be best to communicate to the customers? Who is best to communicate to the suppliers? Who is best to communicate to the financial community? And how are we going to layer all this together in an orchestration the CEO will lead? To say with one voice, here is our overall strategy. It is like the melody in a Beethoven symphony that returns with different instruments.

WHAT I LOOK FOR IN A BOARD POSITION

While I am on the boards of Internet companies, I also recently accepted a seat on the board of a different type of company, Cambridgeport Bank. I was attracted for three reasons:

1. There is an opportunity for this service institution to become a sales and marketing machine.
2. There is a challenge to reposition an old-line economy company into a new economy company.
3. I get to keep my mind a little sharper by not thinking 120 percent of the time about sales and marketing. On this board, I have to think about real estate, mortgages, small business loans, Fed rates, and all the issues that affect banks.

Eclecticism, as I've suggested, is important to a Provocateur. Not that you search it out constantly, but you are open to a healthy variety. I have a close friend who is a physician and a nutritionist. We once went out for lunch, and he ordered a double bacon cheeseburger and French fries. Since I had never seen him eat anything other than the most healthy foods, I asked, "Tim, what are you doing?"

He said, "Larry, as long as I stay on my regime for six days a week, the seventh day I can have whatever I want, and it's not going to hurt. In fact, it's going to help me feel better about the way I live."

Provocateurs do not throw all discipline out the window. It is not how you color outside the lines, but how you create within the lines. Step out of the circle of tradition to select board and inner-circle members and look for an eclectic nature: Have they written? Do they have other interests? Are they broader than their business experience?

When a company invites me to join a board, I think the management is looking for creative marketing and positioning thinking. They want ideas to make the company stand out from its competitors, and they feel I can generate them. They invite me rather than hire a consultant because they want a more intimate relationship than a consultant can give them. The smarter CEOs want a professional family, and they know that even the best consultant still is a hired gun. Also, I think they look for someone who might have one idea so good it could change the face of the company.

They look to me because I understand the media. As the media grows in importance, I can validate the company strategy and direction, and be an increasingly important spoke in the wheel. I am also a counterbalance to the sales-driven people who routinely look too early for things a company shouldn't be attempting: certain sales, certain partnerships, certain achievements.

When I am invited to join a board, I look for focus. A company cannot be everything to everyone. Even if the firm's product looks as if it should have broad acceptance, the company needs focus. Rather than market, say, your email analysis tool to everyone, concentrate for now on financial companies because at the moment they are using technology more effectively than firms in other industries.

I look for an understanding and sensitivity to marketing that many managers do not have. Marketing (with innovation) is, as I said earlier, at the center of everything. It is customer relationship management, which is the CEO's biggest job, and how a CEO handles this is probably the most critical part of the job.

I look for an energy, which is not about making a killing and moving on to the next new thing. It is about becoming the best at something—the best sales automation on the Web, the best email hosting company in the world, and so on.

Another primary objective, whether a company is private or public, should be to set the dialogue agenda. Provocateurs invite thought leaders to set an industry's tone, direction, and agenda. Once a year invite competitors to a seminar on, say, Internet marketing or government relations. Provocateur leaders share their knowledge and, by virtue of such sharing and setting the dialogue, the industry and the press regard them as category leaders.

The company charter determines the board's composition. For early-stage companies, it is financially driven. Whoever has invested seriously gets a board seat. That is why it is very important that Provocateurs look at the outsiders they are allowed to appoint so they can create a more eclectic and integrated complementary group of people and to have informal advisers.

It is healthy when the company charter specifies board terms limited to two or three years. David Hayden, the CEO at Critical Path, says there should be board term limits "so there is a continual ingress of new thought and talent, which is beneficial. Whether you agree with the thinking or not, it's healthy to have new thoughts coming in."

Provocateurs should play Board Survivor. If you had to vote someone off the board, who would go and why? List the reasons and see if they are strong enough to make the change. Leaders must be aggressive because they have to build and protect the company's productive, positive, and profitable environment, and the board plays an important role in creating that environment. If it doesn't, it is the wrong board.

Too many boards take action only when—to exaggerate slightly—they see stockholder suits being filed. That is living reactively instead of proactively. Provocateurs always stay one step ahead of their investors: surprising them in a good way by being innovative, obtaining better than industry average margins, increasing sales. But in addition to a supportive and active board of directors, a leader also needs one or more inner circles.

FORM A VIRTUAL ADVISORY CIRCLE

Actually, Provocateurs at any level in any organization need an inner circle—a group of people you know, trust, and can rely on for their candor, expertise, and ideas. The model for such a group is a dinner party: Surround yourself with people who have thoughts and ideas within the industry but also in areas that may be totally foreign. The goal is discussion and debate, with every idea held to the light (or its feet to the fire) for relevance and crossover potential.

A Provocateur's inner circle is an extension of his or her brain. Today's leader requires experts on customer behavior, on the changing marketplace, and on cutting-edge technologies and business concepts. An inner circle—and one may have several that may or may not overlap—provides a unique vantage point based on their diverse expertise and interests.

Stewart Alsop, a partner at the venture capital firm New Enterprise Associates, says that in looking for an inner circle "you have to maintain outrageous standards, because your success is a direct relationship to how high your standards are. The better the group of people you have around you, the more quality becomes an assumption. It is not an assumption taken for granted, but one that you expect. That's how you control things—by making sure the people doing them are the best."

Booz Allen consultants write that "leadership is no longer the province of the anointed few. The process of promoting select individuals into positions of authority is a relic of a command-and-control culture that paralyzes companies trying to compete in an Internet-enabled environment. The old model of CEO as lone 'star' is no longer relevant. He or she can no longer set agendas and dictate change . . . everyone is a leader, charged with creating an environment for collective gain and success. And the mark of a leader will be to create other leaders within the organization—disciples, of a sort, who are empowered to act. These disciples, in turn, manifest their own leadership skills by translating this vision into a mandate for continued renewal. They create an environment and build management bench strength to achieve change and cascade leadership throughout the organization.

"This model of cascading leadership is not a luxury; it is an imperative in a world where organizations no longer have the time for day-to-day decisions to go up and down a hierarchy, and where knowledge throughout the organization must be leveraged and shared. It's not easy. Market forces continue to rage as companies wrestle with the organizational barriers to institutionalizing this type of entrepreneurial leadership model."

ENGAGE INNER CIRCLES

Experts are spokes that make up an inner circle. They connect to the organization's most critical parts. And a business may have many inner circles that involve employees at many levels: customers, suppliers, reporters, and more.

In the early 1980s, my wife, Dawn, worked at American Greetings in Cleveland, Ohio, a family greeting card business. The CEO decided that, instead of bringing together the top executives to make decisions about new greeting cards, he would have an employee committee meet every Monday morning. This committee was made of employees from all parts of the company: accounting, writing, graphics, and sales. Ten to a dozen people met for about two hours over donuts and coffee to look at the new card concepts and react: "That's good . . . that's not . . . that's good . . . that's not."

What I found interesting was that the CEO invited a cross-section of employees to participate on the committee. I had recently finished graduate school, and she had taken the job because we had moved back to Cleveland. The committee's go/no-go decisions may sound arbitrary, but Dawn says the group went to the core of what made a good card, one that crossed social and vertical boundaries. American Greetings would then send the approved designs out for further tests before they went into full production, but the committee was a good first screen.

Cross-fertilization also exists at CMGI, according to David Wetherell. "A couple of us sit in on both the CEO meetings and the @Venture meetings"—CMGI's venture capital division—"so we are sure to alert the different groups of opportunities between the groups. There is a lot of communication going on like that, a lot of leveraging of opportunity. Every week we discover new opportunities, but that's the nature of the number of interactions you have between 70 companies."

Inner circles may include outside advisers as well as different levels of employees. They can give you the everyday cross-section of what the firm is accomplishing. Outsiders can often bring fresh thinking and objectivity to a complacent organization.

Several years ago eight independent appliance/TV retailers who were attending an industry management seminar at American University agreed to form a critique/support group. While their businesses ranged in size from one store to five, they were all sales and servicing dealers and none were direct competitors. They agreed to meet for three days in a different dealer's hometown every six months, spend two and a half days analyzing the business and the last afternoon reporting their findings, suggestions, and ideas. The dealers hid nothing; the visitors were free to interview the host's employees, accountant, advertising representative, distributor salespeople, and banker. Participants paid their own trip expenses; the host treated everyone to dinner during the last night.

As the group continued to meet, it became clear that different members had individual strengths. One dealer was particularly strong with internal organization and was able to suggest ways to improve records. Another, who came up through the service department, was particularly astute at service management.

The host taped the afternoon critique and had to sit mute; he could neither defend himself nor explain why the visitors had uncovered a certain problem. The visitors inevitably left the host with an action list that often contained several hundred items and went home with ideas on ways to improve their own businesses.

It also became clear over time that it took an unusual manager to subject himself (or herself) to the critique process. It was one thing to visit another dealer's business, pick it apart, tell him what he was doing wrong, and offer good advice. It was something else to be subjected to your peers' scrutiny and receive their good advice. Some could not take the examination, dropped out, and were replaced.

Those who could tolerate the dissection and actually act on the group's recommendations (not always the case) flourished. Their businesses grew while they found more time for their families. (One critique uncovered a troubled marriage, recommended the host start making more time for his wife and seek counseling. That dealer told me the critique saved his marriage.) They became close friends and were an enduring source of advice and information. The critique group idea is one that leaders in many kinds of organizations can adapt to their own needs. And the Web makes staying in touch between semiannual meetings easier than ever.

The Web is going to offer many opportunities to create virtual advisory circles to chat with like-minded individuals about problems, challenges, and theories. The three to seven people that each Great Harvest franchisee communicates with regularly is an inner circle. As Tom McMakin, Great Harvest's former COO, notes, "if there's a hot recipe or a hot promotion, the network will feed them the information over time through those three or five or seven friends." Create a dialogue about different aspects of the business, products, and services. If you meet a Japanese, Thai, or French executive (or all three) at an international conference, it is now possible and inexpensive to keep in touch.

It is also important to stay intellectually engaged in things outside your market. You need "advisers" that have absolutely no sense of your day-to-day life. It would be interesting if, in building your inner circles, you fill in the wheels as I've talked about with people from different specialties, but also with a farmer, a painter, an educator—someone outside the commercial world. I don't think this idea has been considered seriously, but I think it could be provocative and productive.

Why does today's leader need inner circles that challenge traditional thinking?

It was relatively safe in the era of the Generals to rubber-stamp whatever the boss presented; business was uncomplicated and change occurred slowly. In today's world, a leader needs associates who do not agree with a nod and a stamp. Leaders need people who know what is happening and who regularly challenge their thinking. (And leaders, of course, need to be amenable to such challenges.)

You sometimes run into people who look at the work of the greatest abstract artists—Picasso, Rothko, Franz Kline, Motherwell—and say, "My kid could do better than that." But when you study the history of these painters, you discover that they studied the classics and did early work that was realistic and representational. They developed their own visions based on their understanding of tradition and a desire to express something unique.

Great business thinkers are similar. They know the basics, and they know the tradition. They know how to make a good margin; they know finances; they know how to sell; they know a good business plan; they understand strategy. But they leave that behind because they are self-assured. They surround themselves with people who also have the basics down cold, but can take the business to a higher level. That should be the real goal of building the web of advisers—to create an environment that will move a company forward.

"Companies often confuse talking with doing," says Stanford professor Jeffrey Pfeffer. "They think that talking about something is the same as doing it. That planning is the same as doing. That giving presentations is the same as doing. That making reports is the same as doing. Or even that making a decision to do something is the same as doing it. All of those errors occur with alarming regularity in companies today."

Worse than that, says Pfeffer, "talk can actually drive out action. Studies about the way that meetings actually work demonstrate that negative people are perceived as being smarter than positive people—that is, being critical is interpreted as a sign of intelligence. You see this attitude in business all the time: The fastest way for me to seem smart is to cut you down. So you come up with an idea, and I come up with a thousand different reasons why that idea won't work. Now everyone sees you as dumb and me as smart—and we've created an environment where no one wants to come up with ideas."

It is important that there be creative moments throughout the year that provoke a leadership dialogue. Leaders set agendas within the company, so they constantly have mini swirls of dialogue going around products, customers, partners, sales, products, and corporate innovations.

An example comes from George Conrades, the CEO of Akamai: "You have to be able to argue with conviction, and you need self-confidence because you are with other smart people, and somebody is going to trump your idea. That's why we call each other Titans. When somebody goes to the next level, it's 'Titanesque!' or 'You're a Titan!' That's a way for everybody to relieve the pressure that they just got trumped, and to acknowledge it. It encourages people to jump in. You have to have a keen intellect and an ability to debate and the self-confidence to watch your idea get trumped by one a little better. In addition to smarts, you need energy—high energy—and then you need the ability to get along with others. Because one of the things that keep people in a firm are big ideas, making a difference. By definition those projects are hard. When you get something like that going, you're going to have a lot of arguments because it's never been done before. So, it's important to challenge assumptions to get at the best idea or plan."

That is an example of what I am trying to convey. We are getting things done, but somehow we have built a culture that recognizes that we can take something a step further on a regular basis, and that's when somebody becomes a Titan. As Akamai has said, "Wait, this could be even better." Provocateurs create a culture that allows that to happen and prosper.

I would encourage executives in the company to establish their own inner circles. People should belong to more than one circle, and the circle should include executives from different areas. It is also a good idea to bring a board member into marketing's circle or into research's. The more dialogue, the more likely the company's agenda and business plan will succeed. General Electric's board "has made an almost religious practice of ensuring that directors meet often with lower-level GE execs without [CEO Jack] Welch present—a practice all too infrequent elsewhere in Corporate America." But it is a practice other companies can profitably adopt.

INCLUDE AN INNER CIRCLE OF CUSTOMERS
Finally, companies should establish inner circles of customers. These may be customer panels, user groups, dealer advisory boards, whatever. The company invites them to creative sessions; keeps them at the business's center; communicates with them regularly.

I envision using a secure Web site/intranet/chat room to

foster customer communication with the company, as well as annual (or more frequent) meetings between the company's senior management and the customer advisory circle. In many ways, I see this as an expansion of the beta programs software companies use—sending out an unfinished version of a product for comment. Provocateurs should always be thinking in beta mode—how can we improve the product or service?

This is, I know, not an original or new thought. Five years ago, for example, Tony Carter, a professor of sales and marketing at both Columbia University's Graduate School of Business and Wagner College in New York City, advocated customer advisory boards for business-to-business marketers. "These boards are underutilized, and they are a practical, available, and dynamic way for companies to stay in touch with their most important asset," said Carter.

Carter found that 21 of the 70 *Fortune* 500 companies he surveyed in 1996 had customer advisory boards. "The competitive advantage lies in having an ongoing involvement with your customers. And the fact that many other companies don't have customer advisory boards is a competitive advantage in itself."

Carter recommends that customer advisory boards be made up of 5 to 15 members, ideally senior-level managers with decision-making authority in their own organizations. To avoid any appearance of impropriety, board members should not receive financial compensation. They should meet two to four times per year to discuss company strategy, production, or marketing problems. While they usually do not discuss proprietary data, management should ask board members to sign a confidentiality agreement if they do.

EMC Corporation, a Hopkinton, Massachusetts–based $4 billion supplier of storage systems, software, and services, believes customers can collaborate with the firm to produce better products. To formalize this process, EMC employs customer advisory councils. "These are neither sales meetings nor conventional user groups," says EMC's president and chief executive Michael C. Ruettgers. "Instead, these sessions are about methodically extracting product requirements from customers, validating product concepts and long-term business directions, and above all, creating a climate for collaborative innovation. Twice a year in North America and Europe, and annually in other parts of the world, we bring together 50 to 60 customers to join us for 20 hours of intense discussion spread over two and a half days."

Ruettgers says that EMC chooses these customers carefully. It tries to attract only executives who are their companies' acknowledged visionaries, strategists, and key decision makers. They agree to a minimum 18-month commitment and sign nondisclosure agreements.

At the meetings, EMC first presents "what we believe to be the most troublesome short- and longer-term problems facing the industry and their businesses," says Ruettgers. "Next, we confirm that our perspectives dovetail with their experience, and that the problems we're focusing on are, in fact, the problems they're challenged with. If it appears we're on the same page, we present a detailed look at EMC's 'work-in-process' solutions to these problems."

At this point, the EMC executives probe to learn whether their proposed solutions will solve the problem, and, once solved, whether they will have a meaningful business impact. "Through hours of discussion, we try to discover new requirements and fine-tune our offering. We also talk about how to best implement the solution, including which, if any, strategic partners customers would like us to work with. We feed all of this acquired knowledge back into

EMC and integrate it into a coherent product design," says Ruettgers.

That is not the end of the customer advisory council's involvement. At the very next session, EMC shows how the product has changed based on the customer advice. "In the interval between sessions, they can log on to a special Web site to share information with their customer peers and read updates on the prior session's key topics. But the real key is that these councils are a powerful learning tool for everyone; we help customers plan their IT future, and they help us plan ours," says Ruettgers.

Of course, a company does not have to be high-tech or business-to-business to profitably employ a customer advisory board. Dorothy Lane Markets, a $38 million operator of two upscale supermarkets in Dayton, Ohio, has formed one. "They meet four to six times each year," says Amy Brinkmoeller, DLM's director of information systems, "and they focus on a different department of the store at each meeting." Board members, who serve two-to-three-year terms, have also made benchmarking trips that DLM pays for to supermarkets in Chicago and Atlanta.

By maintaining an inner circle of customers, Provocateurs have a golden opportunity to stay in touch with the people who give the company their money. I am only surprised more companies do not have them.

But there is of course more to being a successful Provocateur than leading a flourishing business. There is also the challenge of leading a rewarding life.

11

BEGIN THE JOURNEY

If you had a 12-cylinder BMW, would you be satis-
fied to run on only three cylinders? Of course not.
You would like to run on all 12 cylinders.

—Michael Dertouzos, director,
Laboratory of Computer Science,
Massachusetts Institute of Technology

After asking the rhetorical question about the BMW, Dertouzos asks his real question: "Are you running on all your cylinders as a human being?"

What are the cylinders on which a human being runs? Dertouzos identifies four: the physical, the spiritual, the emotional, and the intellectual—call it rational. "The Enlightenment in the eighteenth century split the rational away from the others, and we highlighted it and suppressed the church—as we should have because it was screwing things up—and of course we had the industrial revolution and became rich. But now? Are we running on any other cylinder today other than the rational? The physical a little bit. Are we running on the emotional, the artistic? Very little. The spiritual? Not at all."

Dertouzos sees a growing realization that to be a complete person one has to run on all four cylinders. "You are going to be at your best as a human being, not as a religious zealot, not as a rational cold-blooded zombie, not as an artsy-fartsy fop, nor as a physical hunk alone, but as the best combination of whatever God or nature gave you. To me, that is a noble goal, and I would like to suggest that is where we should be going."

I agree that many of the people I know are running on only one and a half cylinders, and I agree that running on all four is a noble goal. When I asked Dertouzos how one reaches that goal, he pointed out that I was asking for a rational answer to a spiritual or emotional question. Nevertheless, he says, "If you have the belief and the faith, there will be a million different ways as you empower people and they find ways to do it." Certainly realizing there *are* four cylinders and that running on all four is a noble goal becomes a start.

On a more practical level, Dertouzos says, "I would destroy the barriers between humanists and techies. I would force them to live together. They could still specialize, but I would expect them to drink coffee and talk together. I would tell company leaders, 'Hey, you better empower your employees to run on all four cylinders.' I am sure a good CEO can figure out a million ways to have employees combine these four things. If people want to do it, then they find ways. It is not being in charge. It is lighting the fire; it is grabbing the soul. The Internet gives me the rational, information side, but who is going to give me the passion?"

Leadership in this new century encompasses everything I have talked about in this book. To lead in a highly educated, exceedingly mobile, easily connected, information-based world demands new thinking and a desire to run on all cylinders. Business challenges are more complex than ever before. Employees want more than an annual review and a raise. Diverse audiences demand constant communication. The global market is always open. New competitors spring up continuously. Most of us want to live long, rich personal lives. The way to thrive in all this blooming, buzzing confusion is to stay on top of emerging trends, become your own brand, carve out reflective time, nurture a creative outlook, and be alert to the signs that it's time to get out.

STAY ON TOP OF EMERGING TRENDS

The best way I know to stay on top of emerging business trends is by reading good writers in the best publications— *The Wall Street Journal, The New York Times, The Financial Times, The Economist, Fortune, Forbes, Business Week, Fast Company, The Industry Standard,* and industry trade magazines. Pick writers, not just the publication. Try to follow writers who have a different take on things. I have found John Markoff in *The New York Times* often gives me an interesting twist on a topic. Bill Bulkeley and Walt Mossberg in *The Wall Street Journal* provide insights into creating better environments for your customer base.

Read material with which you intellectually, emotionally, spiritually disagree—political speeches, business analysis, psychological theories—because they may plant a new idea or offer a new perspective. You may find something useful, but even if not, the (asinine) argument helps throw your own convictions into sharp relief, which may clarify your thinking. If you are liberal, read the *National Review;* if you are conservative, read *Mother Jones.*

I believe in kitchen table surveys, asking people their opinions and objectives. Groundbreaking ideas bubble up from the bottom of organizations. Provocateurs visit the lowest parts of the organization periodically to hear what workers are thinking, what is wrong, what is broken, what needs to be addressed, and the ways people use to solve problems.

Patrick McGovern at IDG feels it is so important to stay in touch with individual employees that every year "I go and personally meet everyone at IDG in the United States. I started the practice when we had 13 people, and now we have 4,000 people in the United States, so it takes about three weeks. But I go at the holiday season and visit every business unit. I talk to each person and ask, 'What did you do that you are most proud of this year, and what ways can we be improving?' I give them their holiday bonus, and I find it, for me, the best experience, because you get to see people's body language, their attitude and enthusiasm, and really know what is happening in that business unit."

The visit sends a message that IDG's values are not just words on a plaque in the reception room. Management practices them. Here is the company founder. He knows your name. He knows what you do. It creates a sense that we're all in this together. The employees feel that if they have a problem, they can always call him. In fact, says McGovern, "almost no one ever calls, but it tells employees that these are not faceless people running the company."

Speaking at universities keeps you in touch with some trends. I have learned a lot through the questions students ask. Speaking at industry events can have the same effect. It's not what you say that is important (although it can be for other reasons; you may learn something preparing your talk), but what you hear. Serving on boards at emerging organizations and as a member of different inner circles has paid me back far more than the time has cost.

There are now thousands of college courses you can take online at your own pace. It is tough for a busy executive to go to a class once a week, but, with online learning, there is a course you can take, whether analyzing Virginia Woolf's *Mrs. Dalloway* or focusing on marketing communications.

Indeed, the University of Phoenix, which has no campus and is only online (www.phoenix.edu), is one of the largest colleges in the United States.

In April 2001, the Massachusetts Institute of Technology announced that it plans to make the materials for nearly all its courses freely available on the Internet over the next 10 years. The Web site for the project will include lecture notes, course outlines, reading lists, and assignments for each course in architecture and planning, engineering, humanities, arts, social sciences, management, and science.

In making the announcement President Charles Vest said, "MIT OpenCourseWare is a bold move that will change the way the Web is used in higher education. With the content posted for all to use, it will provide an extraordinary resource, free of charge, which others can adapt to their own needs. We see it as source material that will support education worldwide, including innovations in the process of teaching and learning itself."

BECOME YOUR OWN BRAND

The leader should be separate from and complementary to the company's brand and position. She needs to develop her own platform and position on issues that complement the company's core competency and differentiation. It is a higher, more visionary direction than what the company does every day. The CEO really brands herself as a visionary around certain core competencies and where the firm will be in the future and how it will migrate or evolve its customer bases to that future. Provocateurs look at themselves as actors who need thoughtful scripts on a regular basis, vehicles that evolve and move forward.

How does a leader know when she's reached brand status? She is making her numbers. People respect and follow her.

All the old-fashioned things are working. She has a clear and thoughtful leadership connection to the media. Reporters call for comment on a specific area. Her relationship grows, and more and more people see her as an expert in a category or a field such as Jack Welch on management, Steve Jobs on graphical technologies, John Chambers on Internet infrastructure, Lou Gerstner on e-business and e-services, or Charles Schwab on financial services.

Leaders who come to mind when you think of an industry have achieved brand status. If you think of an industry, the name that comes immediately to mind is the brand. Think of the energy industry . . . Jeffrey Skilling at Enron. He took a commodity and achieved a brand. By also building himself as a brand (even if inadvertently and unconsciously) and having a separate brand with Enron, Skilling has built a successful community.

Other brand status CEOs would include Herb Kelleher at Southwest Airlines, Michael Dell at Dell Computer, Larry Ellison at Oracle, Orville Redenbacher and his popcorn, Frank Perdue and his chickens, and Paul Newman with his line of popcorn, salad dressings, and sauces. Newman is an interesting example, an entertainer going into product development, giving the profits to charity and so attracting a community's interest.

CARVE OUT REFLECTIVE TIME

Is reflective time important? I think it is, but everybody is different. I use planes, cars, and going for walks for my reflective time. A simple recommendation: Most good hotels have a map of walks around the hotel and the city. I get up a half hour earlier than necessary to walk around the city or a park and think quietly. Again, read books outside of business, and think about how they apply to business. Watch little television.

Pete Wakeman, who founded the Great Harvest Bread Company with his wife Laura, says that from the early days of the business they had some simple rules, "but we followed them like religion." They took a two-day weekend every single week. They did not talk about work at home. And they took a three-week vacation, often wilderness camping trips, every year. "Sometimes longer than three weeks, but never less; we *never* skipped them. We loved our work, but we worked so we could take trips. Later, as the business became more intense it was easy to get confused and begin to think the trips were to refresh us so that we could work better. We fought that like the poison that it is. The trips were and are their own justification."

Aside from the physical, spiritual, emotional, and intellectual refreshment the trips gave the Wakemans, there were other benefits. Their inviolate nature forced the Wakemans "to hire right and train right and invent systems for our people as the business grew. It grew up around that belief system, accommodated to it. Of course, that was fabulous for the business—imagine a little bakery, or a just-beginning two-employee franchise company, whose people *knew* they had to do Sundays alone, Mondays alone, August alone—and that there was no way to call if they got into trouble."

Pat McGovern says that "if people feel trusted, they feel responsible and are diligent. When I say, 'You people are doing a great job; I'm going away for two months,' they say, 'Wow! He really thinks we can do it. He's willing to pass the total responsibility on to us.' I find they do an outstanding job. They make the decisions when they should make them and move ahead. I find it's very important to devote the time to your family and develop that relationship, because if you don't it comes back to haunt you. You wind up with children who recognize you didn't give them the time, and they have problems with their lives."

Jeff Bezos, the CEO of Amazon.com, says, "it's easy to let the inbox side of your life overwhelm you, so you become a totally reactive person. The only remedy I know of is to set aside some fraction of your time as your own. I use Tuesdays and Thursdays as my proactive days, when I try not to schedule meetings. I let the other three days of the workweek be completely scheduled, meeting with different general managers in our businesses. That works pretty well for me. And I try to travel about a third of the time. If I travel much more than that, I lose my Tuesdays and Thursdays."

Dr. Charles Vest says that when he was first asked to take the job as president of MIT, "I called up three other university presidents, who I happened to know a little bit. I asked, 'What is your advice?' Every one of them said, 'The most important thing is that you've got to carve out time to sit and think and read, and clear the cobwebs out of your mind.' To each of them I said, 'Well, how do you schedule that?' And they each said, 'When you figure out how to do it, call me back.' But I run along the banks of the Charles River every morning, and you would be amazed how much that helps to keep things in perspective. I love to hike. I usually try to do a lot of reading that has nothing to do directly with work on airplanes and a little bit at the holiday season and vacations. You grab the time where you can."

NURTURE A CREATIVE OUTLOOK

A creative outlook comes about through curiosity, enthusiasm, and a sensitivity to the unexpected. Provocateurs notice when something does not happen as expected, or a new incident contradicts in some small way their picture of reality. The enemy of such an outlook is boredom.

Boredom comes in many different forms, from lack of innovation or doing the same thing all the time to confusion, because so much is happening the mind turns everything off. Provocateurs must be sensitive to business boredom and its roots so they can avoid it.

The flip side of boredom is illustrated by the entrepreneur who can't focus on one thing long enough to accomplish much of anything. We once had a client who became angry because he did not want to give the same speech over and over. He finally demanded a new talk for every occasion, but in fact the way to get his message across was to give the same speech to different groups for six months or a year. Varying his speech actually deflated his message.

Too many entrepreneurs or executives, bored with their own business, will jump into something completely different. An insurance firm will buy an HMO. A photography film manufacturer will buy a drug chain. A toy company will buy a software developer. Poor acquisitions may come out of boredom or from the idea that the firm must simply grow bigger . . . period. The real question should be: How do we use our energy and intellectual intensity to improve our core competency?

Provocateurs must have some criteria of what they focus on as knowledge that will help the business's core competency evolve. These are ideas, features, benefits, and options that make the firm's products or services more interesting, more valuable, and more essential to customers who buy them.

Information about competitors suggests where their strengths and weaknesses are evolving. Information about innovative technology makes products better and easier to buy. Market information shows how the firm is doing. Partner information tells which firms are developing complementary core competencies that will help the company do better.

The companies that grow the fastest and do best are ones where customers, employees, suppliers, reporters, and shareholders want to be part of the community. There should be fun with a purpose. The purpose can be anything—do the best possible marketing communications and PR for a client . . . design and manufacture the most reliable, responsive cars on the road . . . give every passenger a sense that the airline intends comfort and on-time arrival.

Bob Metcalfe at Polaris Venture Partners warns that one should not fall prey to millennialism. "That's the idea that the World Wide Web is so dramatically different that all the old rules are gone, so we have to reinvent intellectual property, commerce, accounting and taxation, and privacy. We don't, so avoid believing that the Internet is so different from anything that has existed previously that you have to start from scratch in your thinking."

If a company has a position and a business model and costs, says Metcalfe, the trick is to map the Web onto that model and see where it has any impact at all and take advantage of that. People—and by extension, companies—develop cultures that succeed at a certain time and then they can't change them. If you are aware of this tendency to stick with what worked in the past even as circumstances change, you can resist it.

Jeff Taylor at Monster.com says you should put your current business out of business. "If you coast, you only coast one way—downhill. If you think you are coasting in business, you absolutely are. If you have to question it, you know you're coasting. You can't drive straight up all the time, but ease up. It's like anything on a hill; if it actually stops, it can only stop for a second, then it starts rolling backward."

We are no longer the old economy or the new economy. We are in *the* economy. Too many leaders of what one might call traditional economy companies are still thinking in terms of black and white—us/them, employee/customer, management/labor. Leaders of new-economy companies tended to think that all the rules had changed, that "first-mover advantage," that "share of market/share of mind," "click-throughs," and "stickiness" were more important than gross margin, free cash flow, and profitability. This new world integrates new technology and communications tools to turn everything into shades of gray.

SIGNS THAT IT'S TIME TO GET OUT

What are the symptoms that it's time for the Provocateur to get out of the company or out of business in general?

It is time to get out when you don't think you can add any more innovation within the core competencies that you bring together. If you don't get excited about the job anymore, if you can't feel passion or excitement about what you're doing every day, it's time to get out. Some fortunate people apparently never reach that point.

I was once in a plane with Sir Richard Harris, the actor, who was on his way to play King Arthur in *Camelot* once again. He was chatting with one of his aides and said, "I'm so excited about this role again."

She asked why, which would have been my question.

Harris said, "Well, there's a whole new way we can look at his character—from a modern perspective." Here was an actor who still had a passion for a role he must have played several hundred times. Think of Mick Jagger. How does he get up on stage and sing "Jumpin' Jack Flash" one more time? He does it, and the audience loves it.

It is time to get out when you cannot devise a new way

to do or present what might be old and comforting. Once you have lost passion, it is probably time to look for a new passion, one that will get you excited about using all your skills and abilities. Sir Laurence Olivier said at the end of his life that he had never given the perfect Hamlet performance because he kept learning more about himself as the character developed. I think that is true for good leaders. They continue to learn about themselves as they try new things.

One problem I saw with a lot of the dot-com companies was that the founders did not feel passionate about what they did for customers or for society. They were merely looking at an opportunistic moment to make a pile of money.

By contrast, my friend V.A. Shiva, the founder and inventor of EchoMail, is passionate about email and its possibilities. But he has a lot of difficulty with people because he is so direct, intelligent, and overbearing. His passion started with a Westinghouse high school science award for the first electronic mail in 1979. All through MIT and up to today, Shiva has remained passionate about how email might evolve. (It will even be more effective, he says, as it becomes more visual.) Shiva is not going to get out at any time in the foreseeable future.

I see two kinds of passion. There is your own, driven by your individual wants, needs, and desires. But there is also an environment that allows for a passionate response, one that evokes enthusiasm in other people. In both, it has to be deep-seated and thoughtful, not a sham.

A business may seem boring from the outside, but the leader who is passionate about the company must attract people who he can infect with his passion for building, creating, and extending. I think often of my father's work as a high school coach. He was passionate about high school football, but it didn't cross my mind until I reflected on it in college that it really didn't matter to him whether we ran the play right or that we won the game. What mattered was that we believed in ourselves, that we could do something, that we built self-esteem, and that we were passionate about playing the game, not about winning. That was a great lesson.

BEGIN THE JOURNEY

The world of business is shifting beneath our feet. We are at the beginning of the truly borderless economy. As George Colony at Forrester Research says, "The moment you turn on your Web site, you are instantly global."

The niche-within-a-niche trend will continue to spiral. Companies are going to find ways to customize their products and services, in some cases to produce a unique item for each customer. Customers will want to know that a company is the best at whatever it offers, which may be quality, safety, design, price, or some other element. Customers will become more and more knowledgeable, and companies will have to respond to that sophistication or wither away. The General who believes "They'll always buy from us because they've always bought from us" is a danger to himself, his employees, and his stockholders.

Sales on the Web will grow. Individual dot-com retailers may fail, but for ordinary customers the trend is obviously toward more convenience and innovation. You want theater tickets in London, a bed-and-breakfast in Syracuse, a Handspring Visor delivered to your house? They're only a few clicks away.

Markets for different products—steel, paper, plywood, office supplies—will develop on the Web if they are more efficient than the existing arrangements. David Wetherell at CMGI observes, "Trillions of dollars will flow through the

Internet, but it doesn't happen overnight. It takes a while to develop the systems, to get the critical mass of suppliers and buyers, and support system to work optimally."

Recruitment and retention, as Jeff Taylor at Monster.com points out, will not get easier, although technology may make it easier for companies to find employees and for job seekers to locate jobs. Companies will have to create environments that keep people as long as possible.

Technologies that help facilitate service will continue to grow more complex and more integrated. To stay on top of these technologies will be a major challenge, which starts by being aware of the possibilities.

Headquarters workers will not always be working at headquarters. They will be wherever they want to be, although not to the extreme we thought five years ago when it seemed everyone would be working in robe and slippers at home. There has to be a human connection, so people will be in the office at least some of the time. But managers will be a lot more tolerant of an employee's desire to work at home.

There will be more and more kinds of partnerships—no business can do everything by itself. It needs partnerships to develop products: it needs to develop customer sets to manage data. It is not optimal to own everything, which was the General's model. Generals wanted control, to be able to order people around. As companies started getting bigger, they worked the wrong way in community building. They went almost communistic with the state/corporation owning everything, from the company cafeteria to its own trucking company and airline.

All these currents and more mean organizations require a new kind of leader to succeed. Provocateurs understand that their job is to build communities rather than companies, communities in which all stakeholders are welcome and comfortable. Customers may have become nomadic and gained power through information, but they will respond positively to companies that genuinely care about them. The product or the service is no longer at the heart of the company; the relationship with the customer is.

To triumph in this new world, leaders will be more teachers than managers. They will, through their enthusiasm, self-confidence, and ability, become the face of the company. They will lead others along an uncertain path, developing individual skills and strengthening commitment. They are curious and intellectually vibrant, reading widely and embracing the arts. They know what customers and other stakeholders desire, and they know where to find it.

Provocateurs understand that technology is more than infrastructure or simply a tool to do jobs the firm has always done faster, cheaper, and more accurately. The best technology allows the firm to do something it could never have done before (or would have been too time-consuming and expensive to be worth doing). Provocateurs watch for those opportunities, since those can offer competitive advantages and growth.

Provocateurs recognize that just as power in the form of knowledge is shifting from the manufacturer or the retailer to the customer, so too is power shifting from company to employee. Job seekers can learn about careers, companies, and industries quickly and easily. It means that good employees have less reason to tolerate a company or a manager that does not respect their abilities or give them opportunities to grow.

Provocateurs also realize they cannot lead alone. They need inner circles made up of associates who will challenge their thinking, provide different perspectives, and suggest original alternatives.

Organizations led by Provocateurs that put the relationship with the customer at the center, that routinely engage customers with innovative products, services, features, and benefits, and that use technology wisely will prosper. It will not be easy or always clear (what does it mean to use technology "wisely"?). But for those who want the fun and rewards of being a Provocateur, it is time to begin the journey.

NOTES

CHAPTER 1

Phil Jackson has said: Frank Deford, "Father Phil: The High Priest of the Triangle Offense," *Sports Illustrated,* November 1, 1999, p. 82.

Knight, says Bill Walton, is a coach: Bill Walton, "Basketball's Tarnished Knight," *Time,* May 29, 2000, p. 96.

In 1997, BU dropped: Gerry Callahan, "Death BU Not Proud," *Sports Illustrated,* November 17, 1997, p. 148.

Trotman was secretive: Alex Taylor III, "The Fight at Ford," *Fortune,* April 3, 2000, p. 144.

Michael Dertouzos, the director of MIT's Laboratory for Computer Science: Michael Dertouzos, a dear friend and colleague, passed away unexpectedly on August 27, 2001.

CHAPTER 2

Yang and Filo: Based on "The Customer Is the Decision-maker," *Fortune,* March 6, 2000, pp. F84–F86; Brent Schlender, "How a Virtuoso Plays the Web," *Fortune,* March 6, 2000, pp. F79–F83; Kristi Heim, "Yahoo! Inc. Succeeds on Internet with Unique Business Methods, Philosophy," *San Jose Mercury News,* April 3, 2000, http://www.lexis-nexis.com (April 18, 2000).

Some companies . . . are appointing "chief community strategists": Sean Donahue, "New Jobs for the New Economy," *Business 2.0,* http://business2.com/magazine/1999/07/19788.htm.

Michael Bonsignore, former chairman and chief executive of Honeywell International: Carol Hymowitz, "Managers Often Miss

Notes

Talent Lurking on Their Own Staffs," *The Wall Street Journal,* May 9, 2000, p. B1.

Jill Barad, the former CEO of Mattel Inc: Kelly Baron, "What Was She Thinking?," *Forbes,* November 1, 1999, p. 54; "Mattel Puts Unit on Block," *Los Angeles Business Journal,* April 10, 2000, p. 40.

General Motors . . . is making its Supply Chain Data Warehouse available: Beth Davis, "Data Warehouses Open Up—Sharing Information in Your Company's Data Warehouse with Suppliers and Partners Can Benefit Everyone," *Information Week,* June 28, 1999, p. 42.

CHAPTER 3

"Now you need to establish far deeper": Marcia Stepanek, "Tell Me a (Digital) Story, *Business Week,* May 15, 2000, p. EB91.

Lawrence McNaughton, . . . of Corporate Branding: Ronald Alsop, "Blue Chips Lose 'Brand Power' to Lower-Tier Firms, Survey Says," *The Wall Street Journal,* March 21, 2000, p. B8.

Small toy makers, as one example: Rachel Backap, "Tiny Toymakers Hitting It Big on the Web," Associated Press, November 23, 1999.

George F. Colony, chairman of the board: George F. Colony, "Hollow.Com—More Forrester.com Thoughts," Forrester Research, Cambridge, MA, April 18, 2000.

Debra Goldman wrote in *Adweek:* Debra Goldman, "Consumer Republic: E-mail Marketing Is a New Medium with an Old Message," *Adweek,* March 20, 2000, p. 24.

C.K. Prahalad, coauthor of *Competing for the Future:* Fred Andrews, "Ideas into Action," *The New York Times,* February 9, 2000, Sec. C, p. 10.

Honeywell's $5.2 billion air-transport business: Steve Hamm and Robert D. Hof, "An Eagle Eye on Customers," *Business Week,* February 21, 2000, p. 70.

CHAPTER 4

Jeff Hawkins, the former CEO of Palm Computing: Paul E. Teague, "Father of an Industry," *Design News,* March 6, 2000, p. 108; Ephraim Schwartz, "Jeff Hawkins, Handhelds," *InfoWorld,* October 9, 2000, p. 56.

Kareem Abdul-Jabbar, who played at UCLA: Kareem Abdul-Jabbar, "Appreciating the Wisdom of Wooden," *The New York Times,* December 10, 2000, Section SP NE, p. 11.

Notes

GE met a serious challenge: Matt Murray, "General Electric Mentoring Program Turns Underlings into Web Teachers," *The Wall Street Journal,* February 15, 2000, p. B1.

Pete Wakeman, who with his wife Laura: Pete Wakeman, "The Good Life & How to Get It, *Inc.,* February 2001, p. 44.

The executive who was head of corporate communications: Scott Bass, "Blood, Sweat & Fear: Are You a Bad Boss?," *Inside Business,* December 2, 1998, http://www.insidebiz.com/hamptonroads/cover/cover120298.htm.

CHAPTER 5

Howard Schultz, now the chief global strategist for Starbucks: Scott S. Smith, "Grounds for Success," *Entrepreneur,* May 1998, p. 120; and Terry Lefton, "Schultz Caffeinatated Crusade," *Brandweek,* July 5, 1999, p. 20.

Pepsi-Cola is spending around $1.2 million: Ellen Neuborne, "Pepsi's Aim Is True," *Business Week,* January 22, 2001, p. EB 52.

CHAPTER 6

Doug Burgum, CEO of Great Plains Software: "Great Plains Software CEO Studies Past to Learn Future," *The Wall Street Journal,* November 21, 2000, p. B1; Ronald B. Lieber, "Beating the Odds," *Fortune,* March 31, 1997, p. 82.

Durk I. Jager, by all published accounts: Emily Nelson and Nikhil Deogun, "Change Was Too Fast at P&G; Jager Goes, Pepper Is Reinstalled," *The Wall Street Journal,* June 9, 2000, p. 1; Robert Berner, "Can Procter & Gamble Clean Up Its Act?," *Business Week,* March 12, 2001, p. 80.

CHAPTER 7

An executive . . . a master at . . . is Herb Kelleher: Hal Lancaster, "Kelleher's Main Strategy: Treat All Employees Well," *The Wall Street Journal,* August 31, 1999, p. B1; J. P. Dutton, "Air Herb's Secret Weapon," *Chief Executive,* July–August 1999, p. 32; Anne Bruce, "Southwest: Back to the FUNdamentals," *HR Focus,* March 1997, p. 11.

In 2000, IBM Global Services hired: IBM Annual Report, 2000, p. 8; "IBM Announces Relationship Marketing Solution for Insurance Industry," www.ibm.com.

Notes

Vernon W. Hill II, the CEO of Commerce Bancorp: James R. Peterson, "A Bank Where the Customer Is Always Right," *ABA Banking Journal,* March 2001, p. S16.

Dr. Joshua Hauser, a medical ethicist: Holcomb B. Noble, "Hailed as a Surgeon General, Koop Is Faulted on Web Ethics," *The New York Times,* September 5, 1999, p. 1.

CHAPTER 8

V.A. Shiva, the founder of EchoMail, Inc.: Deborah Shapley, "Dr. Email Will See You Now," *Technology Review (Cambridge, Mass.),* January 2000, p. 42.

CHAPTER 9

As David Ogilvy, who built: David Ogilvy, *Ogilvy on Advertising,* Crown Publishers, New York, 1983, p. 47.

Ford's vision, says Jason Vines, head of public relations: Jason Vines, "Effectively Communicating Corporate Vision and Beliefs," a speech given at The Conference Board and reported in *Inside PR, Executive Edition,* May 22, 2000, p. 3.

Yet, the story of the uninspired student: David Leonhardt, "Makes Sense to Test for Common Sense. Yes? No?," *The New York Times,* May 24, 2000, Sec. C, p. 1.

The Container Store, a $214 million retail chain: Daniel Roth, "My Job at the Container Store," *Fortune,* January 10, 2000, p. 74.

Mukesh Chatter, the founder of Nexabit Networks: Justin Hibbard, "Branching Out," *Red Herring,* September 1999, p. 66.

A Gallup study: Amy Zipkin, "In Tight Labor Market, Thoughtfulness Is Wisdom," *The New York Times,* May 31, 2000, Sec. C, p. 1.

Randy Hodson, a sociologist at Ohio State University: Sherwood Ross, "Managers Switch from Control to Empowerment," Reuters, Reut11:22 11-01-99.

Employees complain that: Carol Hymowitz, "Managers Often Miss Talent Lurking on Their Own Staffs," *The Wall Street Journal,* May 9, 2000, p. B1.

Bob Metcalfe, who is now a venture partner: Robert M. Metcalfe, "Invention Is a Flower, Innovation Is a Weed," *Technology Review,* November 1999, p. 54.

Notes

CHAPTER 10

The Rite Aid Corporation . . . Camp Hill, Pennsylvania: John A. Byrne, "The Best & Worst Boards," *Business Week,* January 24, 2000, p. 152.

Jack Welch invited Scott McNealy: Brent Schlender, "The Odd Couple," *Fortune,* May 1, 2000, p. 124.

Booz Allen consultants write: Gary L. Neilson, Bruce A. Pasternack and Albert J. Viscio, "Up the (E) Organization!: A Seven-Dimensional Model for the Centerless Enterprise," *Strategy & Business,* 2nd Quarter 2000, http://www.strategybusiness.com/strategy/00106.

"Companies often confuse talking with doing": Alan M. Webber, "Why Can't We Get Anything Done?," *Fast Company,* June 2000, p. 176. See also Jeffrey Pfeffer and Robert I. Sutton, *The Knowing-Doing Gap: How Smart Companies Turn Knowledge into Action,* Harvard Business School Press, Boston, MA, 2000.

General Electric's board "has made an almost religious practice": John A. Byrne, "The Best & Worst Boards," *Business Week,* January 24, 2000, p. 148.

Tony Carter, a professor of sales and marketing: "Judith A. Ross, "Market Research: Why Not a Customer Advisory Board?," *Harvard Business Review,* January–February 1997, p. 12.

EMC Corporation, a . . . supplier of storage systems: Michael C. Ruettgers, "From Customer Satisfaction to Allegiance," *Chief Executive* (U.S), September 1999, p. 60.

Dorothy Lane Markets, a $38 million operator: Scott Kirsner, "Dorothy Lane Loves Its Customers," *Fast Company,* July 1999, p. 76.

CHAPTER 11

Pete Wakeman, who founded the Great Harvest: Pete Wakeman, "The Good Life & How to Get It," *Inc.,* February 2001, p. 44.

Jeff Bezos, the CEO of Amazon.com: George Anders, "Bezos Shares His Ideas for Time Management," *The Wall Street Journal,* February 7, 2000, p. B1.

INDEX

Educators:
versus guides, 131–132
Provocateurs as, 14, 79–102
e-GM, 119–121
80/20 rule, 174
Electronic customer relationship
management (eCRM),
192–195
Ellison, Larry, 1, 213
Email:
advantages of, 188
attitudes toward, 34–35, 185,
186
levels of use, 184
use in customer service,
184–186
EMC Corporation, use of customer advisory boards,
248–250
Employees:
ability to work at home, 264
as advisers, 242–243
average tenure of, 198
communities of, 35–36
dress codes for, 222
education of, 85–86, 90–94
Generals' attitudes toward,
200
hiring criteria for, 208–209
importance of listening to, 25,
253–254
likes/dislikes of, 211–212
loyalty of, 11, 199–200,
210
motivation of, 3–4
physical environment of,
221–222
priorities of, 211
recruiting of, 197–224
retention of, 11, 264
shift of power to, 11, 197–200,
210–211, 265
titles of, 204–205
training of, 90–94

Entertainers, Provocateurs as, 14,
103–129
Entertainment:
at Amazon.com, 123–124
as customer education, 111
and customer loyalty, 125
future of, 121–122
as marketing, 109
at Monster.com, 103–106
at Novell, 110
at Staples, 109
at Starbucks, 115–116
e-tailing, 29–31
advantages of, 63
future of, 55
E*Trade, use of technology to
create a customer commu-
nity, 116

Farmers Group, 167
Fast followers, 76–77
Figgie, Harry, 99–101
management style of,
xi–xiii
Figgie International, corporate
culture of, xi–xii
Filo, David, 18
Ford Motor Co.:
communication priorities at,
223
cooperative endeavors with
competitors, 43
corporate vision of,
201–202
Four Seasons Hotels, 160
Franchising, changes in, 16

Gates, Bill, leadership style of,
26
General Electric (GE):
board of directors practices at,
247
employee education at, 94
plastics division of, 173

ABOUT THE AUTHOR

Larry Weber, widely recognized as a visionary in the converging worlds of technology and communications, is the founder of the world's largest public relations firm, Weber Shandwick Worldwide. He is also chairman and CEO of the Advanced Marketing Services group at The Interpublic Group of Companies, the world's largest organization of marketing communications and services companies. Mr. Weber is a founder and chairman of the board of directors of the Massachusetts Interactive Media Council and sits on the boards of several technology start-ups and nonprofit organizations, including the Boston Symphony Orchestra, the Museum of Science, and the Council on Competitiveness.